Critical thinking is a major and enduring aspect of higher education and the development of criticality in students has long been a core aim. However, understandings of criticality are conceptually and empirically unclear.

The book combines a well developed conceptual discussion of the nature of criticality appropriate for the twenty-first century, the extent to which it is attainable by arts and social science undergraduates, and the paths by which it is developed during students' higher education experiences. Drawing upon empirical accounts and case studies of teaching and learning in different disciplines, this book critically analyses higher education curriculum and policy documentation to explore higher educational processes, encouraging a re-evaluation of practice and educational values, and enabling the development of curricula which incorporate systematic attention to the development of student criticality. This book proposes a rounded conceptual vision of criticality in higher education for the twenty-first century.

Also available from Bloomsbury:

Consumer Experience of Higher Education, Deirdre McArdle-Clinton
Pedagogy and the University, Monica McLean
Rethinking Universities, Brian J. Brown and Sally Baker
University in Translation, Suzy Harris
Work-based Knowledge, Pauline Armsby and Carol Costley

Developing Student Criticality in Higher Education

Undergraduate Learning in the Arts and Social Sciences

Brenda Johnston, Rosamond Mitchell,
Florence Myles and Peter Ford

Continuum Studies in Educational Research

BLOOMSBURY
LONDON · NEW DELHI · NEW YORK · SYDNEY

Bloomsbury Academic
An imprint of Bloomsbury Publishing Plc

50 Bedford Square	175 Fifth Avenue
London	New York
WC1B 3DP	NY 10010
UK	USA

www.bloomsbury.com

First published by Continuum International Publishing Group 2011
Paperback edition first published 2012

© Brenda Johnston, Rosamond Mitchell, Florence Myles and Peter Ford, 2011

All rights reserved. No part of this publication may be reproduced or transmitted in any form or by any means, electronic or mechanical, including photocopying, recording, or any information storage or retrieval system, without prior permission in writing from the publishers.

Brenda Johnston, Rosamond Mitchell, Florence Myles and Peter Ford have asserted their rights under the Copyright, Designs and Patents Act, 1988, to be identified as Authors of this work.

No responsibility for loss caused to any individual or organization acting on or refraining from action as a result of the material in this publication can be accepted by Bloomsbury Academic or the author.

British Library Cataloguing-in-Publication Data
A catalogue record for this book is available from the British Library.

ISBN: HB: 978-0-8264-4117-1
PB: 978-1-4411-3787-6

Library of Congress Cataloging-in-Publication Data
Developing student criticality in higher education / Brenda Johnston . . . [et al.].
p. cm.
Includes bibliographical references.
ISBN: 978-0-8264-4117-1 (hardcover)
ISBN: 978-1-4411-0651-3 (ebook pdf)
1. Critical thinking–Study and thinking (Higher) I. Johnston, Brenda. II. Title.
LB2395.35D48 2010
378.1'7–dc22
2010033352

Typeset by Newgen Imaging Systems Pvt Ltd, Chennai, India
Printed and bound in Great Britain

In memory of
Christopher Brumfit

Contents

Acknowledgements viii

Chapter 1: Introduction 1

Chapter 2: Conceptualizations of Criticality in Higher Education: Philosophical, Field-Specific and Political Engagement Approaches 14

Chapter 3: Conceptualizations of Criticality in Higher Education: Psychological Approaches 40

Chapter 4: A Proposed Framework for Criticality Development 68

Chapter 5: Criticality Goals in the Undergraduate Curriculum 97

Chapter 6: Becoming Critical: Teaching and Learning Processes 126

Chapter 7: Student Writing and Criticality Development 153

Chapter 8: Experiential Learning and Criticality Development 178

Chapter 9: Conclusions and Implications 204

References 229

Index 243

Acknowledgements

We would like to thank the Economic and Social Research Council, UK, for funding the original research in 2002/04, *Development of Criticality among Undergraduates in Two Academic Disciplines: Social Work and Modern Languages* (ESRC Project R000239657), on which this book is based. We would also like to thank the Social Work and Social Policy Subject Centre of the Higher Education Academy, UK, for funding further analysis of the data in 2005/06.

We are also very grateful to a number of people for their invaluable assistance with this book. First thanks must go to our research participants. This study would not have been possible without the lecturers and students of 'Westford University'. They were both generous with their time and brave in allowing us into their classrooms and academic lives. We are grateful to the Modern Languages and Social Work departments for allowing us access. Various others made the research project possible: our ever-patient transcribers (especially Gillian Browne and Debbie Griffiths) and Eleanor Lutman and Susan Lees, our dedicated and capable administrative assistants. Our research students have contributed to our ongoing thinking about criticality in higher education: Sukanya Kaowiwattanakul, Patricia Romero de Mills and Pornrawee Thunnithet.

Mary McKeever and Sir William Taylor have read and made many helpful comments on sections of the manuscript. Alison Williamson has painstakingly and with endless good humour read our manuscript and prepared it for publication.

We would also like to acknowledge Christopher Brumfit's invaluable contribution to the project prior to his untimely death in 2006. His inspiration and many of his ideas live through the finished manuscript.

Chapter 1

Introduction

Employers report repeatedly that many new graduates they hire are not prepared to work, lacking the critical thinking, writing and problem-solving skills needed in today's workplaces.

(A Test of Leadership, p. 3)

My opinion? Does it matter? . . . I don't think you write down what you think. I don't think your opinion matters, as a person.

(Student interview)

Higher education and criticality in the twenty-first century

The unprecedented expansion of higher education in recent decades and its resulting incorporation into mainstream society (as distinct from being an elite preserve), have focused attention sharply on the processes and outcomes of higher education, including criticality. By criticality we mean critical thinking, critical self-reflection and critical action, but much more on this later in Chapters 2, 3 and 4. In this context of expansion, discussion about criticality exists within a wider debate over the purposes of higher education and its future direction. Policy makers focus differentially on higher education as a promoter of economic effectiveness, as an agent of social justice, or as a means through which responsible citizens can be created. A range of views is expressed, for example, in a number of UK policy reports: *Higher Education in the Learning Society* (National Committee of Inquiry into Higher Education, 1997); *The Future of Higher Education* (Department for Education and Skills, 2003); and *Higher Ambitions* (Department for Business, Innovation and Skills, 2009). Similar variability can be found in international policy documents such as *Engagement as a Core Value for the University* (Association of Commonwealth Universities, 2001); *Learning for Life* (Commonwealth of Australia, 1998); *Review of Australian Higher*

Education (Commonwealth of Australia, 2008); and *A Test of Leadership* (US Department of Education, 2006).

Such policy documents and initiatives reflect a shared desire to increase the effectiveness of teaching, learning and assessment in higher education at the same time as meeting the needs of an increasingly diverse student body at a time of educational, social and economic change. They make widely varying reference to different aspects of criticality, in line with their differing emphases on economic, social and moral goals. Generally however, governmental and employer policy statements present 'critical thinking' in some form as necessary for graduates in the twenty-first century, sometimes expressing concern about their failure to achieve it (e.g. Commonwealth of Australia, 2000). We analyse a selection of such policy documents more fully in Chapter 5, and also show how the concern with 'critical thinking' is reflected in various current forms of curriculum guidance and quality audit, in the UK context in particular.

In addition to economic, social and political uncertainties surrounding higher education, the intellectual climate is unsettled. Post-structuralist theories have challenged the certainties of knowledge, the production and stewardship of which was a central *raison d'être* of higher education in the early and mid-twentieth century. Indeed, it has been argued (e.g. by Gibbons et al., 1994) that the nature of knowledge and the manner of its production have been undergoing radical development, changing the traditional contribution of universities to these processes.

Within this unstable context, higher education theorists argue for new or revised roles for higher education in the modern world. Delanty (2001) and Barnett (1997, 2003), for example, see the university as a key site in the modern world for communication and technological advance, which can occupy a leading role in making sense of change and uncertainty while also exploring these further. Readings (1996) argues that universities must continue to provide a space where it is possible to question models, and also to question society and its intellectual configurations. Graham (2005) argues for a balanced role for universities where they 'recover' a distinctive identity, displaying 'credentials as genuine modes of social and personal enrichment' (p. 168) and offering 'a place in which the pursuit of the truth and understanding are given special protection, [although] not to the exclusion of useful or social relevant subjects, but not principally in their service either' (p. 165). These arguments affect the type of criticality that might be required of higher education, and how different parts of higher education relate to these overarching agendas adds further complexity. Universities themselves are not homogeneous bodies. There are differences between universities and other higher education institutions as well as multiple constituencies within universities: senior management, senior academics, junior administrators, junior academics, postgraduate students, undergraduate students and disciplinary groups. Each of these constituencies will relate differently to the overarching agendas proposed by higher education theorists, and this is likely to affect the nature and extent of criticality they exert. A book like this can address such issues only in part.

Among these different theoretical, political, policy, epistemological and pedagogic agendas, criticality has multiple meanings (ranging from the instrumental to the transformatory and emancipatory) in twenty-first century higher education and the broader society as discussed in Chapters 2 and 3. Here we briefly consider these meanings within a wider historical and cultural context.

Historical and cultural contextualization

The development of critical thinking in undergraduates has long been 'a defining concept of the western university' (Barnett, 1997, p. 2) or at least claimed as such. However, many aspects of higher education are historically, culturally and geographically specific, and criticality is no exception. While Western-style universities and models now dominate higher education worldwide (Altbach, 1998; Readings, 1996), Levin (2010) and others have highlighted the unprecedented expansion and success of Asian universities in recent years. This may well affect the balance of influence in future years, in terms of conceptualizations of the overall goals of higher education, criticality included. It is worth exploring some historical complexities in intellectual traditions to contextualize current practices, concerns and policies.

Historically, some have argued (as we will do in Chapter 2) that certain elements of criticality were to be found as far back as the Ancient Greek idea of higher education: critical examination of knowledge; devotion to the truth, and the importance of rhetoric (Barnett, 1990; Burbules et al., 1999; Kerr, 1972). However, the Greek tradition was complemented by extensive intellectual activity in other parts of the world, both before and contemporaneously, for example in Ancient Egypt, Mesopotamia, India and Ancient China (Axelrod, 2002). In the post-Roman period, when transmission of Greek intellectual traditions was disrupted in much of Europe, intellectual activity continued elsewhere (p. 14). If we go back 1,300 years, well before the foundation of Western universities, it was Islamic scholarship and the great Islamic universities which were leading the world in a wide range of disciplines (Halstead, 2004, p. 517). No single intellectual tradition possesses a monopoly of rational inquiry and critical thought. Moreover, as Johnston et al. (2005) described, in European universities created in the medieval period, 'study focused largely on utilitarian professional preparation together with appropriate socialisation within a feudal, but increasingly complex, society' (p. 355). In Rudy's words (1984), '[The universities] were in business primarily to train civil and ecclesiastical administrators, lawyers, and medical doctors, not philosophers, pure scientists, or literary scholars' (p. 31).

One major cultural divide which affects perceptions of criticality in education has to do with the position of religion. For example, Halstead (2004) identifies fundamental differences between Western liberal and traditional Islamic notions of education. He argues that education in Islam focuses on the certainty and unity of all knowledge with religion at its heart while Western liberal education today focuses on the uncertain and contingent nature of knowledge and posits a split between religious and secular matters.

We note that this split has not always been so, and may not be so now, even in the Western tradition. Halstead himself points out that other philosophical traditions in the West such as that of Fichte do not posit such a split (p. 527). For Fichte, God was 'immanent' in the world (Leighton, 1895) and even a cursory glance at Newman's (1899/1996) great work on liberal education illustrates the emphasis he placed on the relationship between religion and education. He believed, unlike many of his time, that there was little conflict between religion and science and that the two could and should operate in unity in universities.

In Europe and North America, while most higher education now has a secular liberal character, many universities continued to have religious associations until quite recently (Axelrod, 2002). For example, even in the early nineteenth century, Oxford and Cambridge in England were under Anglican control. In the United States (US) today, many universities and colleges have strong religious affiliations which affect their curriculum, ethos and operation to varying extents (Farrell, 2005; Fuchs, 2004; Riley, 2004).

Brookfield (2003) is another commentator who points out the cultural situatedness of critical thinking models. His own 'values rational analysis and posits the possibility of meta-cognition – standing outside oneself to observe one's cognitive operations in action'. In this case, Brookfield is highlighting an individual–collective divide. He describes his model as 'grounded in traditions of critical theory and the Enlightenment', and points out that 'to aboriginal and native cultures that value cooperative and collective ways of working, the independent, self-directed ethic that undergirds much adult educational writing [in the West] on critical thinking will be experienced as alien' (p. 160). One may think this is interesting, but not really important given that 'aboriginal and native' cultures play a relatively small role in the twenty-first century world. However, questions can also be raised about the cultural compatibility of Western-style individualistic 'critical thinking' with the intellectual traditions of countries such as India, China and Japan.

One cannot, for example, assume that criticality will transfer unproblematically for the three million international students (Wildavsky, 2010) who study outside their home country. Volet (1999) discusses the challenges faced by groups of students from Confucian heritage cultures in Hong Kong and Singapore when studying in higher education in Australia. Although many learning traits and skills transferred well (such as high levels of motivation and peer group learning), other aspects did not because students' previous experience had focused on depth of understanding, rather than questioning, and on learning from the teacher rather than independently. However, as Volet pointed out, many of the Confucian heritage culture students whom she investigated eventually achieved highly in the Australian university context, suggesting successful adaptation by well-motivated individuals.

In many contemporary education contexts, current underlying philosophies of education are hybrids in practice, the product of interactions between intellectual traditions such as Confucianism, Buddhism or Islam, and Western thinkers ranging from John Dewey to Karl Marx, Pierre Bourdieu and Jurgen Habermas (see relevant discussions in, for example, Shenghong et al., 2004; Saito et al., 2004; Burden-Leahy, 2009). Universities from such 'hybrid' traditions around the world are having great social impact, for instance in producing internationally competitive engineers and scientists (e.g. in India: Grigorenko, 2007) or in promoting women's move into professional employment (e.g. in the United Arab Emirates: Burden-Leahy, 2009). How far such higher education systems need or want to promote the type of criticality valued currently in Western universities is debatable. Levin (2010) believes that the current focus on 'mastery of content' in many Asian countries, rather than 'the capacity for independent and critical thinking . . . may be highly functional for training line engineers and mid-level government officials, but [is] perhaps less well-suited to educating elites for leadership and innovation' (p. 8). He argues that this has been recognized, in China for example, which is now supporting curricular and pedagogical revision in a small number of elite universities to encourage creative and independent thinking. But the future evolution of attitudes and criticality practices in such 'hybrid' contexts is unknown.

The intellectual context of criticality changes over time, even within 'heartland' Western educational institutions. For example, anyone reading the account of intellectual development of young male students at Harvard in the 1950s and 1960s offered by Perry (1968/1999) must be struck by the less complex, less flexible intellectual and cultural context existing at that time in that place than is typical now in most Western universities. Perry, in turn, finds his students more flexible than students of previous generations. He claimed that students in the 1850s were far more homogeneous socially and intellectually than the students of the 1960s whom he was studying. He says that the 1960s students in his study could not have come to university with very simplistic moral and intellectual ideas because of the pluralistic culture and society with which they were surrounded (p. 67).

Finally, even within such 'heartland' institutions today, commitment to criticality cannot be assumed unproblematically. Certainly, 'the quest for truth' was a founding cognitive principle of the university in liberal modernity from the end of the eighteenth century (Delanty, 2001), but even during this period the role of the university and its relationship to criticality has been ambiguous and changing. As Delanty argued, nineteenth- and early twentieth-century universities may have been largely autonomous intellectually, but 'the institution was primarily designed to serve the national state with technically useful knowledge and the preservation and reproduction of national cultural traditions' (p. 2). Neave (2002) supported this view: 'The purpose of higher education in the "regulated order" [of the nineteenth and early twentieth centuries] was to ensure continuity, stability and cohesion by ensuring the renewal of the political and administrative elites within the nation' (p. 29).

The recent expansion of higher education and its incorporation into mainstream society, itself in a state of post-industrial flux (Barnett, 1994; Reich, 1992; Scott, 1995), have further changed this situation. As Neave (2002) has argued:

> Massification [of higher education] and – more to the point, the decision of governments to make provision for it – placed a very particular premium on change, on adaptation by higher education to the pressures of demand and access on the one hand and to the exigencies of the national labour market on the other. Higher education was construed henceforth as an instrument for social and economic mobilisation – radical change indeed, and one not easily compatible with the earlier version of higher education as a vehicle for political stability. (p. 29)

Among other outcomes, 'massification' means greatly increased diversity among students, and it cannot be assumed that all will want to respond to the higher education institutional agenda of learning 'deeply' and are able to do so. Haggis (2003) argues that learners cannot be viewed passively as amenable to restructuring by higher education institutions:

> People who are learners may be resisting, or unable to engage with, what higher education assumes, for reasons to do with a sense of alienation (Mann, 2001), perceived risk or personal cost, or contrary philosophical or cultural perspective. In the new higher education, 'the learner' may be a person who is experiencing tremendous difficulty in the face of unexplained norms and values; he or she may not know, for example, that facts are seen by many lecturers as the vehicle for the more abstract forms of conceptualization that are expected but not modelled or defined. In addition, he or she may be exhausted from part-time work or parenting, distracted by family or financial problems, or lacking the fundamental confidence, self-esteem or health to engage in the ways that are assumed to be both desirable and possible. (Haggis, 2003, p. 98)

We wish to avoid making similar assumptions or to construe students as passive and usually in deficit according to an ideal, but inappropriate, model of (in this case) criticality. Instead we take a student-centred perspective and set out to interpret criticality development as an interaction between the individual with their personal learning history, cultural capital and predispositions, and the expectations of the higher education context. (See especially the student case studies presented in Chapter 7.)

In sum, a sense of historical and cultural context is important when thinking about criticality. We should remember these various shapes of higher education in different ages and places when thinking about higher education today, both to debunk 'golden age' stereotypes and to recall alternative scenarios to those with which we are presented today. Criticality is not a neutral characteristic, viewed as necessary and desirable in all contexts.

That criticality is contextualized raises questions for us when writing about it. Should we advocate criticality in contexts where it is not necessarily valued as an unquestioned social and intellectual good? Is it so necessary for survival, prosperity and well-being in the twenty-first century that we should advocate its development at all costs in all cultural contexts, because not to do so would deprive nations and individuals of the means of achieving those benefits and rights? Or does the enthusiasm for critical thinking represent the practice of cultural hegemony through education? Are there ways forward which build on hybrid traditions and develop new types of criticality practice? We cannot answer all these questions in this book. However, the issues we discuss are relevant to these debates.

Aims of the book

We have just argued that criticality exists in shifting and contested territory, certainly within the world as a whole and even within Western higher education where it is supposedly 'a defining concept' (Barnett, 1997, p. 2). Against this backdrop, an investigation of what *is* happening as regards the teaching, learning and assessment of criticality in higher education for undergraduate students, and a discussion of what *should* happen can make a useful contribution both to teaching and learning and also to broader debates about criticality.

We shall argue that within the context of twenty-first century higher education in the West criticality is desirable, although we write with an awareness of other cultural and historical contexts and do not claim universality for our conclusions and findings. We shall argue that society needs active and responsible citizens who are able to cope with decision making and living in a world that is fast changing – socially, economically, politically and educationally. Not only do people have to cope with technological changes and their application in employment, public life and private life, but there are also complex new moral and ethical dilemmas to face and new social configurations developing which have to be adjusted to and perhaps resisted. We argue that a broad conception of social, moral and intellectual critical development within the modern world and within education is required. Thought about *how* it can be achieved is also necessary. Critical people as citizens and employees are desirable, although how people should exercise their criticality, and in which situations, are questions with slippery answers and where governments, employers, academics, and other individuals may arrive at different answers.

Currently, the processes by which criticality may develop in undergraduates are under-researched and poorly understood. This book illuminates how criticality is developed and practised in one part of higher education today. This will enable underlying principles, applicable in other higher educational situations, to be identified and discussed. In this way the book will contribute to both conceptual and empirical knowledge. Specifically it will offer a well-developed conceptual discussion of the nature and development of criticality, appropriate for the twenty-first century. It will also include rich empirical descriptions, aligned with this theorization, of the extent to which criticality is attainable by arts and social science undergraduates, and the paths by which it is developed during students' higher education experiences.

The book addresses the following questions:

- Why is criticality desirable in twenty-first century higher education?
- How can criticality most usefully be conceptualized?
  - What are its component parts?
  - How does it transfer between different areas?
  - What shapes does its development take?
- What kinds of criticality, if any, are undergraduates learning in their courses? How do the types of criticality developed relate to our conceptualizations?
- How do the types of criticality actually learned relate to stakeholders' perceptions and policy aspirations (institutional and national)?
- How can the teaching/learning of 'criticality' be made more coherent and transparent?

The empirical data on which the book draws were collected during a two-year research project funded by the UK Economic and Social Research Council from July 2002 to June 2004, *Development of Criticality Among Undergraduates in Two Academic Disciplines: Social Work and Modern Languages* (ESRC Project R000239657). This project investigated the development of criticality among undergraduates in Modern Languages and Social Work Studies at the 'University of Westford' (a pseudonym), a large research-intensive university in the United Kingdom (UK). The authors of this book, together with our colleague the late Christopher Brumfit, were the investigators. Additional analysis of the Social Work data was funded by the Social Work and Social Policy Subject Centre of the UK Higher Education Academy in 2005/06.

The investigation draws on empirical data in two contrasting fields: one a traditional arts subject (Modern Languages), the other an applied social science subject with a strong professional training element (Social Work). These fields are powerful exemplars in that the multidisciplinary Modern Languages degree included a wide range of traditional humanities courses in literature, history, linguistics and film, as well as language. The Social

Work degree included a range of social science courses including sociology, social policy and statistics, as well as social work. Both degree programmes involve significant periods of study in out-of-university environments. The Modern Languages programmes offered a wide range of optional courses, so that students could specialize to some degree in fields such as literature, culture, or linguistics. In contrast, the Social Work students had to follow prescribed courses (in social work, social policy, sociology and law) to receive professional accreditation. The Modern Languages degree involved four years of study, the third spent abroad. The Social Work degree had involved four years of study, but was changing over to three years at the time of the fieldwork. The students in our study included students from the first two years of the new degree and final-year students from the old four-year degree, reflecting as far as possible the composition of the new three-year degree in terms of exposure to practice and academic input.

The project involved a wide-ranging programme of data collection. We observed 12 courses, two for each of three years of study in the two departments. We collected data for 20 case study students, 9 in Social Work and 11 in Modern Languages. The students were selected rather than being volunteers. In Social Work, the students were selected to represent a range of abilities. In Modern Languages, the students (who studied on a wide range of optional courses) were selected from among those enrolled on similar groups of options, to facilitate classroom observation. All students were free to say that they did not wish to participate and several did. For each student, we have multiple interviews and various related presentations and pieces of academic writing, including notes, drafts and final assignments, and examination scripts. We conducted interviews with 18 members of lecturing staff, and collected policy and other official documents at a national, institutional, departmental and course level. In this way we collected multiple data types, including contextual information relevant to the acquisition, learning and teaching of criticality.

The analysis was conducted qualitatively and included microanalysis of students' talk, reading, writing and thought as dynamic social and learning activities. We also conducted documentary analysis of the official documents we gathered. We have developed holistic understandings of the individual students' engagement in their social, educational and institutional contexts. These analytical methods have given us access to localized meanings of events, processes and changes (Miles et al., 1994). A major feature has been the analysis of ongoing processes of criticality construction, both collaboratively in class/group settings, and individually through production of written assignments and spoken presentations.

In reporting on our data, we have changed the names of the students, lecturers and courses as well as that of the university in which we conducted the research to disguise their identities. We have used the term 'programme' to indicate the degrees for which students were enrolled (e.g. Spanish and History) and the term 'course' to indicate one of the many semester-long units of study which make up a degree programme. We are aware that there is variable terminology in the world for such matters, as there was at Westford, the university in which we carried out our fieldwork.

The theoretical framework we propose has been arrived at by drawing on existing strands of thought in related literatures and analysis of our own primary data. We aimed to draw out commonalities and contrastive elements in critical development in the two fields. Through analysis of our own data and related theorization, we aimed to propose a framework to describe criticality development, suitable for wider application in the humanities and social sciences. We have carried out an iterative, analytical process of moving backwards and forwards between theoretical concepts and our data, rather than starting with application of theory to data, or alternatively building up theory completely from data analysis. The theory helped us see patterns in the data, and close scrutiny of the data helped us refine the theoretical framework we were developing. Our coding was partly intuitive, reflecting themes emerging from the data, and partly theory driven. Through a series of student case studies and iterations of the theory, a theoretical framework has been reached which is elaborated in this book. We have thus tried to build a theoretical framework with considerable explanatory power and which is faithful to a wide spectrum of our data.

We have worked on a number of conceptual fronts. The major theoretical background informing the research is that of criticality development; the various relevant literatures are reviewed in Chapters 2 and 3. The framework we propose includes elements relating to definition, context, discipline, resources, development and curriculum. Throughout the book, we explore how disciplinary and higher education traditions influence the teaching of criticality and related assessment practices, and what the underlying values and implications of such traditions and practices are. The book is distinctive in its focus on criticality as a social practice, its emphasis on the different levels and domains of criticality, and on the resources students need to be critical. It is empirically based yet theoretically oriented. It is also distinctive in offering detailed empirical descriptions of criticality development.

Brookfield (2003) points out that there are very few studies of how students feel when going through the 'situated struggle' of learning to be critical in higher education (p. 149). By offering a detailed empirically based examination of how students experience criticality, this book gives students something of a voice about the educational process they undergo, which is often denied them in research on and rhetoric about criticality. The investigation also gives other principal actors involved, that is, their lecturers, a voice.

We will not address the issue of criticality in school contexts as this is not our empirical field, but critical development in children and teenagers is clearly an issue of importance and closely related to what is happening in higher education. Equally, our account stops at graduation while clearly the practice of criticality and, we hope, the development of critical capacities does not.

Although the study focused on a research intensive university in the UK, we believe the proposed theoretical framework has wide applicability in a variety of settings as it is based on underlying educational principles. However, we suspect that its application to scientific disciplines, given well-documented disciplinary differences (see for example Becher, 1989; Becher et al., 2001; Donald, 1986, 1995; Neumann et al., 2002), is unlikely to be straightforward and we plan to do further research on criticality in science disciplines in the future.

Structure of the book

Chapters 2 and 3 provide an overview and critical evaluation of current theoretical perspectives and empirical research on criticality and critical thinking in higher education.

In Chapter 4, we propose our own theoretical framework for understanding criticality development. We ask what the essential elements are for understanding how undergraduates experience and learn criticality and for understanding how teachers might facilitate the development of criticality.

In Chapters 5 through 8 we discuss our data. This discussion relates to the theoretical proposals in Chapter 4.

Chapter 5 analyses the place of criticality/criticality development in the undergraduate curriculum at Westford, with special attention to its place in the Modern Languages and Social Work curricula. The chapter draws on a range of sources: official documentation (international and national policy and quality assurance documents, in-house Westford documentation, national professional standards documentation for social work), lecturer views, and assessment procedures.

Chapter 6 analyses teaching and learning processes relating to criticality development as exemplified in face-to-face classes in Modern Languages and in Social Work at Westford.

Chapter 7 concentrates on student criticality development as reflected in student writings and other outputs, plus accounts in student interviews of how these outputs were produced.

Chapter 8 discusses student criticality development through the 'special', out-of-class experiences of the Year Abroad (Modern Languages) and practice placements (Social Work).

Chapter 9 draws together threads from the preceding chapters, discussing their implications for criticality development, pointing out the limitations of our account, and discussing practices likely to encourage criticality development. It points to ways forward in terms of both research and practice.

Chapter 2

Conceptualizations of Criticality in Higher Education: Philosophical, Field-Specific and Political Engagement Approaches

Introduction

In this chapter and the next, we explain and critique existing conceptualizations of criticality and related literatures, probing their limitations and usefulness for providing a pedagogic vision of criticality for twenty-first century higher education. In Chapter 4 we set out our own principled framework to describe criticality development in undergraduates and how it might be enhanced.

We have located a range of relevant literatures: broad philosophical and educational visions of higher education; sociological and pedagogic approaches; criticality as political engagement; and psychological accounts. Some are largely conceptual while others include empirical research. The different approaches are evolving, rather than static, partly in response to wider intellectual movements such as postmodernism and feminism. The approaches arise from different epistemological and ontological bases, some view knowledge as objective, verifiable and accretive while others view it as subjective, consensual and (re)constructed.

The literatures reviewed are complex and extensive, and often isolated from one another. Some address criticality directly, but for others it is only an implied interest. Each has its own terminology. This review is necessarily selective.

For each section of the literature, we focus especially on two questions raised in Chapter 1:

(1) Why is criticality in twenty-first century higher education desirable?
(2) How can criticality most usefully be conceptualized?

For the first question, we focus on perceived benefits arising from criticality and their underlying values.

The second question has three main parts. First, we ask what criticality's component parts are, including: where is it perceived as being located; whether it is perceived as a matter of individual thinking or of social construction; whether it is considered as relating just to formal academic knowledge or as also including aspects of the self, the world, emotion, motivations and dispositions; and how far criticality is viewed as being analytical, how far as creative.

Secondly, we ask about conceptualizations of and empirical evidence about transfer of criticality. If someone is critical in one area, is this criticality transferable? How far is criticality embedded in field-specific knowledge and how far is it field-independent? What might the nature of field-specific knowledge be, if it exists, and what are the implications of these answers for the transfer of criticality and so for the teaching and learning of criticality? The questions relate not just to different fields in the domain of formal knowledge, but also to criticality transfer to other areas of life. Brookfield (2003) poses the question of whether someone 'can be critically aware of oppressive political structures and dominant value systems, yet be entirely uncritical of the repressive features of his or her behaviour in intimate relationships?' (p. 160).

Thirdly, we ask how criticality is perceived as developing and whether and how it is viewed as being teachable (although not every approach is interested in criticality and education).

We now discuss various approaches, drawing out what each can offer in answer to the questions outlined above. We describe each approach then discuss its limitations and contributions to the development of a pedagogically useful vision of criticality in the twenty-first century.

In this chapter, we deal with approaches arising from philosophy, sociology, education and those with a strong political focus. In Chapter 3 we deal with those arising from cognitive psychology.

In higher education, fields are often known as disciplines, but disciplines are often restricted in meaning to formal knowledge and often to particular branches of formal knowledge. To avoid such restrictions of meaning and as our review of criticality goes beyond formal knowledge, we often refer to fields rather than disciplines, unless the literatures themselves refer to disciplines.

Philosophical approaches

These approaches usually rely on logical reasoning, rather than empirical research.

Liberal academic views

The approach

The modern concept of liberal education, concerned with the pursuit of truth, the development and fulfilment of the mind and so an understanding of how to live as an individual and a social being, is descended from Ancient Greek philosophical doctrines about the relationship between knowledge and the mind (Hirst, 1974/1998). Axelrod (2002) traces the heritage of these ideas over the centuries and through various cultures, including the contribution of Islamic scholars in the European 'Dark Ages'. He traces their intermingling with Christian theological concerns from medieval times. The Enlightenment focus on rationalism had some influence on university curricula, but it was not until the nineteenth century, especially in Germany and France, that secular ideas for higher education gained influence (pp. 14–22).

As Delanty (2001) explained, 'the neohumanist university, such as the Humboldtian university in Germany or the liberal arts college in the Anglo-Saxon world, was based on the idea of the autonomy of knowledge' (p. 22). In this view, 'the pursuit of knowledge or truth [is] an end in itself' (p. 38). This Humboldtian ideal also stressed the development of the whole person, and of self-cultivation through the ideal of '*Bildung*'; this was echoed in the Anglo-Saxon liberal ideal of self-development and personal care (Johnston et al., 2005). Newman (1899/1996) was a strong advocate of the liberal university, based on the principles discussed above, in the Anglo-Saxon world. He mainly focused on intellectual empowerment for individuals through education.

The traditional Anglo-Saxon liberal position had little time for instrumental skills or professional training which it despised as trivial, narrow, related to 'training' rather than 'education' and lacking in self-criticism (Newman, 1899/1996; Nussbaum, 1997). In Germany, however, *Ausbildung*, a German concept which can be translated as the 'formation of professionals' and entailing a constructive synthesis of education and training, is a powerful concept.

In summary, the historically influential liberal approach, in which truth and knowledge are seen as objective and obtainable, views education as intrinsically worthwhile. (Higher) education is about (1) the pursuit of 'truth', through critical investigation; (2) the expansion of the student's outlook; (3) the development of the student's capacity for social and civic interaction; and (4) the development of the student's general intellectual capabilities (Newman, 1899/1996; Whitehead, 1932a, 1932b; Nussbaum, 1997; Oakeshott, 1950/1989; Jaspers, 1960; Shils, 1997).

There has, however, been longstanding controversy over the exact curricular content of a liberal education. Recently, this disagreement has focused on issues such as the degree of specialization within degree programmes. Hirst (1974/1998), for example, argues that students should sample knowledge across different disciplines, not aiming for comprehensive understanding or specialist knowledge, but developing a broader knowledge. This view can be traced in contemporary curriculum models such as that of the American liberal arts college, or the so-called 'Melbourne model' (Devlin, 2008).

Newer liberal visions of higher education revise some aspects of traditional views. For example, Gallo (1994) argues for recognition of the importance of empathy in reasoning, as well as critical and creative thinking. Nussbaum (1997) argues for a liberal education based on the Socratic tradition, which would prepare students for world citizenship by teaching them to reach out to people of different traditions, to ask questions and to argue rigorously and critically. Martin (1998) focuses on an education with space for emotion and action as well as 'rational thought'. The Association of American Colleges and Universities (2002) argues for a liberal education that is both intellectually enriching and practically oriented; the Melbourne 'attributes' refer to 'active global citizens' who are 'attuned to cultural diversity' (University of Melbourne, 2007).

Limitations and contributions

Liberal views of criticality are open to question on several grounds. First, traditional liberalism is often discussing the education of a small governing elite (usually male), not the diverse student body found in mass higher education for whom the focus on self-development, independence and disregard of vocational education may be less appropriate (Nussbaum, 1997). Secondly, it has been suggested that obliging students to 'think/write critically' has often, in practice, been a means of exercising control over members of disciplines who adopt academically controlled, cognitively based disciplinary modes of inquiry, argument and communication in their search for disciplinary recognized 'truths' (Bartholomae, 1985; Barnett, 1990, 1997; Grant, 1997; Lea et al., 1998). Thirdly, liberal visions usually focus on the domain of formal knowledge/critical reason, with some focus on the development of the rational self, rather than considering emotional or practical aspects (Barnett, 1990, 1994, 1997; Martin, 1998; Walker et al., 1999). Fourthly, intellectual movements such as postmodernism have undermined positions which accept objectivity and 'truth' as obtainable (Barnett, 1990). Fifthly, liberalism has some difficulty in dealing with collectivist thinking such as in academic disciplines, apart from seeing disciplinary members as individuals who gather together to think about similar issues. Sixthly, the transferability of critical thinking between different specialist domains is insufficiently problematized.

These criticisms are substantial, but nonetheless liberal views of higher education offer an important contribution to our conceptualization of criticality in terms of their underlying philosophical, moral, social and educational vision. Accordingly, we shall place our proposals broadly within such understandings, as distinct from, for example, a Confucian or Islamic or Christian tradition.

Liberal values form the bedrock of much Western higher education, and the remaining approaches discussed in this chapter usually lie within a liberal educational framework, tacitly if not explicitly.

Critical being

The approach

Barnett's book, *Higher Education: A Critical Business* (1997), an invaluable text for us, provides a theoretical conceptualization of criticality; a vision of what criticality should be in higher education today. He also makes a powerful case for why criticality is desirable and necessary today. Barnett (1990) started from a base of liberal education, but critiqued it (as indicated earlier) and proposed strategies for moving beyond it.

Barnett relates criticality to his wider concerns about the purposes of higher education. He suggests that higher education, especially in its mass form, can have a powerful influence within society by promoting the critical capacities of university graduates. He proposes that criticality be understood over a range of domains (knowledge, self and the world), and that there are three forms of critical being: 'critical reason, critical self-reflection and critical action'. While there is no 'determinate boundary' between these (p. 7), Barnett argues that focusing attention on the three domains 'highlight[s] the varying objects that critical thinking can take *and the purposes it can fulfil*' (p. 66). He suggests that these domains have to be brought together 'if a unity of critical outlook is to be achieved' (pp. 114–15). The underlying purpose of higher education and educators, in this vision, is to develop 'the capacities to think critically . . . to understand oneself critically and to act critically' and so to form 'critical persons who are not subject to the world but able to act autonomously and purposively within it' (p. 4). The traditional liberal focus on mind only is insufficient.

Table 2.1 Levels, domains and forms of critical being

Levels of criticality		Domains		
		Knowledge	Self	World
4	Transformatory critique	Knowledge critique	Reconstruction of self	Critique-in-action (collective reconstruction of the world)
3	Refashioning of traditions	Critical thought (malleable traditions of thought)	Development of self within traditions	Mutual understanding and development of traditions
2	Reflexivity	Critical thinking (reflection on one's understanding)	Self-reflection (reflection on one's own projects)	Reflective practice ('metacompetence', 'adaptability', 'flexibility')
1	Critical skills	Discipline-specific critical thinking skills	Self-monitoring to given standards and norms	Problem-solving (means-end instrumentalism)
	Forms of criticality	Critical reason	Critical self-reflection	Critical action

Source: Barnett (1997), p. 103.

Barnett also suggests a range of levels, from instrumental criticality through to transformatory critique. He suggests that we would wish students of today to become critical transformers, critical beings, located towards the top of his table, rather than those who are instrumentally and partially critical, located towards the lower levels. Table 2.1 summarizes his proposals for domains and levels.

Barnett suggests that higher education should seek to develop students as critical beings across the three domains and to the highest level within each, for 'the full potential of critical being' to be achieved. Through this integration 'critical but creative persons will result, capable of living effectively in the world' (p. 8). The purpose of achieving 'critical being' for a broad swathe of the population is 'social wisdom', which would offer 'a significant reflexive capacity . . . bent on understanding, on enlightening and on improving in every sense society and its changes' (p. 8).

Barnett also addresses the difficult issue of how criticality relates to critical standards. He asks (p. 24) whether there are 'any critical standards that we can hold on to?' and 'if so, are they simply expressions of different forms of life, embedded in contrasting languages games (the postmodern position)' as espoused by Lyotard (1984). According to such a position, 'higher education [would] simply [be] a collection of discrete academic sub-cultures with their own languages, values and relationships to the wider world of work' (p. 29). Alternatively, there might be 'universal critical standards which might also inform our practices in, and our understanding of, higher education (as implied by critical theory)' (p. 24), as espoused by Habermas (1987, 1991). A third position, which Barnett adopts, draws on Habermas's idea that 'critical thought could operate at different *levels*'. He argues that it is possible to be 'both locals and cosmopolitans with respect to critical thought' (p. 33). By this, he means that we can both use critical standards within our own local field and apply standards from other areas. That is, 'through metacritique, we could step right outside our frameworks of thought and bring to bear the firepower of alternative critical frameworks' (p. 33). Here, Barnett supports the view of Habermas that we are not prisoners of postmodern local frameworks.

Limitations and contributions

Barnett's framework is not a psychological theory of cognitive development, suggesting instead a view of what it is to be a student and the kind of critical tendencies we would wish students to develop (p. 71). Barnett is primarily, although not exclusively, interested in speculating about the uses of criticality, rather than its detailed structure and components *or* development *or* relationships to empirical evidence with regard to undergraduates. He does not address disciplinary differences in criticality. Nor does he suggest developmental paths or the intellectual and personal resources that people will need to proceed to higher levels of criticality. Issues of transfer go to the heart of the kind of cross-domain criticality advocated by Barnett (1997), but he does not discuss these. These are not his purposes. In contrast, we are interested in at least some of those issues and so seek additional conceptual support elsewhere.

Criticality in Barnettian terms provides a broader conceptualization than 'critical thinking'. This is a highly significant contribution. The idea of domains and levels of criticality also helps to clarify much confusion in the field. We question, however, whether higher education should or could develop students across all domains to the highest level, and in later chapters we explore which of Barnett's domains and levels can be traced empirically in student criticality development.

Critical thinking approaches: general skills and dispositions

The approaches

Arising out of analytical philosophy, critical thinking is a major approach to criticality particularly favoured in the US (e.g. Dauer, 1989; Ennis, 1962, 1987; Facione, 1990; Fulkerson, 1996; Paul, 1984; Siegel, 1988), although with some UK adherents (e.g. Fisher, 1988; Fisher et al., 1997). It is often linked with the informal logic movement and frequently associated with critical thinking in education, although, logically, not necessarily so (Johanson, 1987; McPeck, 1981; Scriven, 2003; Siegel, 1988). As Siegel (1988) points out, and as is clear to anyone reading this literature, there are wide (and frequently somewhat acrimonious and arcane) differences among those associated with 'the movement', expressed in an ongoing dialogue (e.g. McPeck, 1981; Paul, 1994).

Critical thinking authors operate within a general framework of liberal education, often tacitly rather than overtly, assuming the desirability and possibility of developing rationality in individuals. They focus on training of the mind and the search for the truth. For example, Siegel (1988) argued that critical thinking is 'principled', 'consistent', 'impartial' and based on 'standards' which are taken to be 'universal and objective' (p. 34). Dauer (1989) claimed that 'critical thinking might be taken as the art of assessing truth claims according to certain general principles or canons' (p. 3).

Critical thinking approaches usually assume that students are deficient in their ability or disposition 'to discern certain kinds of inaccuracies, distortions, and falsehoods' (Burbules et al., 1999). With proper training, the appropriate skills and dispositions will develop. As Paul (1982) explains, '. . . the reader is encouraged to look for formal and/or informal fallacies, conceived as atomically determinable and correctable "mistakes". Irrationality in human reasoning is implied thereby to be reducible to complex combinations of atomic mistakes' (p. 3).

Frequently, critical thinking writers provide taxonomies of necessary skills and dispositions, sometimes including 'dispositions' and 'tendencies'. Recognition of the importance of the latter has grown. Ennis's early work, from which much current interest in this particular critical thinking tradition may be traced, focused on skills, abilities and proficiencies, developing a taxonomy of those required in critical thinking (Ennis, 1962). Ennis (1969) offered teachers a breakdown of logical thinking to follow when training their students to reason analytically. Later, he included creative aspects of thinking. Ennis (1987) listed 14 'dispositions' (e.g. seeking reasons, trying to be well informed) and 12 'abilities' (e.g. focusing on a question, analysing arguments), each sub-divided into several sub-points, which are involved in the process of 'reflectively and reasonably deciding what to believe or do' (pp. 12–15); however, his taxonomy has remained largely focused on evaluation of arguments, rather than their creation.

Siegel (1988) regards critical thinking 'as an educational ideal which involves dispositions, habits of mind, and character traits as well as skills' (p. 8). He writes about the disposition of 'critical spirit' (p. 39) and thinks it important to consider underlying purposes of critical thinking such as validation of truth, intellectual honesty and attention to evidence. Other dispositions identified in the critical thinking literature include, for example, tolerating ambiguity, being open-minded and being inquisitive (McBride et al., 2002).

Paul (1982, 1987) focuses on 'weak' and 'strong' conceptions of critical thinking. The 'weak' focuses atomistically on components of arguments and avoidance of mistakes in the use of critical thinking techniques. However, Paul (1982) argues that:

> any student studying critical thinking at the university level has a highly developed belief system buttressed by deep-seated uncritical, egocentric and sociocentric habits of thought by which he interprets and processes his or her experience, whether academic or not, and places it into some larger perspective. (p. 3)

Therefore a 'strong' conception of critical thinking is necessary. This includes consideration of world views, awareness of potential self-deception and of both egocentric and sociocentric components in one's thinking, emotional investment, ethical issues and the relationship of these to thinking processes.

Writers in this tradition have also provided practical texts to encourage the development of these skills and dispositions (e.g. Van den Brink-Budgen, 2000; Browne et al., 2007; Cottrell, 2005; McDonald, 1989; Reid, 1988; Smalley et al., 1986). Fulkerson (1996) synthesizes various approaches to developing argument in the critical thinking tradition, including fallacy theory and Toulmin's model of argumentation where six interrelated components for analysing arguments must be mastered. Fisher (1988) shows how to deconstruct and assess arguments made by such writers as J. S. Mill and Karl Marx. Such tools are typically taught through courses on critical thinking or informal logic, and influential tests have been constructed (e.g. the Cornell Critical Thinking tests; the Watson-Glaser Critical Thinking Test).

Moseley et al. (2004) describe and evaluate many of the thinking skill taxonomies and teaching approaches arising out of philosophy.

The focus in critical thinking approaches is on the processes and skills of reasoning, rather than substantive content. Some writers discuss the issue of transfer (e.g. Ennis, 1989; Facione, 1990), but most focus on isolating particular thinking skills which it is assumed will be transferred between domains relatively unproblematically. However, Facione (1990) does discuss the relationship of domain-specific and overarching critical skills, arguing that critical thinking skills transcend disciplinary boundaries, but that 'learning and applying these skills in many contexts requires domain-specific knowledge' which might include knowledge of methodological principles and the ability to carry out practices according to standards prevalent in the relevant discipline to reach judgements acceptable in that context (p. 5). He argues that 'too much of value is lost if CT [critical thinking] is conceived of simply as a list of logical operations and domain-specific knowledge is conceived of simply as an aggregation of information' (p. 5).

Cognitive approaches, discussed in Chapter 3, and critical thinking approaches draw on one another at times (e.g. McGuinness, 1993). Quellmalz (1987) proposes that the critical thinking focus on definitions of reasoning types (that is, on products) and the cognitive approach on underlying cognitive operations (that is, on processes) overlap and may be mapped onto one another.

Limitations and contributions

Critical thinking approaches have been heavily criticized. Given their popularity and our broad agreement with the critiques, we will discuss them in some detail.

First, from an educational viewpoint, the approach is overly complex. Few teachers or students know the relevant logical rules from analytical philosophy. Teaching students (and their teachers) these rules would be time consuming and probably confusing. Fallacy theory illustrates these problems. Over the years, informal logicians have identified and named various argumentative fallacies. Fulkerson (1996) has identified 11 major fallacies: hasty generalization, poor analogy, fallible sign, *post hoc*, *argumentum ad verecundiam*, accident, *argumentum ad populum*, *argumentum ad misericordiam*, *argumentum ad hominem*, the straw man, and ignoring context (pp. 96–130). Each fallacy is then divided into sub-types. Learning to apply such a complex system is challenging, and in practice this approach usually operates as a separate sub-discipline.

Secondly, and compellingly, cognitivist psychologists argue that logical mental models, where people work through all logical possibilities to reach a conclusion, require effort and place a heavy load on working memory. Therefore, with experience people draw on schemata in long-term memory to reach conclusions rather than relying on logical thinking from first principles (Markman et al., 2001, pp. 228–31).

Thirdly, the relationships between knowledge and argument are not straightforward. As McPeck (1990b), an analytical philosopher, points out, the critical thinking approach assumes that the aspiring critical thinker has only to learn some clear rules and apply them rigorously to easily acquired and understood facts (pp. 27–8). However, in reality knowledge is often incomplete, contested and complex.

Critical thinking approaches view rational thinking as separated from social and intellectual contextual knowledge. They offer general intellectual rules which can be transferred between disciplines and do not offer a shared knowledge base or understanding of key principles of particular disciplinary areas, crucial elements in the application of intellectual rules (Bailin et al., 1999b; Barrow, 1999; McPeck, 1990b). We discuss the role of domain-specific knowledge more fully in the section 'Criticality Embedded in Specific Fields', (p. 28) and in Chapter 3. Advocates of a social emancipatory and critical pedagogy perspective (see p. 36) such as Giroux (1988) have criticized critical thinking approaches because they fail to recognize (1) the frame of reference or the particular theoretical perspective which underlies any facts; and (2) the relationships between the selection and ordering of facts and values, interests and norms (pp. 62–3). Walters (1994) argues that 'first wave' critical thinking advocates such as Glaser et al. reduce critical thinking from 'good thinking' in a broad sense to a minimal focus on logical operations (p. 11).

Critical thinking approaches have also been criticized for favouring a masculine Western mode of thinking. As Burbules et al. explain:

> Theories of education that stress the primary importance of logic, conceptual clarity, and rigorous adherence to scientific evidence have been challenged by various advocates of cultural and gender diversity who emphasize respect for alternative world views and styles of reasoning. (pp. 49–50)

Fourthly, critical thinking processes focus on deconstruction and evaluation of arguments, rather than construction of arguments or formulation of critical actions. For example, fallacy theory is a checking tool applied to an analytical product. It gives students little guidance on how to reach a non-fallacious argument (and indeed, given its complexity, is more likely to convince them of the impossibility of ever doing so). Informal logic approaches usually focus on dissection of relatively short texts on different topics, pre-selected for the students. Walters (1994) argues that this has been harmful pedagogically in that:

> standard textbooks and courses in critical thinking typically concentrate on exercises and lectures that drill students in the mechanics of logical argumentation (inductive and deductive reasoning, fallacy recognition, quantitative and statistical calculation, evidence assessment, and problem solving), while ignoring or at best minimally attending to modes of thinking that emphasize imaginative creativity, personal commitment, self-inspection, or a sensitivity to contractual styles of discourse and persuasion. (p. 4)

The risk is that potentially 'good thinkers' become transformed into 'mechanical logic-choppers' (p. 10), potentially intolerant of other more flexible and perhaps discovery-oriented thinking approaches. Ruggeiro (2003) points out that there has been little input from the field of creative thinking in terms of 'insights and strategies' (p. 375) into critical thinking. He argues that advocates of creative thinking (which focuses on encouragement of 'imaginativeness', 'originality' and 'ingenuity') and students of critical thinking (which focuses on evaluation of the ideas of others) operate with little cross-fertilization (p. 375). Creative thinking is discussed in Chapter 3. As Gallo (1994) points out, the focus in critical thinking is on convergent thinking, that is, 'inference and evaluation against articulated standards', which homes in on the best response (p. 46). The student has no opportunity to build up in-depth field knowledge or to practise information gathering or evaluating which information is worth collecting.

Fifthly, as Burbules et al. (1999) point out, it is unclear what the relationship is between dispositions, social relations and institutional contexts. Critical thinking approaches focus on the individual but do not consider how to foster appropriate dispositions (p. 49).

Additionally, although there are many related practical teaching and testing materials, there is little empirical research on the effects of these.

In seeking a vision of criticality suitable for the twenty-first century, this general thinking skills approach is useful for reminding us that there are universal rules of logic which cross disciplinary boundaries and for highlighting various aspects of thought in taxonomies. It is useful to be aware of the tools developed for deconstructing arguments, if difficult to apply them in practice. However, the limitations of critical thinking approaches must be recognized.

In terms of Barnett's (1997) framework, although focused on general life problems as well as specific academic problems, informal logic/thinking skills approaches usually prioritize the domain of formal knowledge. They usually operate at Barnett's lower levels as the primary interest is in deconstructing existing arguments according to logical rules, rather than transforming argument. Paul's (1982, 1987) interest in 'strong' and 'weak' conceptions of critical thinking comes closest to approximating Barnett's interest in domains and levels.

Resources

The approach

Another theoretical framework, also arising from philosophy, was proposed by Bailin et al. (1999a) and focused on the intellectual resources needed to achieve critical thinking/criticality. The authors note the limitations of approaches which essentially propose taxonomies of skills and attitudes, with little indication of how students might achieve them. They point out that 'such lists imply nothing about the psychological states, capacities or processes that enable critical thinkers to have the requisite accomplishments, and nothing about the kinds of instructional procedures that are likely to be efficacious in bringing them about' (p. 290). Bailin et al., therefore, propose a range of intellectual resources necessary for critical thinking to happen, and also instructional approaches to encourage their development.

Bailin et al. (1999a) suggest that someone has to have access to the following intellectual resources to be critical:

- background knowledge: what someone knows or can find out about an issue;
- knowledge of critical thinking standards in a particular field: knowledge of relevant standards and principles (e.g. the credibility of statements made by authorities), including the ability to use them in a non-mechanical way;
- possession of critical concepts: ability to identify and work with, for example, assumptions, arguments, implications of arguments, statements, definitions;

- knowledge of a wide range of strategies or heuristics useful in thinking critically: for example, thinking of counter-examples, or discussing a problem or issue with another person;
- certain habits of mind: respect for reasons and truth and an inquiring attitude.

They further suggest three pedagogic components:

- engaging students in dealing with tasks that call for reasoned judgement or assessment;
- helping them develop intellectual resources for dealing with these tasks; and
- providing an environment in which critical thinking is valued and students are encouraged and supported in their attempts to think critically and engage in critical discussion. (pp. 298–9)

Limitations and contributions

For us, the notion of resources is potentially useful for identifying where difficulties with criticality arise for students and how to address them. However, these ideas have not been developed conceptually or explored empirically. They focus largely on the domain of formal knowledge and assume that knowledge is objective and so obtainable. Criticality is viewed as neutral and transparent. There is no consideration of the political agenda behind criticality as an instrumental or transformatory or emancipatory force.

It would also be useful to understand more about the portability of resources between domains and the relationship between resources and the social and cultural background of students; it may be that certain types of students have access to more resources than others. We draw here on Bourdieu's notion of capital. Capital is essentially a form of power in a given field which may take various interlinked forms: economic, cultural and social. Capital is activated, spent or transferred by individuals in accordance with their *habitus*, which is the subconscious, internalized and tacit interpretation of the world and rules governing one's perceptions, aspirations, preferences and actions (Bourdieu, 1996; Delanty, 2001). It may be that certain students, by virtue of who they are and where they come from, have more resources/knowledge/capital than others, or that some can use their capital more effectively than others, according to their habitus.

Criticality embedded in specific fields

The approaches

Interest in field-specific conceptions of thinking comes from various directions: philosophy, psychology, sociology and, especially, education (e.g. Becher et al., 2001; Biglan, 1973; Bloom et al., 1956; Broudy, 1977; Bruner, 1963; Donald, 1985, 1986, 1995; Hirst, 1974/1998; Kuhn, 1970; Lattuca et al., 1994). Through their focus on field-specific contextual aspects, these approaches make useful contributions to discussions of criticality. Please note that discussions of field-specific differences in expertise, relevant to this section, are in Chapter 3.

One strand within philosophy and education (McPeck, 1981, 1990a, 1990b; Peters, 1966; Toulmin, 1958) perceives key aspects of thinking as field specific, including content, procedures, merit and rationality. Peters (1966) argued that 'it is . . . absurd to think that procedures can be handed on without content. Critical thought is vacuous without anything concrete to be critical about and there are as many brands of "critical thinking" as there are disciplines' (pp. 53–4). Barrow (1999), an educational philosopher, has argued this position:

> To be logical in science requires more than sifting through scientific argument with one's knowledge of logic; it requires understanding the key organizing concepts and methods of science. Putting it at its simplest, it takes an understanding of science to recognise what is contradictory in a scientific argument . . . a person cannot be a critical, thinking scientist without being a scientist, and the same goes for anything else that is an organised type of inquiry or field of endeavour with its own unique organizing concepts. This is why it is so often the case that the distinguished novelist talks idiotically about politics, or the eminent scientist does not seem to understand educational questions, and the lawyer does not understand morality. (pp. 134–5)

Some are influenced by Wittgenstein's work which focuses on the centrality of language in shaping and expressing thought. Each field has its own 'rules' of predication or 'language-game' essential for expressing the concepts and the content of the discipline. Through these language games, 'which govern what can and cannot be thought or said coherently', disciplines can address issues of conceptualization, evidence and rationality (McPeck, 1990b, p. 36).

Others have opposed such field-specific views. Paul (1990) contended that McPeck's view ignored thinkers such as Plato, Freud and Voltaire, whose influential work spanned many spheres (p. 106). He argued that we should consider the totality of our life experience, rather than delegate responsibility to specialists (p. 109). Students should be encouraged to recognize 'that in virtually every area of our lives . . . there are multiple conflicting viewpoints and theories vying for our allegiance, the possible truth of virtually all of which calls for shifts in our global perspective' (p. 110).

McPeck (1990b) himself responded to Paul's argument, recognizing that everyday problems do lie across categories, and that they are multifaceted (pp. 117–18). He placed his approach overtly within a framework of liberal education, as he recognized the importance of developing autonomous thinkers with a broad understanding. He argued that students should develop understandings of the strengths and weaknesses of the structures under-girding particular bodies of knowledge and that they should also be made aware of alternatives (pp. 30–3). He agreed with Paul's emphasis on the importance of worldview (p. 120).

Some have suggested an intermediate position which acknowledges both context-specific and general logical knowledge. Recently, Elder et al. (2006) have argued for certain general critical rules to be pursued within different disciplinary contexts. They consider that to analyse thinking, in whichever context, people have to learn to identify its elemental structures, which are: the purpose of the thinking; the viewpoint of the thinker; the assumptions underlying the thinking; the implications of the reasoning; the information needed to support the thinking; related inferences and conclusions; underlying concepts and theories; and key questions to be answered. These structures will vary in precise content and nature according to disciplinary context.

Ennis (1989) has argued that a continuum of approaches to teaching critical thinking exists, ranging from those which see critical thinking as general (critical thinking principles using everyday knowledge for exemplification) through to infusion (where there is subject matter plus explicit discussion of critical thinking principles) and then immersion approaches (where general critical thinking principles are not made explicit). It seems reasonable to conclude that criticality in our sense is a mix of localized and more general rules.

We now examine what the literature says about the specificity of thinking in different fields, which tend to be categorized according to different criteria.

Some categorizations are based on philosophical speculation and observation (e.g. Broudy, 1977; Hirst, 1974/1998; Kuhn, 1970) and some on empirical research (e.g. Biglan, 1973; Kolb, 1981; Lodahl et al., 1972). Lodahl et al. investigated the structure of scientific fields; Biglan perceptions of academics; and Kolb the learning strategies of students in different fields.

Broudy (1977) argued that all disciplines have a knowledge base but that they vary in several respects:

> it is sometimes difficult to recognize their maps, classifications, and directions as applying to a common territory . . . Some classifications are based on the nature of the subject matter being studied; some on the methods of studying it. Some are characterized by their epistemic status, for example, the differences between opinion, belief, and knowledge; between knowledge by acquaintance and knowledge by description (Russell, 1912) or Gilbert Ryle's distinction between knowing what and knowing how. (Ryle, 1949)

He invited the reader to 'compare the questions that an epistemologist, psychologist, humanist, and educator might ask of a discipline X' (p. 1), illustrating the different foci according to discipline:

> Epistemologist: What is the logical structure of X? What are the entities, relations that enter into its laws or generalizations? What are its modes of inquiry, and what are the criteria for the validity of its results?
>
> Psychologist: How does one discover the structure of X? How do people learn this structure? Are there stages in this process? What factors are involved in the success or failure of the process?
>
> Humanist: What is the import of X for human goals? What is its significance for humanity and for individual selves?
>
> Educator: How does what the psychologist or epistemologist say about the learning of X help in the teaching of X? How does what the humanist says about X figure in the teaching of X or in deciding whether or not X should be taught and to whom? (pp. 1–2)

The literature suggests many aspects of difference between fields. Those most central to understandings of how criticality might work in particular fields, are:

- the nature of organizing concepts and logical structure;
- the truth criteria used and claims made;

- the nature of knowledge, its growth and the specific knowledge base;
- the underlying aims and major cognitive purpose;
- the particular nature of key intellectual skills, the enquiry methods employed;
- the representation of knowledge;
- the nature of teaching, learning and assessment;
- values and ethical codes; and
- social and cultural characteristics (including intra- and inter-disciplinary relationships).
  (Bailin et al., 1999a; Becher, 1989; Becher et al., 2001; Bloom et al., 1956; Braxton, 1995; Bruner, 1963; Donald, 1985, 1986, 1995; Elliott, 1998; Ford et al., 1964; Grossman, 1990; Hirst, 1974/1998; Kolb, 1981; Lattuca et al., 1994; Neumann et al., 2002; Shulman, 1986; Ylijaki, 2000).

In order to function effectively in a specific field, students must understand and be able to operationalize the relevant aspects.

We now discuss some of these aspects, including consideration of how they might operate, according to the literature, in the two academic fields examined in this book: Modern Languages and Social Work. Often, the starkest contrasts drawn are between the sciences and humanities, rather than between social sciences and the humanities, our main areas of interest. A common categorization found in the literature, deriving from the work of Biglan (1973), describes disciplines as (1) hard or soft and (2) pure or applied. The first is based on the degree to which a disciplinary paradigm exists, as defined by Kuhn (1962), that is, as 'a body of theory which is subscribed to by all members of the field' (Biglan, 1973, p. 195). The second is concerned with the degree of application of the field. Disciplines will be more or less 'convergent' and homogeneous in terms of these patterns, and will change and develop over time (Becher et al., 2001).

Modern Languages (soft, pure) is a wide-ranging humanities-based field which includes the study of languages, literature, culture, history, film and linguistics. Social Work (soft, applied) is a broad-ranging, professionally oriented Social Science, which includes the study of sociology, social policy, law, human development, and ethics alongside social work itself, and involves practice and professional reflection.

Donald (1986), an educationalist, gives examples of key *organizing concepts* underpinning different fields. She suggests that in the psychology of thinking the most important organizing concept is that of theories, which are 'symbolic systems, summaries that allow one to predict, understand, explain'. In law, the most important concept is that of common law methodology, 'a system of analysis by which litigation is determined and which entails the observance of precedent in that determination . . . ' (p. 275). As Donald pointed out, organizing concepts vary from concrete to abstract, from theory to methods (p. 275).

Donald (1986) suggests that *truth criteria*, the standards by which we 'measure truth or validity constitute a . . . level of analysis' which interacts with the logical structure in a field' (p. 269). She suggests that in science, the focus is on coherence, reliability and consistency over time and goodness of fit to a particular explanation or concept. In the humanities, the truth is uncertain and dependent on individual critical judgements because divergent and creative thinking is valued (p. 269). Social scientists depend somewhat on logical structures and specific criteria in making judgements, but these structures and criteria are far less developed than in the sciences. Social scientists suggest and observe general patterns which can be validated through general agreement (p. 276). These differences are echoed by Lattuca et al. (1994). Kolb (1981) also points out internal differences within fields, arguing that some include 'considerable variation in inquiry norms and knowledge structures' (p. 244). For example, 'sociology can be highly abstract and theoretical (as in Parsonian structural functionalism) or concrete and active (as in phenomenology or ethnomethodology)' (p. 244).

The literature suggests characteristics we may find at a local level. Donald (1986) compares history and literature, two of our Modern Languages sub-fields: 'Although history can quote sources, literature tends to be judged in terms of its expressive effect and the imagination underlying its production. The thought structures and processes are their own validation' (p. 276).

Elder et al. (2006) compare history and sociology, another two of our sub-fields. In history, for example, the underlying purpose of thinking is 'to create a "story" about the past that captures its dynamics and helps us make decisions about the present and plans for the future' (p. 32). In sociology, the underlying purpose of thinking is 'to learn how and why people act in the way they do as a result of living with others in groups' (p. 33).

In terms of *the nature of knowledge,* Lattuca et al. (1994) argue that 'the softer fields [both Modern Languages and Social Work in our case] acquire knowledge more often by recursive patterns of research than by systematic accretion'. They 'use multiple perspectives and pursue knowledge in several directions simultaneously, leaving room for curricular diversity' (p. 419).

Becher et al. (2001) suggest that in such soft fields knowledge is 'reiterative; holistic (organic/river-like); concerned with particulars, qualities, complication; personal, value-laden; dispute over criteria for knowledge verification and obsolescence; lack of consensus over significant questions to address' (p. 36). Elliott (1998) argued that 'some disciplines . . . are as much concerned with considering every plausible mode of understanding a topic as with achieving a true understanding of it', whereas others 'seek to build solidly truth on truth' (p. 98).

In applied social sciences such as education, law, social policy – or, by extension, social work – Becher et al. (2001) suggest that knowledge is 'functional; utilitarian (know-how via soft knowledge); concerned with enhancement of [semi-] professional practice; uses case studies and case law to a large extent; results in protocols/procedures' (p. 36).

In terms of *main cognitive purpose*, Neumann et al. (2002) argue that in fields which emphasize soft pure knowledge [such as Modern Languages] the emphasis is typically 'on a broad command of intellectual ideas, on creativity in thinking and fluency of expression'. Thinkers are expected to consider issues in broad terms, and students to undergo considerable personal development and growth of critical capacities during their courses. This relates strongly to the liberal conception of education (p. 410). In contrast, soft applied programmes [such as Social Work], have a 'vocational slant'. 'Their knowledge base tends to be more eclectic'. However, they share with soft pure fields the emphasis on 'personal growth and intellectual breadth'. The importance of 'a growing base of knowledge . . . a necessary condition for making meaning of professional experience' is emphasized. Involvement in professional activity therefore tends to be a gradual development in the undergraduate degree (pp. 410–12).

Methods of enquiry also differ between fields. Bloom et al. (1956) argued that 'each subject field has a body of techniques, criteria, classifications, and forms which are used to discover specifics as well as to deal with them once they are discovered' (p. 68).

At a more specific level, Donald (1986) highlighted differences between subfields. Citing Rosenberg (1979), she suggested that '. . . the historian is tied by sensibility and socialisation to the particular', whereas 'the models which social scientists create can be tested and verified and their logical structure can therefore be defined or at least represented' (Donald, 1986, p. 276).

In terms of *representation of knowledge* (either spoken or written), Donald (1987) argued that 'the truth strategies, or sets of rules which guide the search for knowledge, are more explicit and systematic in the physical and biological sciences. It follows that representation should be more feasible in disciplines which have clearer procedures for validation' (p. 191).

Some have suggested a relationship between *the nature of teaching* and specific fields. Dewey (1902) argued that teachers must learn to 'psychologise' their subject matter, that is, to rethink disciplinary topics and concepts to make them accessible to students. Shulman (1986) talked of pedagogical content knowledge, 'a second kind of content knowledge . . . which goes beyond knowledge of subject matter per se to the dimension of subject matter knowledge *for teaching*. I . . . speak . . . of the particular form of content knowledge that embodies the aspects of content most germane to its teachability' (Shulman, p. 9). Jan Parker (2001) argued that:

> The humanities are bound together . . . by their common tradition of teaching as a mutual rather than one-way, top down activity. This mutuality is fundamental to teaching and learning the humanities, affecting both the way that knowledge is acquired and understood and the development and kinds of skill required to utilise and communicate that knowledge. (pp. 22–3)

In terms of classroom practice Braxton (1995, pp. 60–1) cited various studies which suggest that in soft disciplines, lecturers focus on the following aspects:

- 'student growth and development, preparation and needs' and 'a more discursive approach to teaching' (Stark et al., 1990);
- discussion of 'points of view other than one's own, discussion of issues beyond those covered in course readings, and the relating of course topics to other fields of study' (Graff et al., 1971);
- 'oral and written communication skills, critical reading skills, and active learning as methods of pedagogy' (Lattuca et al., 1995);
- 'lecturing on topics derived from current scholarly books, assigning research activities, and assigning current journal articles as required course reading'.

These views suggest that students will learn to function in disciplines according to modelling and practice in the classroom and in texts they read.

Kolb (1981) suggested differences in *learning style* according to discipline. He posited differences between disciplines on continua such as abstract to concrete approaches and active to reflective approaches. He suggested ongoing links between a student's choice of subject and their development:

> The student's developmental process is a product of the interaction between his or her choices and socialization experiences in academic

disciplines. That is, the student's dispositions lead to the choice of educational experiences that match those dispositions, and the resulting experiences further reinforce the same choice dispositions for later experiences. (p. 245)

Kolb also proposed that students who choose a discipline where their learning styles are not appropriate will perform less well, will feel their workload to be higher and may feel less well adapted to the university (pp. 246–7).

In terms of disciplinary socialization, as Becher et al. (2001, p. 48) describe, possible approaches are twofold. Some constructivist approaches emphasize 'the role of individual agency in identity and cultural construction' (e.g. Tierney, 1997). Other 'situated practice' approaches emphasize 'socialisation and learning within "communities" of practice' with the focus on 'historical and social context' (e.g. Lave et al., 1991).

Limitations and contributions

This literature contributes useful understandings of the structure and functioning of disciplines, and the shape that criticality takes in each. Recent work by philosophers on links between general thinking skills and specific domain knowledge and skills suggests how Barnett's view of the importance of cross-domain thinking can be realized. It accords with work done by cognitive psychologists on transfer, as discussed in Chapter 3.

In terms of limitations, the disciplinary literature does not add anything to the general liberal position on *why* it is important to think well. In Barnettian terms, it relates largely to the domain of formal knowledge and does not specify differences in levels of thinking. It assumes that functioning effectively within disciplinary rules is desirable and unproblematic. However, disciplines have two aspects; on one hand they are enabling, allowing knowledge to exist and to grow, questions to be asked and knowledge to be circulated and challenged. However, they are also constraining (Barnett, 1997; Grant, 1997). Questions can only be asked and knowledge expressed in certain ways. As Barnett (1997) wrote:

> Bodies of knowledge are also sites of organized power (Foucault, 1980). Their definitions of the world impose themselves on those who fall under their sway. Those who inhabit them rarely experience their oppressive character, but even those distinguished in their fields can feel that burdensome weight if they dare to step outside the presupposition of under-

standing and the sanctioned forms of inference and presentation of 'evidence'. Both the social sciences and the natural sciences brook no dissent from the uninitiated: the non-expert are expected to accept the definitions of the world that are imposed on them. (p. 17)

Criticality as political engagement

Criticality can also be viewed in the context of political engagement. This usually takes one of two forms: (a) social emancipatory approaches or (b) citizenship education.

Social emancipatory approaches

The approaches

Rather than viewing educational systems as liberating and democratizing, social emancipatory approaches view educational systems as supportive of the ideological hegemony of capitalism and of the status quo, through such means as 'the rhetoric of meritocracy, . . . testing, . . . tracking, . . . vocational training or college preparatory curricula, and so forth' (Burbules et al., 1999, p. 50). Freire (1970/2000) argues that education is a major instrument for the creation and maintenance of the 'culture' of silence because those who are oppressed cannot achieve critical awareness or respond effectively. Instead there is ignorance and lethargy.

Freire (1970/2000) argued for the development of *conscientização*, that is, 'critical consciousness' or 'learning to perceive social, political, and economic contradictions, and to take action against the oppressive elements of reality' (p. 35). He deplored what he called the 'banking' concept of education where students passively receive, file and store knowledge from their oppressors who hand knowledge to them as a gift (pp. 72–3). He argued that teachers and students should work together permanently to re-create knowledge through common reflection and critical action (p. 69). As Burbules et al. explain, in these approaches 'the object of thinking critically is not only against demonstrably false beliefs, but also those that are repressive, partisan, or implicated in the preservation of an unjust status quo' (p. 51). Knowledge, in this view, is part of power relations within society (p. 47).

According to writers such as Freire (1981) and Giroux (1983), learning to think critically is a matter of an oppressed social grouping learning how to resist and liberate itself from social shackles, or of others working to liberate such a group. Collectively, human beings have sufficient agency to struggle, resist and transform society, and education is a potential space for resistance. Critical thinking is embodied in the critical consciousness of the masses. It is normed according to the values and interests of social groups, typically the oppressive group but potentially the oppressed. A critical person is 'one who is empowered to seek justice, to seek emancipation. Not only is the critical person adept at recognising injustice but, for critical pedagogy, that person is also moved to change it' (Burbules et al., p. 50).

Shaull (2000) argues that the ideas applied by Freire in poor areas of Latin America are also applicable in the first world where the advanced technological society is making us into objects and 'subtly programming us into conformity to the logic of the system. To the degree that this happens, we are also becoming submerged in a new "culture of silence"' (p. 33). Macedo (2000) points out that many Schools of Education in the US ignore the ideas of Freire, a form of censorship by omission (p. 16).

Giroux (1988) advocates non-hierarchical classroom relationships where the students have a considerable amount of power and are encouraged to critically examine their lives and question the teacher, rather than viewing him/her as 'the expert, the dispenser of knowledge,' which is likely to 'crippl[e] student imagination and creativity' and 'promote passivity, docility, and silence' (p. 64).

Giroux claimed that critical scholarship is linked to oppositional struggle outside the classroom and should involve the role of public intellectual (p. xviii). He argued for 'transformative intellectuals' for whom 'thinking and acting are inextricably related' (pp. 100–1). Giroux distinguished between 'a language of critique' and 'a language of possibility' (Burbules et al., 1999, p. 51), saying that educators should provide hope for change, rather than just acceptance of the inevitability of oppression (p. 51).

Limitations and contributions

Accusations have been made that critical pedagogy comes close to indoctrination, and that there is insufficient space available for people to disagree with its conclusions (Burbules et al., p. 54). Some have accused critical pedagogy of ignoring the claims and concerns of women and other groups, that is, of being another means of oppression (e.g. Ellsworth, 1989; Gore, 1993).

In addition, the work of critical pedagogists does not usually engage at the level of undergraduate courses. Those interested in criticality as emancipation are most interested in encouraging students to challenge the status quo but beyond that do not say much about, for example, transfer or development.

These approaches operate near the top of Barnett's (1997) table, across all domains. Unlike some other approaches, the 'world' is central in critical pedagogy. From our perspective, this literature is useful for raising awareness of the need to be conscious of and, in some way, to address oppressive practices in various shapes and at various levels of operation, including in the classroom itself.

Citizenship education

The approach

Political engagement can also take the form of citizenship education. Barber (1992) claims that a major issue facing civil society is that of providing citizens with:

> The literacy required to live in a civil society, the competence to participate in democratic communities, the ability to think critically and act deliberately in a pluralist world, the empathy that permits us to hear and thus accommodate others; all involve skills that must be acquired. (p. 4)

These views are often associated with 'civic republicanism' which focuses on civic rights, responsibilities and participation as the best defence of liberty (Annette, pp. 78–9).

In this tradition, Schneider (2001) argues for renewal of civic education through higher education, which can encourage and develop the knowledge and dispositions necessary for a vibrant public sphere, where civil engagement means 'becoming more active on unsolved challenges both at home and abroad' (p. 18). She thinks that this is happening as new fields of study (e.g. Women's Studies, Deaf Studies, Gay and Lesbian Studies) have opened up active engagement with social issues (p. 20). These fields oblige students to think about issues such as social justice, power and identity (p. 20). Schneider thinks that 'learning communities' where students take topically linked courses such as 'global hunger' and 'sustainable change' indicate the emergence of 'an engaged academy' (p. 21) and promote the goals of 'justice, equity and democratic accountability' (p. 25). She believes such engagement should become central to the academy's role; in different fields of study, students will need different kinds of preparation for 'democratic involvement' and 'social responsibility' according to their likely different employment spheres. She calls for 'a far-reaching conversation about education for citizenship as an actively owned commitment of the American academy' (p. 27).

Mattson and Shea (1997) write about 'service learning' (active learning based in the community) in the US, and the civic role of universities. They argue that universities have become a training ground for professional competence, downplaying citizenship and engagement in public life. Instead, higher education should aim to develop public citizens as well as private employees who are willing to engage both in their communities and in national and international affairs (p. 3). Universities should ensure that students become engaged in community issues, and then examine these issues critically in the classroom (p. 7). They argue that such involvement 'makes abstract lessons about politics and ethics more concrete' and increases students' 'reflective, critical engagement in the everyday activities of public life' (p. 8); they become more aware of issues outside their own 'private worlds' (p. 13). These views are echoed by Annette (2000) who argues for critical thinking about values which can be fostered by work within different communities (p. 78).

Limitations and contributions

Civic responsibility is in the liberal tradition of public service, and it can be argued that it is missing from many recent policy documents, which consider citizenship largely in the shape of economic participation in the economy in an era of ever-growing economic competitiveness (e.g. DfES, 2003; DBIS, 2009).

Citizenship education clearly relates to Barnett's concern for interaction between the domains of formal knowledge, the self and the world and is therefore a useful aspect of criticality for us to bear in mind. However, the level at which critical links are made is somewhat unclear.

In Chapter 3, we continue our review of the literatures of criticality.

Chapter 3

Conceptualizations of Criticality in Higher Education: Psychological Approaches

In this chapter, we continue to review literature criticality with an examination of psychological approaches, before drawing this and the previous chapter to a conclusion.

Psychological approaches

Approaches to thinking in cognitive and developmental psychology work within a positivist paradigm, assuming universal norms and the objective, verifiable and accretive nature of knowledge. They are often closely associated with empirical research and usually work tacitly within a liberal educational framework.

Cognitive approaches to thinking

The approach

We explore the role of cognitive approaches in conceptualizing (1) cognition, including the nature of expertise; (2) transferability of thinking; and (3) development of thinking.

1. Cognition, including the nature of expertise

Information-processing models dominate in cognitive psychology, focusing on how the individual mind represents, organizes and processes knowledge (McGuinness, 1993). Cognitive psychologists are interested in cognitive architecture and phenomena such as long- and short-term memory, language, problem-solving, reasoning, decision-making, cognitive development and individual differences (p. 307). 'These cognitive structures are assumed to underlie such phenomena as problem-solving and transfer ability' (Palinscar, 1998, p. 347). They also consider the relations of cognitive processes to intelligence and the outcomes of thinking (Halpern, 2003, p. 8).

Cognitive psychologists usually talk of 'thinking skills' rather than 'critical thinking'. Thinking is viewed as a multi-skill activity rather than a unitary tendency or stage, with each skill individually teachable (Bereiter et al., 1987; Bernstein, 1995; Halonen, 1995; King, 1995; McBurney, 1995). Thinking is located in an individual's cognitive processes unlike in a socio-cultural approach, which would assume that individual 'cognitive processes are subsumed by social and cultural processes' (Palinscar, 1998, p. 371).

McGuinness (2005) describes how thinking skills include 'higher-order thinking', that is:

> the need for learners to go beyond the mere recall of factual information to develop a deeper understanding of topics, to be more critical about evidence, to solve problems, to think flexibly, and to make reasoned judgements and decisions rather than jumping to immediate conclusions. (p. 107)

Higher-order thinking is effortful, complex, yields multiple solutions and 'involves nuanced judgements and interpretations' (p. 110).

Cognitive psychologists (e.g. Costa, 2000; Perkins et al., 1993) also discuss dispositions, comprising motivations, attitudes, values and habits of mind related to thinking well, which they view as separate from cognition, their main focus of interest. Usually dispositions refer to qualities such as open-mindedness, curiosity, scepticism and reflection. Perkins et al. (1993) developed a taxonomy of seven dispositions, each comprised of abilities, inclinations and sensitivities. The *disposition to be planful and strategic*, for example, has three components. Thinkers need to have the *ability* 'to formulate goals and to evaluate alternative models of approach; the ability to make and execute plans and to forecast possible outcomes'. They need also to have the *inclination* 'to set goals and to make and execute plans; the tendency to approach things in a calculated and/or stepwise fashion; a desire to think ahead'. Additionally, they need to have the *sensitivity* to be alert 'to aimlessness, lack of direction, lack of orientation; alertness to off-hand thinking and sprawling thinking' (p. 9).

In dispositional approaches, there is some consideration of social, cultural and moral aspects by some writers. For example, Perkins et al. (1993) propose that to develop inclinations, 'one must provide learners with frequent opportunities to set goals and make plans for themselves in meaningful contexts' (pp. 17–18). Teachers should encourage students to perceive learning as cumulative and amenable to improvement through their own efforts (p. 16).

A major concern in cognitive psychology is expertise, which relates to criticality, on the assumption that experts might be better equipped to be critical than novices (although experts may identify too closely with their field of expertise to critique it as a novice outsider might). Investigation of experts and novices, two ends of capability continua, highlights differences in types and levels of knowledge, skills and thinking mechanisms. For example, Gobet et al. (2000) focus on particular chunking and retrieval strategies developed by experts.

Some have proposed staged models of expertise (e.g. Dreyfus and Dreyfus, 1986; Lesgold et al., 1988). Raufaste et al. (1998) proposed a category of super-experts who practise (in their case, radiological diagnosis) using conscious effort by reason of their roles as researchers and professors and so continue to develop and practise in a more deliberate fashion than basic-experts, who are busy practitioners.

Expertise varies by field. Earlier research in highly specified fields such as physics (e.g. Chi et al., 1981) and chess (e.g. Chase et al., 1973) stressed the importance of experts possessing a rich base of knowledge and a problem-solving approach to new challenges. Later research in more humanistic areas such as writing and history, similar to the fields in our study, found that expertise more closely resembled a capacity for problem *finding*, with experts spending longer on carrying out tasks because of the complexities and uncertainties involved (Wineburg, 1998, p. 320). Wineburg (1991) suggested that historical thinking does not involve problem-solving because outcomes are usually known, unlike science fields. The historian's responsibility is to construct an *explanation* of the outcome. He argued that expertise for historians lay in three related heuristics: *contextualization* ('the act of situating a document in a concrete temporal and spatial context'), *sourcing* ('the act of looking first to the source of the document before reading the body of the text') and *corroboration* ('the act of comparing documents with one another') (1991, p. 77). Expert historians viewed 'texts not as vehicles but as people, not as bits of information to be gathered but as social exchanges to be understood' (p. 83). In contrast, novice historians assumed that textbooks were unbiased and jumped to conclusions without contextualization through careful reading of documentary evidence (Wineburg, 1991, pp. 83–4).

The level of domain-specific intellectual skills required may vary according to level of expertise. For example, Perkins (1985) argued that 'the higher the level of competence concerned, the fewer *general* cognitive control strategies there are' (p. 348) as domain-specific knowledge becomes ever more important. Perkins et al. (2001) cite the case of chess-playing expertise, supposedly dependent on logical reasoning and planning. However, research reveals that chess skills are heavily dependent on chess-related schemata, that is, memories of patterns. They argue that this is also true for computer programming, mathematics and physics (p. 272). It seems unlikely though, even at these high levels, that general skills, knowledge or dispositions will be redundant.

Novice–expert studies are useful for describing differences between different groups, but usually do not address transition from one group to another, or how such a move could be facilitated by teachers. Raufaste et al. (1998) did suggest that greater expertise could be encouraged through continuing practice and reflection. A few studies (e.g. Nokes et al., 2007; Rouet et al., 1996) have investigated instruction among history students and provisionally concluded that using multiple texts and teaching heuristics to develop history students' capacities to synthesize and evaluate sources was more effective than using single textbooks and focusing solely on historical content.

2. Transferability of thinking

The transferability of thinking skills is a major issue for cognitive psychologists (De Corte, 1999; Halpern et al., 1995; Livingston et al., 2004).

Some cognitive psychologists focus on the general model of thinking skills, viewing cognition as 'driven by a central processor'; they argue that 'intervention at this level is likely to have widespread effects across many thinking domains' (McGuinness, 2005, p.110). This view is closely associated with Piagetian theories of cognition. A domain-specific model is associated with those focusing on disciplinary modes of thinking and expertise (pp. 110–11).

In the early 1970s researchers usually assumed that *general* heuristic knowledge led to good thinking. This position was supported by then-existing understandings of the functioning of memory which viewed abstracted, generalized semantic memories as far more stable and accessible than the fleeting and less important episodic memories (Foertsch, 1995, p. 365; Tulving, 1972). Semantic memories are 'generic items of knowledge that relate to an entire class or entities (like one's knowledge of cars), and "episodic" memories, which is knowledge that is tied to a particular context, a particular episode in space and time (like a memory of going for a ride in your uncle's 1967 Corvette)' (Foertsch, 1995, p. 365). Later, cognitive psychologists developed their understandings of how people think and, as critical thinking programmes designed to teach general intellectual skills proved problematic, scholars became more interested in the role of content knowledge and domain-dependent thinking (Brown et al. 1989; Gallagher, 1994; Glaser, 1984).

The difference between domain-specific and general intellectual skills is now better understood. Some argue that, under certain circumstances, skills relating to general heuristics can be transferred to specific domains (e.g. Voss et al., 1995). Markman et al. (2001) suggest that the distinction between abstract and domain-specific reasoning is best seen as a continuum. They posit strong and weak ways of thinking. In a weak approach, a thinker draws on general cognitive strategies which can operate without domain-specific knowledge, typically when encountering a new area. In a strong approach, a thinker draws on pre-existing knowledge representations and reasons by example (p. 225). Some basic skills and attitudes are common to many fields (e.g. scepticism about information presented, and the need for supporting evidence), although applied in different ways. Perkins et al. (1992) draw attention to the differences between near and far transfer (similar contexts and tasks and dissimilar contexts and tasks, respectively), suggesting that near transfer usually had a higher chance of success than far transfer, but that far transfer was not impossible. Perkins et al. (1993) argued in their conception of triadic dispositions that abilities might be domain specific while some inclinations and sensitivities might be general.

In memory research too, ideas have moved on. It is now thought that 'even the most abstract semantic memories reflect context to some degree' (Foertsch, 1995, p. 368). So we are dealing 'with a continuum, where the vast majority of memories have both some degree of generalisation and some degree of context dependency' (p. 369). This suggests that learning will most usually involve some elements of both general and particular memories.

In sum, current research suggests a flexible, iterative process of movement between general and specific strategies, knowledge and memories where each is implicated and integrally involved in the other when thinking within a particular field.

Volet (1999), an educational psychologist, emphasized cultural aspects of transfer, involving motivational and emotional capacities as well as cognitive aspects. She argued that personal capabilities interact with the surrounding educational context in ways which are more or less effective according to the match between the capabilities and the context.

Wineburg (1998) proposed that the capacity to adapt (transfer) knowledge may be a central characteristic of expertise, suggesting that experts are able to employ various sense-making strategies when without direct knowledge of a sub-field. In a study involving two history experts, one operating in an unfamiliar substantive field, each expert engaged in a dialogue with the textual materials encountered (p. 337). Each understood that they had to create a story from the textual evidence presented to them and that to do so was a complex, demanding cognitive task. The historian who was a non-expert in the specific field was able to bring his general historical strategies and heuristics to an unfamiliar historical field. Novices would not have such resources to draw on. Markman et al. (2001) argue that experts can rely on memories of previous experiences to reach conclusions. This can reduce working memory load as the need to think logically through different possibilities is more limited (although continued use of a past conclusion which worked can limit future abilities to find other fruitful conclusions) (pp. 228–31).

The implications of these understandings of transfer for pedagogy are complex. Given constraints on instructional time, how can students learn to transfer effectively and quickly?

Researchers have suggested low and high roads to developing transferable skills and knowledge. For Perkins et al. (2001) 'low-road' transfer occurs when reflexive, automatic skills, such as driving a car, are transferred to a closely relevant situation, such as driving a lorry. The nearness of the situations provokes automatic responses and memories, making transfer happen. Similarly, reading on one subject can transfer to reading on another (pp. 372–3). Closely related fields such as history and current affairs might facilitate this kind of transfer (p. 376). 'High-road' transfer involves reflective thought and depends on the 'deliberate mindful abstraction of skills and knowledge from one context for application in another' (p. 373). 'High-road transfer is not as dependent on superficial stimulus similarities, since through reflective abstraction a person can often "see through" superficial differences to deeper analogies' (p. 374). In both cases, 'thorough and diverse practice' of transfer performances is likely to encourage skill development (Perkins et al., 1992).

The development of metacognitive strategies, related to high-road thinking, is thought by some to be a powerful way to promote transfer. Perkins et al. (1992) and Foertsch (1995) argued that explicit abstraction of principles by teachers, students, or both is likely to encourage recognition of new situations which are similar in principle. Giving attention to another side of an argument and standing back from an argument to define and explore its nature are examples of relevant abstractions (Perkins et al., 2001, p. 375). Students' attention could also be drawn to patterns of thinking of intermediate generality such as the role of evidence across various hard sciences or the role of categories of style and form in arts subjects; the precise categories and styles will vary, but the general principles will hold in different areas (p. 377). Raising students' metacognitive awareness will expose them to strategies other than those they already use and raise awareness of their own strategies so that they may, if appropriate, be encouraged to try other options. Foertsch also argued that (transfer of) learning is most likely to be effective 'when general principles and reasoning processes are *taught in conjunction with* their real-life applications in varied, specific contexts' (p. 374). Foertsch cites research by Brown et al. (1989) which elaborates the conditions likely to facilitate successful teaching of transfer: the simultaneous use of 'specific examples and general principles'; directing learners' attention 'to the underlying structure and commonalities of related problems; mutual construction of rules; past experience for learners in the substantive problem domain; and a collaborative learning atmosphere' (pp. 374–5).

Another strand of metacognitive awareness consists of increasing student regulation, monitoring and appraisal of their own cognition by increasing their knowledge about what they should be doing (Brown, 1987, p. 66; McGuinness, 2005, p. 108) so that they can evaluate their efforts for efficiency and effectiveness (Flower et al., 1990; Hanley, 1995). Such self-monitoring and mindfulness of the potential of activities are likely to assist transfer (Perkins et al., 1992, pp. 6–7).

In effect, students need both subject knowledge (which will enable strategic reflection) and reflective strategies (or they will just stay with their largely inert subject knowledge) (Perkins et al., 2001, p. 377). Spiro et al. (1987) advocate:

> a cyclical alternation between abstraction-centred presentations, in which cases illustrate or concretise the abstractions, and case-centred presentations, in which the same abstractions are now used in combined form to describe the cases. (p. 13)

They argue that each of these approaches will help the other develop. As knowledge about individual cases increases, this should facilitate understanding of system at the abstract level, which is made up of individual cases. As knowledge of the abstract level increases, this should provide insights into the functioning of individual cases. This can be a cyclical, 'bootstrapping' process (p. 13).

Perkins et al.'s (1993) conception of domain-specific abilities and general inclinations and sensitivities explains how one could teach some general skills within a specific context and suggests the possibility of movement back and forwards between general and specific areas.

Lack of any element – general intellectual strategies, domain-specific strategies, content knowledge of the particular domain or metacognitive awareness – is likely to hamper the general exercise of higher-order thinking. For example, if people have a high content knowledge of a domain but none of the other elements, they will often learn the information as inert ideas only (Whitehead, 1932a). Perkins et al. (2001) report much evidence of 'inert' and 'passive' knowledge in fields such as medicine and computer programming (pp. 371–2).

The empirical evidence on transfer is mixed. There is some evidence of transfer after instruction in real classrooms, usually when instruction has focused on metacognition and has occurred within the same domain (Livingston et al., 2004, p. 24). However, such research often involves looking at areas where limited types of transfers (e.g. of a particular sub-skill) can be measured in ways acceptable to cognitive psychologists. Moreover, De Corte (1999) suggests that the particular theoretical convictions of the researchers strongly influence data interpretation (p. 556).

3. Development of thinking

Cognitive psychologists have also developed thinking skills frameworks which offer possible models for how undergraduates learn.

Moseley et al. (2004, 2005) reviewed 55 such frameworks, devised by psychologists, educationalists and philosophers. Moseley et al. (2005) suggested four family groups for the frameworks:

- models and theories of personality, thought and learning (*the all-embracing family*);
- models and theories of instructional design (*the designer family*);
- models and theories of 'critical' and 'productive' thinking (*the higher-order family*);
- models and theories of cognitive structure and/or cognitive development (*the intellectual family*). (pp. 372–3)

Description of some of these frameworks gives a flavour of how far they can contribute to our understandings of criticality. Those selected are aimed at educators, have an instructional focus and have been developed by psychologists.

Feuerstein's 'instrumental enrichment' programme is one of general thinking skills, intended originally to develop the thinking of slow-learning teenagers (Feuerstein et al., 1980). McGuinness (2005) reports that Feuerstein's theoretical base 'pre-dates "modern" cognitive psychology', and incorporates many ideas from socio-cultural theory, such as Vygotsky's notions of learning mediation and the zone of proximal development (p. 112).

Bloom et al. (1956) made an early and influential attempt to develop a hierarchical taxonomy of cognitive processing and skills, designed to assist assessment in higher education. They subdivided *knowledge* into knowledge of specifics (terminology and specific facts); knowledge of ways and means of dealing with specifics (conventions, trends and sequences, classifications and categories, criteria and methodology); and knowledge of the universals and abstractions in a field (principles and generalizations, theories and structures). They divided *skills and abilities* into comprehension, application, analysis, synthesis and evaluation. Each of these was again sub-divided; these skills and abilities were considered to be of increasing levels of complexity. Moseley et al. (2004) report that this framework is used widely to assist in the design of teaching. Anderson et al. (2001) have updated and revised Bloom's original framework, mainly from the perspective of school level education. They propose six cognitive processes (remembering, understanding, applying, analysis, evaluation, creativity) and four knowledge categories (factual, conceptual, procedural and metacognitive).

Halpern (2003) provides another thinking skills framework for higher education. She proposes that various skills (e.g. argument analysis), cognitive capacities (e.g. memory) and dispositions are necessary for critical thinking. She is interested in metacognition as well as motivation and proposes a four-part model for teaching critical thinking:

- students should explicitly learn the skills of critical thinking;
- students should develop the disposition for effortful thinking and learning;
- teachers should direct learning activities in ways that increase the probability of transcontextual transfer (structure training);
- teachers should make metacognitive awareness monitoring explicit and overt. (p. 14)

Halpern focuses on generic skills, applicable across a range of knowledge domains: reasoning, analysing arguments, hypothesis testing, making decisions, establishing likelihoods. She also suggests six dispositions for critical thinking: willingness to plan, flexibility, persistence, willingness to change your mind, being mindful, consensus seeking (Halpern, pp. 15–18).

Moseley et al. (2005) propose a synthesized model for understanding thinking and learning, drawing on elements in the frameworks they reviewed.

The cognitive skills section of the framework has three components: information gathering, building understanding and productive thinking. Information gathering 'subsumes skills involved in perception, recognition and retrieval' (Moseley et al., 2005, p. 378). Building understanding includes understanding, elaborating and using (p. 376). Productive thinking is 'higher-order' thinking which relates to Bloom's *analysis, synthesis and*

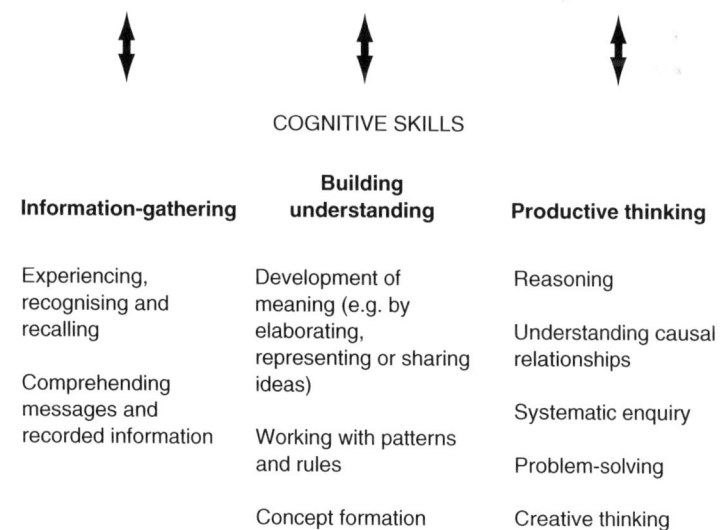

Figure 3.1 An integrated model for understanding thinking and learning (Moseley et al., 2005, p. 378)

evaluation; it 'should result in a productive outcome such as a deeper understanding of an issue, a judgement, solution or decision, or in a tangible product, such as an invention or work of art' (p. 377). Strategic and reflective thinking includes metacognition and self-regulation. It indicates 'conscious purpose, careful monitoring and evaluation' and may happen at any stage during the cognitive processes (pp. 378–9). Progression through the three cognitive stages is likely to be iterative, although with movement in the direction of productive thinking. Cognitive processes may happen without reflective and strategic processes, but learning is more likely to happen when they are involved (p. 379).

There have been various reviews in recent years of research on instructional approaches to the development of thinking skills, similar to those described above, usually with children (e.g. Glevey, 2006). Moseley et al. (2004) report that the effectiveness of such approaches with post-16 learners is not well researched and, indeed, the evidence as described below is inconclusive.

Moseley et al. suggest that 'the value of thinking skills approaches stems from attention given' in associated pedagogic approaches to learner engagement (motivation and beliefs), metacognition (knowledge of how one's cognition works) and self-regulation (the strategic management of thinking through devices such as planning and monitoring) (p. 1). Higgins et al. (2004) conducted a systematic review on the effectiveness and nature of impact of various thinking skills interventions in schools. They commented on the delay likely between input and effects on attainment, and suggested that different groups may respond differently to thinking skills programmes.

Livingston et al. (2004), who focused on post-16 learning, found that there were few studies they considered satisfactory of programmes where thinking skills were taught separately. However, there were several programmes where thinking with specific subject knowledge was the focus; these indicated sound evidence of learner improvement in thinking within the subject. Where programmes focused on incorporating thinking throughout an existing curriculum, there was evidence of students' transfer of particular thinking processes to different parts of the curriculum. However, it was not clear whether this improved thinking could be transferred beyond the curriculum. Halpern (2003) also cites various empirical studies, usually in higher education, which suggest that thinking skills can be improved (pp. 11–12).

McGuinness (1999, 2005) categorizes interventions, mostly targeting schoolchildren, into three types: general thinking skills courses which are add-ons to the existing curriculum; subject-specific thinking; and infusion approaches which provide across-the-curriculum opportunities for work on thinking skills. The general skills enrichment approaches have been evaluated more thoroughly than the others. McGuinness (2005) reports, for example, that because the materials of Feuerstein's 'instrumental enrichment' programme are de-contextualized outside main subject matter, research has found problems with transfer of thinking (p. 113). She also reported on conditions for success for children's thinking skill programmes such as sufficient teacher development, management support for the programmes and prioritization in the curriculum.

McGuinness (2005) has argued that, despite diverse theoretical perspectives on learning thinking, there is a developing consensus on what actually works in encouraging children to think, although one cannot assume that this will transfer unproblematically to adults. She highlighted a growing recognition of the importance of metacognitive aspects for those coming from the cognitive tradition, and of the importance of dialogue and joint construction of meaning for those coming from a socio-cultural perspective.

Limitations and contributions

Cognitive psychologists work within a normative, positivist approach. They usually view critical thinking as being composed of neutral cognitive processes which are individualistic and de-contextualized, rather than as embedded in social practices which vary with culture and historical period. Given our understandings of criticality as contextualized, this focus is problematic. In Barnettian terms, cognitive psychologists usually focus on the domain of formal knowledge and usually have an atomized approach to critical thinking.

Dispositional approaches are problematic in that they acknowledge the importance of social and personality aspects of developing 'good' thinking, but do not acknowledge social and cultural variety. It is unclear exactly what dispositions are (apart from contextual influences, motivation and skills) and whether dispositions are innate or subject to environmental influences. Perkins et al. (2000) acknowledge that 'dispositions may well be noisy social–cultural constructs rather than corresponding to distinct cognitive processes'. Empirically it has not been demonstrated that dispositional approaches can increase the use of appropriate thinking dispositions, as most research focuses on abilities rather than dispositions (p. 287).

Approaches which suggest de-contextualized critical thinking skills can be taught separately from content knowledge are likely to be ineffective because of transfer problems. Overall, the literature on transfer of thinking skills, the role of metacognition and the development of thinking is thought-provoking and suggestive conceptually, but the empirical evidence is as yet inconclusive.

The taxonomies developed in thinking skills frameworks are 'useful for mapping out the "territory"' (McGuinness, 2005, p. 109) and, certainly for us, they are thought-provoking. However, 'they are not always well grounded in cognitive and developmental theories and the pedagogical implications are not immediately obvious' (p. 109).

Cognitive approaches suggest what the thinking of experts in areas such as history and, by extension, other arts and social science subjects might look like. They also make useful contributions in the areas of development and instruction. However, they usually assume that by breaking down skills and giving students practice they will learn to be critical, whereas other learning theories suggest a much more complex relationship between instructional input and learning, as discussed later in this chapter.

Creative thinking approaches

The approach

Creative thinking approaches in cognitive psychology focus on the creation and development of ideas. Cognitive and creative approaches to critical thinking operate separately and communicate little (Ruggeiro, 2003).

Creativity is viewed as contributing to 'individual and societal change and evolution' through the development of original, important ideas (Runco, 2004). Interest in creativity flourished after Guilford's (1950) address on creativity to the American Psychological Association when he suggested a focus on the following factors: 'sensitivity to problems, ideational fluency, flexibility [of mind], ideational novelty, synthesising ability, analysing ability, reorganising or redefining ability, span of ideational structure, and evaluating ability' (p. 454).

Creative approaches focus on 'imaginativeness', 'originality' and 'ingenuity' (Ruggeiro, 2003, p. 375), and sometimes 'appropriateness' (Lubart, 1994, p. 290). Research has focused on issues such as how far creativity is a general or a domain-specific ability. What does creativity mean for a mathematician as distinct from an artist, for example? Research indicates a wide degree of variation across domains, probably because of the nature of relevant cognition, motivation, personality, process, product and environmental factors (Lubart, 1994; Runco, 2004). Runco also discusses the possibility of cultural differences in creativity, suggesting that in Western culture, mathematical and verbal creativity is often highly valued, whereas in other cultural settings, creativity in 'spatial or other nonverbal domains' may be more valued (p. 678). Creativity occurs at different levels: individual, local and societal (Lubart, p. 290).

As Lubart explains, there are different conceptions of the origins of creativity: divine, psychodynamic with focus on inner tensions, cognitive and social-psychological. The *cognitive approach* has dominated since Guilford's work. He focused mainly on divergent thinking, that is, the 'the ability to generate many different ideas in response to a problem' (p. 296). Other psychologists in this tradition focus on perceptual processes, problem-definition skills, insight skills and induction skills (p. 297), or on the structure of the brain (Runco, 2004, pp. 664–5).

Those in the *social-psychological tradition* focus on personality traits associated with creativity: 'independence of judgement, self-confidence, attraction to complexity, aesthetic orientation and risk-taking' (Lubart, p. 298). Further attributes proposed and researched include tolerance of ambiguity, perseverance and openness to new experiences (pp. 309–10). Others suggest that self-actualization is a 'motivational force' which is 'promoted by a supportive, evaluation-free environment' and that 'boldness, courage, freedom, spontaneity, self-acceptance, and other traits lead a person to realise his or her full potential' (p. 299).

Social context is important in this approach. Relevant contextual factors include 'cultural diversity, war, availability of role models, availability of resources (such as financial support), and number of competitors in a domain' (Lubart, p. 299). Runco (2004) mentioned further situational factors identified by research as encouraging creativity: freedom (especially from criticism), encouragement (especially for originality), independence, autonomy, stimulation, zeitgeist, time (as many creative ideas come to fruition only over an extended period), and other people. Discouraging factors are 'a lack of respect (specifically for originality), red tape, constraint, lack of autonomy and resources, inappropriate norms, project management, feedback, time pressure, competition, and unrealistic expectations' (pp. 662–3). Some factors such as competition, however, may be potentially encouraging, according to context (p. 663).

Lubart suggests a range of *intellectual abilities* which encourage creativity and which may be general or domain-specific. Problem finding is an important high-level ability as many significant problems are 'not obvious or are actively ignored by most people' (p. 301). Problem definition and problem representation are related abilities which affect how the problem is understood – at what level and how clearly – and this in turn relates to how easy the problem is to address (pp. 301–2). Strategy selection for addressing problems is another high-level ability, which may involve convergent thinking (homing in on the one best response), divergent thinking (considering a wide range of options), or both. It is likely to involve heuristic search (focus on potential solutions) rather than exhaustive search (consideration of a wide range of unhelpful options) (p. 302). A third high-level ability is that of evaluation which may be continuous throughout creative work (p. 303).

Creativity researchers also suggest basic abilities such as insight and divergent thinking. For example, insight 'involves restructuring the nature of a problem or the elements that contribute to a problem's solution'. It 'may consist of noticing relevant new information, comparing disparate information and finding relevant connections, and combining information in a problem-relevant fashion' (Lubart, p. 303).

The link between general intelligence and creativity has been investigated, showing that 'creative individuals tend to be above average on general intelligence' as measured by intelligence quotient (IQ) tests (Lubart, pp. 305–6). However, the correlations between intelligence and creativity are highly variable across studies and frequently weak (p. 306). Various explanations are offered, including, first, 'the significance of personality traits and maturation rather than an increasing IQ', and, secondly, methodological problems in the tests used (p. 306).

Another component of creativity is *knowledge*. Runco (2004) argues that declarative knowledge has an ambiguous role in creativity. It 'may supply the individual with options when he or she is solving problems, but at the same time can inhibit creative thinking if the individual looks only to established knowledge' (pp. 667–8). However, knowledge also assists creativity in that it facilitates recognition and understanding of problems. It further enables someone to know how to move away from existing thinking, to know what is new knowledge; and to produce well-developed, successful ideas (Lubart, 1994, p. 307). Procedural knowledge, including tactics to encourage creativity, can have an important role (Runco, p. 668). If someone already has basic declarative and procedural knowledge, this allows them to focus on the development of new ideas (Lubart, p. 307). Hayes (1989) found that creative masterpieces in the shape of musical compositions and art tended to be produced only after several years of practice (cited in Lubart, 1994, p. 307).

Yet another potential component of creativity is *thinking style*. As Lubart explains, thinking styles 'exist at the interface between cognition and personality traits. Thinking styles are preferred ways of applying one's intellectual abilities and knowledge to a problem' (p. 308). People who have intuitive, inductive ways of thinking and those who prefer innovation over adaptation may be more creative (p. 308). However, the question of where thinking styles come from remains unanswered.

Creative thinking is heavily researched empirically, and both Lubart (1994) and Runco (2004) offer reviews. In the early years, attention focused more on the relationships between intelligence, personality and creativity. Now, greater attention is given to the social contextualization of creativity, often within the family or educational settings or organizations (Runco, 2004).

There is also discussion about levels of creativity. As Runco (2004) points out, it is sometimes thought about as something approximating to flexibility in response to changes in everyday life in a fast-changing society, which suggests reactivity, whereas others view it as making an extensive contribution to evolution and change.

Researchers have increasingly suggested that creativity *development* requires synthesis of multiple components (Runco, 2004), including an appropriate environment, motivation, relevant knowledge of a domain and creative skills. It has been argued that greater knowledge and skill will lead to increased creativity over time (Lubart, 1994, p. 300). Some have suggested that creativity may slump at particular ages and stages of schooling where conformity to educational norms and convergent thinking may be encouraged, although these slumps are by no means universal (Runco, pp. 668–70). Researchers have tried to link creativity to family background factors, including 'family tendencies and values' (p. 669).

Away from cognitive psychology, the creative element in thinking has also been acknowledged by the educational philosopher John Passmore (1980), who suggests that:

> Our society needs its critics just as it needs its imaginative creators. Within the institutions of science, let us say, those scientists who are prepared rigorously to test hypotheses which other scientists suggest play as vital a part as those more imaginative colleagues who formulate the hypotheses they criticise. (p. 174)

Limitations and contributions

Conceptualizations of creativity and associated research offer us various useful elements in our exploration of criticality such as the emphasis on the importance of context and personality traits, the focus on developing ideas (rather than dissecting them) and the interest in different levels of creativity. Creativity can be viewed through the kind of lens that Barnett (1997) applies to domains and levels, related to purposes.

Also useful are suggestions such as Gallo's (1994) on the advisability of combining both critical and creative thinking, that is, convergent and divergent thinking, together with empathy, in order to achieve effective thinking. For example, if one is to critique a new article, one should certainly evaluate the content of the article in a critical thinking sense of whether the argument is logical and reasonable. However, one should also generate other plausible explanations and note elements which are absent from the article (pp. 47–8).

Intelligence

The approaches

In this section, we consider how far criticality depends on innate intelligence and how far intelligence (and so criticality) can be taught and learned. There is some overlap between the first section, 'Cognitive Approaches to Thinking', p. 40 and this one, with some authors appearing in both.

Intelligence is a complex and contested phenomenon. Researchers disagree over the degree and nature of the heritability of intelligence, the role of nurture and the exact nature of intelligence. Some (e.g. Herrnstein et al., 1996) argue that there is an inherited general intelligence factor, apparently 'no less than 40% and no more than 80%', that education can do little to enhance (p. 23). This is a huge variation, but even the most pessimistic picture suggests a significant role for education.

Contemporary models of intelligence often focus on a complex systems approach, with consideration of both individual biological and social contextual factors. Sternberg's (1985) Triarchic Theory of Intelligence focuses on information-processing skills, abilities to optimize the match between a person's skills and their external environment, and the capacity to use previous experience to process new experiences and information. These three strands are described as analytical, practical and creative intelligence. Gardner et al.'s (1993) Multiple Intelligences theory proposes that different kinds of intelligence (e.g. linguistic, interpersonal, visual-spatial) are initially innate capacities which develop through training and socialization. Ceci et al.'s (1997) Bioecological Model focuses on the interactions between and intertwining of several innate potential abilities and environmental context; this theory is explicitly developmental, as biological predispositions are shaped by interaction with context in the shape of field-specific cognitive processes and knowledge as well as other aspects. These models provide especially useful explanations for how and why intelligence develops over time and in different contexts.

There is considerable controversy over whether musical abilities, kinaesthetic abilities and personal skills may be called intelligence or would be better labelled as 'talents' and 'interpersonal skills' (Herrnstein et al., 1996). Emotional intelligence (e.g. Mayer et al., 2000) is another controversial area.

Some issues in intelligence research parallel those addressed by cognitive approaches to thinking. As Grotzer et al. (2000) explain, some intelligence researchers are concerned not only with the ability to carry out a task, but also the sensitivity to the need to carry it out and the inclination to do it; they are interested in issues of persistence of learning and transfer to other tasks. They talk about the enablers that allow intelligent performance of tasks: knowledge of how to do something, experiential knowledge and neural factors (such as processing time).

Empirical research carried out in classrooms which have tried to enhance 'intelligence' using either the Sternberg or Gardner model, has suggested positive outcomes (Shearer, 2004; McGuinness, 2005). The findings overlap with those discussed in the first section, 'Cognitive Approaches to Thinking', p. 40. After reviewing the evidence, Grotzer et al. (2000) argue that it is possible to foster expert-like strategies, but that it is also important to foster the sensitivities and inclination to do tasks. Transfer of intelligent behaviour to other tasks over a long period of time cannot be assumed, and may best be encouraged by knowledge-building strategies such as memory aids and self-management in learning skills (p. 501). Enhancement of neural functioning to promote greater intelligence remains a remote possibility as research in this area is in its infancy (p. 502).

The cultural and temporal situatedness of intelligence has also been addressed. Sternberg (2000) suggests that Western conceptions of intelligence, which often emphasize 'speed of mental processing', may not be shared by other cultures which value depth of processing and such personal characteristics as unselfishness and social co-operation (pp. 5–7). He also suggests that understandings of intelligence change over time, pointing out that a symposium of experts in 1986 placed far greater emphasis on the importance of metacognition and context in defining intelligence than did a symposium of experts in 1921 (pp. 8–9). Gardner (1993) suggests that conceptions of intelligence have varied over the ages as abilities necessary for survival in particular societies changed (pp. 235–6).

Grotzer et al. (2000) focus on the cultural values of the classroom, the nature of the learning environment and the importance of emotional and intellectual involvement in learning (pp. 503–5). They argue that students should be encouraged to believe in their ability to learn and be intelligent, rather than believing intelligence is limited and beyond their control (p. 507).

Conceptions of intelligence are not ideologically, politically or socially neutral (Sternberg, 2000). For some, education should aim to develop an intellectual elite to lead society. For others, people are equal and interchangeable and so institutions should not favour one over another. For yet others, people should have equal educational opportunities, but some will be able to use the opportunities more productively (p. 12). Different conceptions place greater or lesser emphasis on biological, cultural and social aspects of learning.

Intelligence researchers have also focused on changes or otherwise over the life span. As Berg (2000) explains, a traditional view is that intelligence declines throughout adulthood. However, a contrary view asserts that adult intellectual development instead demonstrates a progressive integration of different types of thought (cognitive, interpersonal and emotional) so that more synthetic understandings of the world are possible. Adult life is more likely to demand skills and abilities in different areas such as social intelligence and professional life (p. 118). The development of intelligence throughout adulthood can be seen as a balance between these two trends (p. 117). This view of intelligence development includes consideration of (socio-cultural, biological and historical) context (Berg, 2000; Sternberg, 1985).

As age cohorts move through the life span, they may display different intelligence characteristics according to factors such as the particular educational experiences of a generational cohort. These characteristics should be associated with historical time, rather than as stages of adult development (Berg, pp. 118–19). Individuals show considerable variation in decline, maintenance or improvement of different intelligence functions across the life span according to a number of factors such as genetic inheritance, illness levels, educational background and the nature of daily activities (p. 122).

Over the life span, we may expect to see differential functioning at different ages according to the types of intelligence developed and required in particular contexts, which may vary.

Limitations and contributions

The intelligence literature has much to offer our understandings of criticality, as many of the discussions are analogous.

The ideological and political implications of different theories of intelligence for society and individuals can be transferred to different understandings of criticality. The importance of context, recognized in modern theories of intelligence, suggests that people may appear, and indeed may be, more intelligent in more familiar environments and their levels of intelligence may be assessed differently according to particular cultural and temporal environments. Biological inheritance plays some role in intelligence, but it has complex interactions with environmental factors. When considering how critical someone is, such factors and interactions should be taken into account.

Many personal qualities (such as persistence and willingness to cooperate) attributed to intelligent people in various cultures (Sternberg, 2000) are often recognized as being important aspects of criticality. Whether or not we recognize 'emotional intelligence' as a kind of 'intelligence' or as a 'disposition,' it, too, is likely to play an important role in effective critical functioning.

Understandings of intelligence across the life span provide useful insights into how we might expect critical abilities to function.

Intellectual development approaches

The approaches

Although there is overlap with the thinking skills frameworks discussed previously, the frameworks described below are more concerned with describing developmental stages which lead to more sophisticated and mature thinking.

Traditionally, intellectual development approaches have focused on children. *Cognitive constructivists* such as Piaget et al. (1969) have argued that children progress through well-defined developmental stages of thinking, as individuals move in a discrepancy-producing environment which requires them to 'assimilate' and 'accommodate' new knowledge. Piaget argued that the stage (usually age 11 upwards) where children can think about 'formal operations', that is, can think abstractly, emerges naturally and systematically after an individual has passed through the stage of concrete operations, that is, where children can think logically, but only about objects and events. Critical thinking is potentially enabled if individuals have reached the stage of formal operations. In a cognitivist constructivist approach, the educational focus is on the provision of an appropriate learning environment rather than teaching specific skills. Learning is viewed as an external process following the internal process of intellectual maturation to particular levels (Palinscar, 1998, p. 352).

Scholars such as Gardner (2006) have questioned the notion of a general intelligence which develops uniformly across domains, arguing that Piaget underestimated the importance of cultural, social and individual factors in learning. Gardner also argues that Piaget has an impoverished view of adult cognition, associating it with logical-rational thought only, rather than creativity, intuition or the type of mental processes employed by people such as artists or writers. Gardner's criticisms are consistent with the account of the development of intelligence given in the previous section, and with the account of creative thinking presented earlier (see 'Creative thinking approaches', p. 52).

Social constructivists, also interested in child development, have focused more on learning as a dynamic social activity, gradually internalized by the individual (e.g. Vygotsky, 1978). In this approach, children learn through interaction with teachers and peers, with language playing a central role. Vygotsky (1978) talked about the zone of proximal development, which he defined as:

> the distance between the actual developmental level as determined by independent problem solving and the level of potential development as determined through problem solving under adult guidance or in collaboration with more capable peers. (p. 86)

Vygotsky argued that the learner, through structured learning activities undertaken in interaction with the teacher or more capable peers, would progress through the zone of proximal development, for example acquiring an operation or concept. However, this is only the beginning of the development of the child's capacity to use the operation or concept. As Vygotsky (1962) explained:

> Instruction has its own sequences and organization, it follows a curriculum and a timetable, and its rules cannot be expected to coincide with the inner laws of the developmental processes it calls to life. On the basis of our studies, we tried to plot curves of the progress of instruction and of the participating psychological functions; far from coinciding, these curves showed an exceedingly complex relationship. (p. 101)

The central role of the teacher, according to Vygotsky, is to provide a structured learning environment. This involves building tasks through instruction, modelling, questioning and feedback until the learner can operate independently (McCarthey et al., 1992, pp. 17–18). Palinscar (1998) reports that the particular types of discourse engaged in affect the type of learning that takes place. 'Specifically, talk that is interpretive (generated in the service of analysis or explanations) is associated with more significant learning gains than talk that is simply descriptive' (p. 365). Teachers play a crucial role in promoting discourse which may push students' thinking and encourage group activity 'so that responsibility is shared, expertise is distributed, and there is an ethos for building preceding ideas' (p. 365).

Needles et al. (1994) investigated what a social constructionist approach to writing might be and how it might work in contrast with a skills-based or whole language approach. They suggested that writing should incorporate skills in context, be meaningful and authentic, connect with the writer's background and experience, involve interaction with others, be approached as a problem-solving task, and that writers be given many opportunities to write extended text (cited in Palinscar, p. 369).

Vygotsky (1978) argued for the importance of social and cultural influences in development. For social constructivists, as Palinscar (1998) elaborates, 'thought, learning and knowledge' may be viewed as 'internalised discourse', that is, socially and culturally shaped thought, arrived at through interaction with others (p. 349) and then 'transformed in idiosyncratic ways in the appropriation process' (p. 365).

Social constructivist thinking has implications for assessment practices. Rather than perhaps focusing mainly or solely on summative assessment of what the learner knows, interest moves towards formative assessment where the concern is with how learners can be moved forward by appropriate feedback from their teachers or peers (Palinscar, 1998, p. 366).

Some developmental concepts used by child psychologists and educators have been useful when applied to adult learners. However, as well as differences between the intellectual development of children and that of adults, researchers have argued that adult students of different ages behave differently in terms of approaches to studying and confidence levels (Reed, 1998).

Others have developed stage models related to adult intellectual development, with a focus largely on the period of young adulthood, usually in a formal educational environment such as college or university. These models, based on empirical research, suggest that thinkers' understanding of the nature of knowledge and themselves as knowers develops over time (Reed, 1998). We will discuss some of the major frameworks here.

Perry (1968/1999) applied the notion of staged development to college years, doing extensive empirical research on young (largely male) students at Harvard in the 1950s and 1960s. As White (1999) reported, Perry was interested in exploring whether there was 'any substance to the familiar claim that a liberal education means learning how to think' (p. xxxix). Perry suggested that students move through nine stages of development, ranging from an uncritical acceptance of a right–wrong position on issues, through an acceptance of multiple points of view, and finally to a stage where they can evaluate competing claims and commit to a position. Usually students move through these stages in the same order, although some become locked at one stage for a long period, some regress and some rebel. This framework built on Piaget's work. Perry suggested that students moved through the stages as they were exposed to experience and diversity, which challenged existing beliefs and understandings, and that students in the lower levels of the model were more likely to need structured input. Students at higher levels often valued experiential learning, but did not need as much instructor-guided structure.

In addressing the moral elements of development, Perry argued that courage was required:

> Since each step in the development presents a challenge to a person's previous assumptions and requires that he redefine and extend his responsibilities in the midst of increased complexity and uncertainty, his growth does indeed require courage. In short, the development resembles what used to be called an adventure of the spirit. (p. 49)

Perry was strongly aware of the pressures to conform, and that learning to reason in an independent way as required in higher education could lead to 'independent-*like* thought to get good grades (p. 113). He asked, 'Can one learn to think independently out of obedience to Authority's demand?' (p. 112).

Belenky et al. (1986) proposed a categorized framework of knowledge and voice, based specifically on the voices of women. Unlike Perry, their participants came from a variety of urban and rural locations, social classes, ethnic backgrounds, ages and educational histories. They grouped women's ways of knowing into five categories. The lowest of these was silence, where women felt themselves to be voiceless. By the highest level, women felt they could be creators of knowledge and recognized and valued both objective and subjective ways of knowing. Belenky et al. drew on Perry's scheme, although they did not recognize his stages as relating to the women in their study.

Based on a study of largely young, white, middle- and upper-class students at Miami University, Baxter Magolda (1992) argued for four patterns of knowing: absolute knowing, transitional knowing, independent knowing and contextual knowing. Development through the different ways of knowing happens as students progress through their years of higher education, although men and women exhibit somewhat different behaviours.

Following Perry's work, King et al. (1994) developed a seven-stage model of reflective judgement for adolescents and young adults, sitting within three overarching periods of development: pre-reflective thought, quasi-reflective thought and reflective thought. Knowledge becomes increasingly provisional as the stages advance and is arrived at through a process of reasonable enquiry. King and Kitchener argue that people pass through the stages in order, but that they may operate at a variety of stages at any point in their lives. Moseley et al. (2004) point out, however, that the model leaves questions about cultural transferability, the nature of maturation and development, and transfer of reflective capacity from one domain to another (p. 37).

Some adult education writers (e.g. Brookfield, 2003) have argued that critical reflection develops throughout adulthood with experience, as adults ask whether the rules and norms of personal, work, political life and gendered existence conform or otherwise to what they learned to expect as children. Reflection on these issues is induced on exposure to a variety of broad, deep and differentially intensive experiences over a long period of time (pp. 146–7). Brookfield (2003) argues that 'a context-free critical thinker is conceptually and empirically absurd' (p. 159).

Limitations and contributions

Probably the findings related to developmental stages depend on the age, gender and educational background of the group included in the empirical research. One particular factor likely to be relevant in a university context to the shape of intellectual development and usually not mentioned in developmental models, is field of study.

The critiques of general stages models such as of Piaget are useful for reinforcing our developing understandings of the variable nature of intelligence and development. It is useful to remember the empirical finding that students may be at different stages of intellectual development at different times during their degree programmes, and there may be students at different levels of development within one class. Students may be confused about what the teacher wants because of their developmental stage. Alternatively, Reed (1998) suggests that a variety of levels of development within a class may actually assist learning as people learn about a variety of ways of processing knowledge and of reasoning, which may add to their own repertoire.

The interest in moral and intellectual development and the personal qualities required, shown by researchers such as Perry, is useful for reminding us that criticality is not a neutral, painless process end product.

Vygotsky offers valuable insights into how minds mature and how to structure the environment to promote learning. His interest in the complexity of the links between instruction and full development of the capacity to use concepts being taught is useful. His work, together with that of developmental models, such as those of Perry and Baxter Magolda, indicates the prolonged nature of intellectual development.

Conclusions from the review of existing literatures

In Chapters 2 and 3 we have reviewed existing conceptualizations of criticality and related literatures, probing their limitations and usefulness from the perspective of our starting questions:

- Why is criticality in twenty-first century higher education desirable?
- How can criticality most usefully be conceptualized?
    - What are its component parts?
    - How does it transfer between different areas?
    - What shapes does its development take?

Existing approaches to the conceptualization of criticality and to empirical research on the subject offer elements that are helpful in answering all these questions, despite differences in underlying epistemological and ontological stances.

Why is criticality desirable?

If we are thinking about why criticality is desirable, there are several suggestions in the existing literature. Traditional liberal thinking offers us an intellectual and moral vision of an education that is intrinsically worthwhile, devoted to a rational pursuit of 'truth' for the benefit of society and individuals within it. Citizenship education is a practical political manifestation of one aspect of liberal education. Barnett (1997) offers us a conceptualization of criticality focusing on the development of critical beings in higher education, able to think and act independently (after appropriate critical reflection) for the benefit of society as a whole. Social emancipatory approaches call on us to develop critical awareness of repressive elements and to act to resist them. While these sources occupy somewhat different ontological and epistemological spaces, and place a greater or lesser emphasis on the need for resistance or alternatively working within existing systems, they all provide a profoundly moral vision of where higher education should aim. They all focus on a search for what is true, on independence of thought and action, and on the quest for the greater good.

Component parts

The literature offers several useful conceptualizations of the component parts of criticality. At an overarching level, Barnett (1997) conceptualizes criticality as existing in three domains (formal knowledge, the self and the world) and over several levels. This is consistent with the understandings of why criticality is important, and suggests that higher education may potentially focus on any or all of the domains. Creativity offers us a conception of the generative aspects of criticality: the need to conceptualize problems, to envision solutions and to use divergent thinking. This could be connected to Barnett's domains and levels. Cognitive psychology offers us a breakdown of skills and dispositions as well as a focus on micro-cognitive processes. Critical thinking advocates from analytical philosophy offer us taxonomies of critical skills. The notion of intellectual resources provides a conceptualization of the factors which enable criticality to happen. Subject-specific work from sociologists and educationalists suggests the different shapes that thinking takes in different subject fields.

The role of knowledge as distinct from the role of thinking skills is discussed, especially in cognitive psychology; consideration of both these aspects is important. Most approaches emphasize the importance of personal characteristics or dispositions in criticality, although they differ about how such qualities can be developed and what they consist of. Criticality is perceived variably as being located within the individual or within the interactions of the individual with society and their cultural environment.

Transfer of criticality

Cognitive psychology, and to some extent field-specific approaches, offer insights into issues of transfer of critical skills and knowledge from one context to another. Transfer is clearly problematic, but possible under certain conditions. Cognitive psychology also sheds useful light on the functioning of memory and on issues related to metacognition, illuminating in some detail how transfer might occur. Empirical research on the way that people think and resolve issues makes it clear that we rely heavily on memories of similar scenarios previously encountered, in combination with some logical thinking from first principles.

Development of criticality

Intelligence research suggests how nurture and context affect the development of intelligence. These ideas are applicable to the development of criticality, along with their implications for society and individuals. Intelligence research also suggests that what counts as intelligence may vary across cultures. This is also applicable to criticality and is consistent with our observations in Chapter 1 about geographical and historical variability in understandings and manifestations of criticality. Research on the changing nature of intelligence over the life span relates to people's ability to be critical at different stages of their lives. Developmental theories such as that of Perry offer us understandings of the shape intellectual development might take for someone going through higher education. The idea of different stages and a prolonged period of learning is useful. Cognitive psychology offers us descriptions of differences between novice and expert performance, as well as an account of underlying factors. It also highlights the importance of metacognitive strategies in thinking and suggests that these might be encouraged through instruction. The resources approach to criticality emphasizes the need to foster the intellectual and personal resources which will enable criticality to develop. Dispositional and intelligence approaches emphasize the importance of sensitivities and inclinations to do tasks, as well as strategies. Work on domain-specific and general thinking suggests that development of criticality requires focus on the skills and knowledge attaching to both. McPeck talked about the central role of language in learning.

Social constructionist perspectives suggest that a curriculum to encourage critical development should focus on tasks which are contextualized, meaningful and relevant to the doer as well as involving interaction with others, including feedback from peers and teacher.

Going forward

There is little empirical research on the key question of what is actually happening in terms of criticality development across the higher education curriculum in ordinary undergraduate classrooms. Research is needed which displays awareness of the wider social, political and educational context in which these classrooms are operating and which is framed by a theoretical understanding of what criticality might be or how it might develop.

In Chapter 4, we set out to provide such a theoretical framework, drawing on elements arising out of Chapters 2 and 3. In later chapters, we relate the framework to empirical reality as we found it in our case study of Westford University.

Chapter 4

A Proposed Framework for Criticality Development

Introduction

In this chapter, we propose a framework for understanding the nature of criticality, its development and how it is learned. As discussed in Chapter 1, the framework has been arrived at through an iterative process of drawing on existing strands of thought in related literatures (discussed in Chapters 2 and 3) and analysis of our own primary data (as discussed in following chapters). We present the theoretical framework here in Chapter 4 to assist the reader to make sense of the complex data generated in the project, but equally it could have followed the data-based chapters, since the framework and the analysis were developed concurrently. Our framework offers a vision to aim for in terms of critical development. In Chapter 9, we make some concluding comments about the relationship between the framework and the data analysis.

Our unique contribution to criticality debates is to draw together existing strands in the literature in a novel way. Our emphasis on the contextualized nature of criticality and the resources necessary for criticality to take place is unusual. The firm grounding of our framework in longitudinal empirical, naturalistic data is also a valuable contribution.

We argue that a clear understanding of the type of criticality developed in higher education has implications for both undergraduate and postgraduate students in a broad range of social science and humanities fields, and for schoolchildren's development into adults in their professional and civic lives. These implications will be discussed in Chapter 9.

In this chapter, we first present our understanding of the nature of criticality, including its moral vision. Secondly, we explore aspects of context which are relevant to the practice and development of criticality. Thirdly, we move to the intellectual and personal resources needed to function critically, elements often absent in discussions of criticality. Fourthly, we propose a developmental framework, including three broad levels of criticality development, each requiring different levels of intellectual and personal resources. Finally, we consider how people move through this developmental framework and acquire critical resources.

Understandings of the nature of criticality

Barnett's (1997) conceptualization of criticality is invaluable as a heuristic tool to distinguish the kinds of criticality students develop. We share Barnett's concern with the need for critical being in the modern world. We accept his view that criticality can usefully be understood over three domains: formal knowledge, the self and the world.

Our research investigates how students function in all three domains. Barnett suggests different forms of knowledge which operate in each of these domains: critical reason, critical self-reflection and critical action. We share Barnett's argument that we are not prisoners of postmodern local critical discourses, but that critical standards may be applied from our own field and others in a process of metacritique. This is more satisfactory for developing critical persons than focusing on only one domain and/or focusing on over-simplistic conceptualizations of universal critical standards as in many approaches described in Chapters 2 and 3.

We share Barnett's concern with levels of criticality. His levels are essentially different *types* of criticality, hierarchically arranged, rather than a developmental framework. Each type may presumably be performed with greater or lesser degrees of effectiveness. We too are interested in types of criticality, mainly transformatory criticality (his highest level) and, to some extent, instrumental criticality (his lowest level). These levels are conceptually clear, whereas we find the intermediate levels, *Reflexivity* and *Refashioning of traditions,* somewhat unclear.

In *transformatory criticality,* the basic premises of a situation in any of the three domains may be questioned rather than accepted. This might entail questioning the basic shape of a field or the self: importantly, transformatory criticality moves towards the *construction* of an alternative shape, avoiding the 'logic-chopping' approach of some critical thinkers. Creative thinking, as discussed in Chapter 3, will probably be required and may lead to critical action where appropriate. Consideration of the values and underlying implications of different positions and theories is integral to transformatory criticality. Technical expertise, as discussed in Chapter 3, is a necessary but not sufficient condition for transformatory criticality. Here the approach converges with other traditions in the literature such as liberal thought and views of criticality as political engagement, which also operate with a strong moral vision. For us, this value position will generally encompass notions of human rights, impartial justice and fairness in a largely secular environment. However, we recognize both that this is a position contextualized within the Western university in the twenty-first century and that there are tensions within a criticality which espouses a particular value position, since the point of transformatory criticality is that moral positions have to be open for reflection, analysis and discussion. We also recognize that within this basic value position there will be varying opinions and that values may differ from practices.

In *instrumental criticality*, criticality may be required in any of the three domains, but on terms set by others to achieve pre-existing goals. This may involve problem solving or monitoring to pre-existing standards. The nature of critical moves is limited, but may be performed with a high degree of effectiveness and expertise. Instrumental criticality, even at a high level, is insufficient for a morally based, comprehensive conceptualization of criticality involving potential challenge to basic premises, although it may be considered sufficient in contexts such as some types of employment (or some classrooms?) where transformatory critical employees (or students?) questioning basic premises may be viewed as a threat to established routines and practices.

Given our interest in a moral and comprehensive vision of criticality, as described below, transformatory criticality is our ideal, but we do not argue that it is always possible or necessary. Neither do we argue that it is either practical or desirable for students (or indeed anyone) to be critical at a transformatory level at all times in all domains. It may be that fully transformatory criticality can only be performed at specific moments in Barnett's domains. At times, problem solving (instrumental criticality) may be sufficient, without consideration of deeper and wider aspects. Practised at an advanced level, transformatory criticality requires high levels of knowledge, skill and experience. It is unrealistic, in most cases, to expect undergraduate students to function at that level. They are more likely to function at less expert levels of transformatory criticality or to use instrumental criticality. Our main interest, as regards levels, is in developmental paths towards transformatory criticality. Educationalists can only aim to facilitate students' progress somewhat along the critical developmental path.

In line with moral visions of education as a means of developing active, constructively critical citizens, we propose that fully effective transformative criticality in social science and humanities fields should be viewed as:

- the motivation and ability to persuade, engage and act on the world and self through the operation of the mindful, analytical, evaluative, interpretive, reflective understanding of a body of relevant knowledge;

- mediated by assimilated experience of how the social and physical environment is structured, combined with a willingness and capacity to question and problematize our shared perceptions of relevance and experience; and
- underpinned by a moral vision and values.

Lesser degrees of criticality are possible, where individuals have partial control over the elements described above.

Our understandings of criticality, as expressed above, incorporate assumptions about context; about the contributions of different types of knowledge and ability; and about dispositions and motivations towards the practice of criticality. These emerged as significant themes in the previous chapters.

We now discuss our framework in greater detail.

Contextual aspects of criticality

Broad context

In Chapter 1, we argued that the nature of criticality varies by historical period and cultural context. Many traditions have recognized the role of context as discussed in Chapters 2 and 3. Here, we argue that any study of criticality has to examine the micro-practice of individuals as they interact with their cultural, historical, social and educational context. Our study of criticality is firmly placed in the early twenty-first century, in a university in the UK, and this contextual information should be remembered when interpreting our concerns.

Sociologists have complex and overlapping conceptions of the relationship between social structure and individual agency (see for example Beck, 1994; Bourdieu, 1996; Bourdieu et al., 1992; Giddens, 1984). Similarly, according to developmental psychologists such as Vygotsky (1978), culture is experienced especially through language, re-enacted by individuals and internalized.

Accordingly, we argue that any critical act will take place in a context comprising cultural, social, educational, developmental, disciplinary/field-specific, emotional, ethical, physical, cognitive and political elements which will themselves be in dynamic interaction and which will be mediated and (re-)created by the choices of individuals. Criticality is practised both individually and collectively; the two elements are inseparable. The individual self is central in this process.

Field-specific aspects

As described in Chapters 2 and 3, field-specific aspects of thought are considered important in various areas of the literature. The relationship between field-specific knowledge and general critical thinking skills is contested. We argue that there are general critical dispositions, intellectual (and other) rules, values, qualities and abilities necessary for criticality as outlined in this chapter (see 'Understandings of the Nature of Criticality', p. 69), but that local manifestations of criticality in the shape of local social practices will differ widely. As Darling (2001) explains of social practices:

> [A] practice [is] a complex human activity governed by rules, standards of excellence that are considered in the light of certain virtues, and initiated through a particular intention or set of intentions (MacIntyre, 1984). These are carried out within a community in which understandings about certain practices are shared (Benhabib, 1992). Every practice needs to be considered in the light of these features: rules, standards, virtues and intentions. (p. 108)
>
> Darling argues that understanding social practices through these aspects provides in-depth understandings of a wide range of activities from sports to music, and that without such understandings these activities would be incomprehensible. (p. 108)

In higher education, the shape and nature of criticality itself is socially constructed and contextually permeated (with localized sub-field, institutional, departmental and other variations), but mediated by individuals. Our students are attempting to perform social and intellectual practices of particular fields, the rules of which they may only partially understand. Indeed, as Barnett (1997) points out, undergraduate students often do not encounter the 'fundamental theoretical conflicts that drive a chasm through the research community in a discipline' (p. 78). Their lecturers are full members of the social practice community attached to the field who enforce its rules and standards. Fields function as communities of practice, as mentioned in Chapter 2.

Field-specific differences relate to what is understood to be the body of relevant knowledge; to what is accepted as mindful, analytical, evaluative, interpretive and reflective understanding of it; and to perceptions of how the social and perhaps physical environment is structured. They also affect perceptions of how to persuade, engage and act on the world.

As we saw in Chapter 2, writers such as Becher (1989) and Biglan (1973) suggest division of disciplines into 'hard pure', 'soft pure', 'hard applied' and 'soft applied'. In this book, according to this classification, we are focused on a soft pure field (Modern Languages) and a soft applied field (Social Work).

We have already argued that higher education should educate students to function critically within the three domains proposed by Barnett. However, the shape of criticality will vary according to field. The domain of the world will be more prominent in applied fields such as Social Work than in pure fields such as Modern Languages, where the domain of formal knowledge is likely to be more important. In applied fields the main focus will be on making critical connections between domains.

There are tensions between free expression and the demands of specific fields for criticality to take certain forms. Higher education should encourage the development of criticality in particular fields because, as Barnett (1994) points out, if the student is not engaged in the habitus of one particular discipline, they may seem free to form their own models of thinking but in reality will only be able to bank unconnected knowledge and be unable to engage in a meaningful dialogue in any disciplinary context (p. 64). However, encouragement of criticality within specific domains does entail field-specific controls over the range and nature of criticality that is judged acceptable.

Given the difficulties of transfer of criticality discussed in Chapters 2 and 3, we expect transfer between fields to be somewhat problematic.

Context to encourage critical development

The importance of providing an appropriate context for student criticality development is widely addressed in the literature, as discussed in Chapters 2 and 3. Barnett (1997) argues that students need appropriate cognitive, personal and practical space and guidance in order to develop as critical beings across all three domains (pp. 114–15). Social constructivists such as Vygotsky have suggested the careful structuring of learning environments to enable individuals to function in their zone of proximal development. Bailin et al. (1999a) proposed that students should be given appropriate tasks in an appropriately supportive environment (pp. 298–9).

Those researching field-specific approaches to learning have suggested that socialization through the use of field-specific guidance and pedagogical content knowledge will assist the development of field-specific thinking. Intelligence researchers discuss the importance of motivation, culture, experiential knowledge and procedural knowledge alongside field-specific knowledge in the performance of tasks. Some cognitive psychologists suggest that awareness-raising through explicit discussion of general rules, together with field-specific examples and practice of thinking including meta-cognitive strategies, will also assist the development of thinking. We support these arguments and investigate their operation in our data.

We now discuss the intellectual and personal resources necessary for criticality.

Resources aspects

We accept that people are able to exercise criticality largely according to the intellectual, knowledge and personal resources available to them (Bailin et al., 1999a; McPeck, 1990b, p. 20). These resources can be acquired, to some extent at least, in an appropriate nurturing environment according to the literature on intelligence and various other areas as discussed in Chapters 2 and 3 and will be, we hope, deliberately cultivated at university.

Bailin et al. (1999a) offer a valuable conception of critical thinkers in the domain of formal knowledge as those with 'intellectual resources [such] as background knowledge, operational knowledge of appropriate standards, knowledge of key concepts, possession of effective heuristics, and of certain vital habits of mind' (p. 285). We extend their notion of resources to the domains of the self and the world, as outlined by Barnett (1997) and also to the idea of different levels of resources for different developmental levels, as proposed by us in the following section ('Developmental Aspects', p. 81). Functioning at each successive level of criticality will require a higher level of resource than the previous level.

We suggest that the resources needed to be critical across the three domains (formal knowledge, the self and the world) involve distinctive types of knowledge and certain personal qualities and values. Close consideration of the resources necessary for criticality to take place is uncommon, so here we draw on a range of sources additional to those discussed in Chapters 2 and 3. Below, we outline the knowledge resources we propose as necessary for criticality and in Table 4.1 suggest examples of these in Social Work and Modern Languages.

Different types of knowledge

The different types of knowledge are complex, fuzzy, overlapping and contested. We propose a simplified schema covering the broad areas in which we would expect people to have some knowledge resources to carry out criticality. Without these, criticality would be impossible. A person may have lesser or greater knowledge resources which will affect the type of criticality exercised. The ability to synthesize and make linkages between various types of knowledge is important.

The types of knowledge described below are often field specific, but there are general aspects. The work of cognitive psychologists on the nature of field specificity and generic thinking skills is especially useful here. For example, they contrast expert and novice knowledge in a field and suggest that profiles of expert knowledge may differ between fields, as discussed in Chapter 3 ('Cognitive Approaches to Thinking', p. 40).

Declarative knowledge

Often associated with the philosopher Gilbert Ryle, declarative knowledge is about 'knowing that', for instance, London is the capital of the UK (Ryle, 1949). Declarative knowledge relates to theories and data (remote, personal and professional). Such knowledge will often be field specific for students in the domain of formal knowledge but may also consist of general knowledge in the domain of the world. (See, for example, the account of Wineburg (1998) of the field-specific declarative knowledge of an expert historian discussed in Chapter 3.

It has been suggested to us that it is possible to be critical, for example, about some information heard on the news, without having extensive declarative knowledge. However, we argue that criticality is only possible in such cases in the limited sense of initial speculative commentary. Informed, penetrating commentary, let alone action, is unlikely (or unwise or both) without a critical understanding of a body of relevant knowledge. As Whitehead (1932b) wrote, 'Fools act on imagination, without knowledge' (p. 140).

Procedural knowledge

Procedural knowledge, also associated with Gilbert Ryle, is often tacit and involves someone knowing 'how to' do something, such as how to fly an aeroplane or how to carry out a research study in a specialist area. As McPeck (1981) has argued, procedural knowledge can have:

> identifiable *intellectual components,* such as the use or partial use of various methods (research methods, statistical methods, programming methods), *strategies* (for solving problems, winning battles or games, attacking mountains) and *techniques* (crystallography *versus* spectrometry, models *versus* pictures, telling *versus* showing). (p. 11; emphases ours)

Knowing 'how' includes lower as well as higher order skills. For undergraduates in the domain for formal knowledge, lower order procedural skills include basic tasks such as locating information in a library. Higher order writing skills in arts and social science subjects include knowing how to build an academic argument, how to engage with secondary sources and how to read effectively.

Many higher-order thinking skills associated with critical thinking (e.g. interpretation, analysis, evaluation, inference (Facione, 1990)) are aspects of *knowledge how*. To be effective, these must interact with other types of knowledge listed in this section which are largely field specific. One cannot, for example, evaluate effectively without having substantive declarative knowledge of the field or understanding why one is applying particular criteria.

The expert historian described by Wineburg (1998) was able to utilize various aspects of procedural knowledge ('asking questions', 'reserving judgement', 'monitoring affective responses' and 'revisiting earlier assessments') in a complex historical task outside his specialist domain. This enabled him to make a sensitive and intelligent interpretation of various documents, although he could not operate at the same level of sophistication as his colleague who had detailed field-specific declarative knowledge. (See Chapter 3)

Knowledge why

It is also important to know *why* it is useful or desirable to do something, for example, to listen empathetically (Reimer, 1998). Arguments for the importance of *knowledge why* focus on the internal logic of a thought or action system and its underlying values, beliefs and implications. They relate to the notion of social practices discussed earlier (see 'Contextual Aspects of Criticality', p. 71).

Reimer, a philosopher of music education, argues that knowing why something should be done in a particular way provides a value structure – 'a logically consistent system of examined beliefs – within which the other knowings can be experienced as meaningful' (p. 165). In relationship to art, Reimer argues that *knowledge why* enables us to understand:

> why art exists; why all cultures have developed arts in some ways like and in some ways different from arts of all other cultures; why standards for judging art might be both general and also dependent on particularities of this and that art, style, genre; why the experience of arts and why

creating art seem to be so important for people; why different groups of people have different beliefs about art, what it is good for, and how it should be used; why philosophers of art have debated for centuries every conceivable issue related to art, its nature, its value, why some people think education in the arts is essential for all; why some students to engage themselves in special efforts to develop creative capacities in an art. (p. 165)

More generally, Giroux (1988), a critical pedagogist, argues that students should be aware of the underlying social and political implications of what they are learning, and criticizes purely technical approaches (pp. 55–6).

Being critical at anything beyond a basic level requires *knowledge why*, both to understand the internal logic of the field and to assess how deserving it is of critical evaluation.

Knowledge of what it is to be

Knowledge of what it is to be relates to personal and professional experience (Berlin, 1980). It can be achieved through memory or imagination, that is, through some process of immersion. It concerns the capacity to conceive of 'more than one way of categorising reality, like the ability to understand what it is to be an artist, a revolutionary, a traitor, to know what it is to be poor, to wield authority, to be a child, a prisoner, a barbarian. Without some ability to get into the skin of others, the human condition, history, what characterises one period or culture as against others, cannot be understood' (Berlin, 1980, pp. 106–7). It is 'the knowledge of the actors, as against that of the audience, of the "inside story" as opposed to that obtained by some outside vantage point' (p. 117).

This type of knowledge probably assists in the development of *knowledge why* and *how*. It will clearly be required for critical action in the domain of the world. Students in professional subject areas will need knowledge of the professional environment and of the diverse participants within it. Students who graduate without experience in a field and so without *knowledge of what it is to be* are unlikely to be effectively critical until they have such knowledge. In the domain of formal knowledge it is necessary to understand what it is to be a member of a field in order to know how to engage, construct and critique.

Arguably, *knowledge of what it is to be* could in some cases decrease criticality, in that a person might come to over-identify with a field. It is also not always necessary to have first-hand knowledge of what it is to be in a direct sense (e.g. of drug abuse, alcoholism) to be critical. However, a close indirect acquaintanceship with such conditions and with people who do have first-hand experience is probably necessary for effective criticality.

Knowledge of and how language is used

Knowledge of and how language is used is also a central resource for criticality (see 'Criticality Embedded in Specific Fields', Chapter 2, p. 28 and 'Intellectual Development Approaches', Chapter 3, p. 59). Language has a central role as the medium of the ongoing dialogue between individuals and their environment, for the process of socialization and for the expression of individuality (Bakhtin, 1986). Through describing reality, language also shapes reality and promotes learning. It is through the existing forms of language that individuals come to know their world, although they in turn can reshape reality by their use of language (Goodwin et al., 1992, p. 17).

Without control over the language of academic discussion and understanding of the sub-genres within it, writers will be unable to participate fully in the ongoing dialogue between writing, reading and thinking.

Philosophers have highlighted the importance of language in shaping worlds of understanding. Peters (1966) wrote that:

> It is a grave error to regard the learning of language as a purely instrumental matter, as a toll in the service of purposes, standards, feelings, and beliefs. For in language is distilled a view of the world which is constituted by them. In learning a language the individual is initiated into a public inheritance which his parents and teachers are inviting him to share. (p. 53)

Problems with the language of academia can have a range of consequences for a student. As Goodwin et al. (1992) point out, 'The role of language and dialogue is critical since it is through speech and social interaction that the learner acquires new abilities' (p. 17). However, novice writers often have problems in understanding what they read, expressing ideas appropriately and expressing individuality, as they are unfamiliar with the specific meanings, linguistic preferences and inferences of academic dialogue (Bakhtin, 1986, p. 80). It may be difficult to grasp basic concepts, often expressed in complex language, especially as the student usually does not have a well-developed knowledge base into which new ideas can fit. Lack of control over appropriate academic genres may have serious consequences ranging from failing a course or not getting good grades, to accusations of plagiarism, and so on. Indeed, Mercer (1996) writes that research

Table 4.1 Types of knowledge in modern languages and social work

Types of knowledge	Modern languages examples	Social work examples
Declarative	Theories (e.g. of race) Contents of novels and plays	Psychosocial theories Content of relevant legislation
Procedural	How to write a literary commentary, make an effective translation	How to do a social work assessment for care required, advocate for a service user
Knowledge why	Why the study of literature is important	Why certain values are important, why reflection on practice is beneficial
Knowledge of what it is to be	A Modern Languages student, a resident in another culture	An (apprentice) social worker
Language	One or more target foreign languages, the language of literary critique	Language of legislation, Social Work official language, language of academic social work

on language practices 'supports the view that for students, "becoming educated" is very much a matter of linguistic socialization, of learning how – and when – to use language in special, contextually-specific ways' (pp. 30–1). Those who have better control over language in academic genres will find it easier to learn, to express themselves, to keep to unspoken rules and generally to participate in academic discussion.

Examples of the different types of knowledge in the two fields we investigated, Modern Languages and Social Work, are given in Table 4.1.

The necessity of knowledge for criticality

The above types of knowledge are necessary for criticality to take place, although the balance will vary according to domain and field context.

Knowledge levels as well as space and time to construct knowledge often relate to motivation. For example, Tobias (1994, p. 50) argues that broader and deeper knowledge of a field in general and a topic in particular is likely to relate to sustained interest levels.

The discussion of developmental models in Chapter 3 indicated the prolonged nature of intellectual development. One reason for this is that the overall construction of a knowledge base is a slow process of building links between data, theory and personal understandings. The students may already have this knowledge at the start of a criticality task, or they may seek to construct knowledge during the task. Acquiring, selecting, managing and focusing knowledge in order to exercise criticality is a complex, multi-layered business. Going through the process of constructing and developing a personal knowledge base leads to intellectual development of itself.

Students do not arrive in class with uniform levels of knowledge. In modular degrees, where students can choose modules with different starting levels of declarative knowledge about a topic, some will be ahead of others in terms of understanding. So we would expect very different patterns of knowledge levels in a more unitary degree such as Social Work compared to Modern Languages, where students may choose from a wide variety of film, literature, history and linguistics modules. Students' knowledge resources develop over time differentially according to various factors such as starting level of knowledge which interacts with labour and time invested, as well as personal capacities to process knowledge. For example, mature students might be expected to have more 'knowledge of what it is to be' in various situations. However, the use they make of this knowledge depends on their capacity to process it, that is, to reflect and to relate it to formal knowledge. Individuals will have different combinations of the types of knowledge, and in some ways good knowledge in one area can compensate for poor knowledge in another but only to some extent.

Often, students are accused of being uncritical, and an audit of their knowledge resources illustrates why this might be the case.

Personal qualities and values

Many of the literatures reviewed in Chapters 2 and 3 (philosophy, sociology, psychology and education) discussed the resources of personal qualities and values, under different names (dispositions, values, traits of character, attitudes, motivations and habits of mind). We argue that to be critical, an individual has to have:

- a well-developed, robust, confident and aware self, able where necessary to challenge and reconstruct existing understandings and modes of operation;
- an awareness of the values, priorities and power structures implicit in a context and a capacity to be constructively critical of them;
- appropriate values such as respect for reasons, an inquiring attitude, open-mindedness, independent-mindedness (see Bailin et al., 1999a for a more extensive list of appropriate values, p. 294).

The lower levels of criticality require somewhat fewer of these qualities and the higher levels more, although it is important to remember that qualities such as courage and confidence are required even for the lower levels of criticality.

Some approaches discussed in Chapters 2 and 3 argued explicitly that to some extent, such qualities and values could be developed rather than being innate: a viewpoint with which we concur.

Concluding comments on resources

We view resources as described above as necessary prerequisites, but not as sufficient indicators of criticality. For example, a student may have knowledge, but that knowledge may be 'inert' and involve the passive reception of over-detailed, disconnected ideas (Whitehead, 1932). Similarly, a student may be courageous and confident, but may lack the knowledge and skill needed to be critical. Moreover, the possession of resources does not necessarily indicate criticality; motivation and opportunity are also needed.

Resources and values are not neutral categories. The kinds of knowledge and values favoured and encouraged relate to the kinds of criticality being developed. A strong focus on procedural knowledge without emphasis on knowledge why, for example, may indicate a preference for instrumental criticality. A strong focus on confidence without emphasis on questioning aspects may have the same emphasis.

Without appropriate resources in terms of knowledge, skills and personal qualities, students will be unable to practise criticality. Those concerned with undergraduate education need actively to encourage students to develop all these types of critical resources, and create appropriate learning environments for this.

Developmental aspects

Following in the tradition of thinking skills' frameworks (e.g. Moseley et al., 2005) and developmental frameworks discussed in Chapter 3 (e.g. Perry, 1968/1999), we propose a framework relating specifically to criticality. This incorporates a developmental view of levels of criticality. It arises partly from our own data analysis and partly from the work of others (e.g. Barnett, 1997, various studies of expertise; Perry et al., 1968/1999).

We are mindful of comments we made in Chapter 1 about the geographical and historical contextualization of criticality, and we recognize that our framework incorporates particular values deriving from our early twenty-first century Western context. We suggest a set of developmental levels which are also not 'neutral', but reflect our interest in and prioritization of criticality. Haggis (2003) warns against 'pathologising' those unable or unwilling to aim at high level performance in such models (pp. 97–8). Therefore, our understanding of criticality development encompasses considerable individual variation in aims and motivation. Students, as do others, have varying motivations and priorities in their lives and, as Haggis points out, many may not want or be able to reach the highest levels of learning. Nonetheless, we believe that many people who may not wish to engage in the effortful process of advanced transformative criticality might benefit as citizens from a degree of criticality in their everyday lives as regards processing the information to which they are exposed by numerous media and official bodies. Economic and cultural survival and well-being in the modern world probably require some criticality.

Attention should be paid to group tendencies, in line with the issues raised in the social emancipatory literature discussed in Chapter 2 (see 'Social Emancipatory Approaches', p. 36) and in the resources literature in Chapter 2, p. 26. For example, if members of particular social groups consistently fail to reach the highest levels of criticality and become societal leaders, we should question underlying social dynamics and issues of equity.

Proposed levels of development

We propose three broad and overlapping levels of criticality development:

- *Early criticality*, where there is a tenuous engagement with and control over critical strategies and knowledge, largely within terms of others' understandings and actions.
- *Guided criticality*, where there is more secure control over critical strategies and knowledge and partial challenges at times to existing understandings and actions of others.
- *Late criticality*, where there is mastery over critical strategies and knowledge and, where appropriate, the person can easily challenge orthodoxies within terms of their own understandings.

Early criticality is itself an achievement. Many people probably do not reach this level, but we have not researched this and so cannot comment authoritatively. *Late criticality* corresponds to the fully effective criticality described in this chapter (see 'Understandings of the Nature of Criticality', p. 69); we did not observe late criticality operating in a sustained way among undergraduates during our fieldwork.

Each level of critical development incorporates both *processes* and *products*. For example, in the higher education context students will read about theories and concepts, listen to others talking about them, reflect on the information, perhaps deconstruct and reconstruct the information through devices such as informal discussion or notes (all processes), and later perhaps present or write about these theories (products).

Aspects of criticality

Activity at each level of the developmental framework incorporates four main aspects: (1) *entry into the critical process*; (2) *solution searching*; (3) *rationale-building*; and (4) *understanding of the territory*. Two of these terms derive from the writing of researchers Walvoord et al. (1990): for them, 'solution searching' is the inventive, creative part of writing and 'rationale building' is the presentation of an argument in writing (p. 13). We extend their conceptualizations to other aspects of the domain of formal knowledge as well as the self and the world.

Criticality development in different fields will vary. For example, making links between domains (knowledge, self, world) will be more developed in 'applied' fields than in 'pure' fields. Constructing a case in an 'applied' field may take the form of a reflective report or plan of action, incorporating links between domains, whereas a 'pure' field may require a more highly developed case in one domain, perhaps that of formal knowledge.

Listed in Table 4.2 are typical capabilities and observable behaviours for each of the levels of critical development we propose. The framework incorporates elements relating to our view of transformative criticality (see 'Understandings of the Nature of Criticality' in this chapter, p. 69). It also includes elements from across Barnett's three domains. We view the aspects of instrumentality and transformation (which Barnett discusses as dispositions or motivations) as applying at any level of criticality, although people's capacity to be transformatively critical will be enhanced when they have various advanced critical resources at their disposal. Someone who is operating at the early criticality level may have a transformative motivation but will lack the resources needed to operate at a higher level. It is unlikely that someone who is instrumentally critical will be able to operate at the late criticality level.

Entry into the critical process

This includes two elements: the nature and degree of engagement with task; and control over definition of topic, question and action.

Table 4.2 A developmental framework for criticality in the social sciences and humanities

		Level of criticality		
		Early criticality	Guided criticality	Late criticality
Entry into the critical process	1. Nature and degree of engagement with critical tasks	1. Tenuous engagement with and control over strategies and knowledge 2. Working within understandings of others	1. More secure control over strategies and knowledge 2. Partial challenges to the understandings of others	1. Mastery over strategies and knowledge 2. Where appropriate able to challenge orthodoxies
	1. Nature and degree of engagement with critical tasks	Active engagement with critical tasks, but other people shape tasks	More active engagement e.g. in understanding purpose of tasks, but within others' understandings	Engages in critical tasks in terms of own understandings
	2. Control over definition of topic, question and action	Works within other people's questions and conceptions of possible actions	Some ability to pose own minor questions and limited autonomy of action	Locates/defines significant problems and actions
Solution-searching process	1. Information location and management	Locates and manages information with guidance	Minimal guidance required	Locates and manages information independently
	2. Use of explanatory frameworks/theory	Uses explanatory frameworks in limited aspects only	Contrasts, synthesizes and integrates theory, limited challenges	Challenges and constructs explanatory frameworks
	3. Use of data/evidence/other voices in the field	Tentative recognition and use of evidence and organizing concepts	More confident use of evidence and organizing concepts, but within recognized parameters	Challenges principles and frameworks of evidence

A Proposed Framework for Criticality Development

4. Linking between domains of formal knowledge and/or the self and/or action	Limited ability to link between domains	More confident linking, some pushing of boundaries	Makes links creatively and confidently, redefines understandings and actions
5. Reflection (on formal knowledge, self and action)	Limited reflection on e.g. immediate competence	Reflection on thoughts, self and action, including underlying purposes	Extensive reflection on thoughts, actions and self, including underlying direction and values
6. Constructing a case (process)	Building of a case uncertain, limited skills and understanding of purposes	More control over case construction, some autonomy	Challenges and shapes rules of case construction where appropriate
Representation of the case/of knowledge (spoken and/or written) (product)	Tenuous, emerging control over forms of representation	Control over rules of representation, ability to build rationale, some pushing at boundaries of established practice	Challenges and shapes rules of case representation where appropriate
Rationale building			
Understanding of territory, including power relationships	Locating legitimacy, authority and rules for action	More confident working within established power relationships and some challenges to status quo	Engagement as active protagonist, ability to reshape the rules of action
Understanding of territory, including power relationships			

1. The nature and degree of engagement with critical tasks

This relates to the extent and nature of reading, listening, discussion, analysis or other action and, of course, thought. We propose a continuum of engagement ranging from:

- *Early criticality*, where people engage in critical tasks in terms of other people's expectations in the shape of, for instance, discussion, analysis, self-analysis, action and so on, as distinct from passive acceptance or unawareness of others' understandings; through
- *Guided criticality*, where some more active engagement with tasks is possible (in terms of understanding of the purpose of the task, interest in the task, pride in the processes and outcomes of the task), but is still constrained within the understandings of others; to
- *Late criticality*, where people are willing and able to engage in critical tasks in one or more domains, within the terms of their own understanding.

Off the lower end of the continuum of criticality, people might not engage with critical tasks on any terms. Those who are instrumentally critical, even at an advanced level, will be unable to move beyond guided criticality in that they always work within the understandings of others.

Issues of engagement relate to various areas discussed in Chapters 2 and 3: liberal views on the imperative to find the truth, philosophical and psychological interest in dispositions, creativity, and social emancipatory interest in critical engagement.

2. Control over definition of topic, question and action

We envisage a continuum of control ranging from:

- *Early criticality*, where people work within others' frameworks of understandings regarding questions and sub-questions it is possible and permissible to ask, and actions it is possible to take; through
- *Guided criticality*, where some autonomy is possible with ability to define sub-topics, pose minor questions, and have limited autonomy of action; to
- *Late criticality*, where someone may be able and willing to locate problems, define topics, pose major as well as minor questions, realign frameworks of understandings and take significant actions.

Off the lower end of the continuum of criticality, people might passively accept or even welcome topics chosen, questions posed and conclusions drawn. Those who are instrumentally critical will be unable to move beyond guided criticality in that they cannot realign the topics chosen or the questions posed.

Such issues of control relate especially to discussions in Chapter 2 on creativity, critical theory and social emancipation.

Solution-searching processes

This aspect includes six elements: information location and management; use of explanatory frameworks and theory; engagement with data/evidence/other voices in the field; making links between the domains of formal knowledge, the self or action; reflection and construction of a case.

1. Information location and management

This includes basic technical functions but also includes advanced location, selection and management aspects (such as those involved in writing this book!). We propose a continuum of control over these aspects ranging from:

- *Early criticality*, where people locate and manage information/knowledge with guidance, perhaps from multiple sources; to
- *Guided criticality*, where people locate and manage information/knowledge with minimal guidance; through to
- *Late criticality*, where people locate and manage information autonomously.

Off the lower end of the continuum of criticality, people might make do with information presented to them in easily available sources such as the media. Those who are instrumentally critical may locate and manage information efficiently but will usually not locate information which challenges existing orthodoxies.

Information location and management relate to discussions of resources in Chapter 2 and earlier in this chapter (see 'Resources Aspects', p. 74).

2. Use of explanatory frameworks and theory

We conceive of theory in broad terms, including formal theory as encountered in academia and also informal explanatory frameworks, as encountered in the broader world. We propose a continuum from:

- *Early criticality*, where people recognize and use theory and explanatory frameworks in limited aspects only. They can somewhat tenuously define

overall theories and explanatory frameworks and select and recognize key points, give examples of theory-driven analysis and recognize the indeterminacy of theories and concepts; through to
- *Guided criticality*, where people have greater control over the use of theoretical and explanatory frameworks. Where appropriate, they can contrast, synthesize and integrate theories and actions, and they may make limited challenges to these frameworks; to
- *Late criticality*, where appropriate, people will challenge theoretical and explanatory frameworks and be able to construct their own.

Off the lower end of the continuum, people might not even recognize theories or frameworks of understanding as such. Those who are instrumentally critical may recognize and use existing theory but will usually not challenge such theories, even when it is appropriate to do so.

Such issues of theory use relate to discussions of resources, field-specific knowledge and some aspects of social emancipatory and psychological approaches in Chapter 3.

3. Nature of engagement with data and evidence and other voices in the field

In different academic fields, data will take different forms (e.g. literary texts, statistical data and various forms of social information). In non-academic settings, it may be various life experiences (personal, professional and general world experiences). Engagement may take the form of assessing evidence, linking different kinds of evidence and understanding the principles behind evidence use. We propose a continuum from:

- *Early criticality*, where people start to recognize the principles of evidence use and the organizing concepts of the field, and where they will identify and somewhat tenuously use data, evidence, and so on from various sources (e.g. academic coursework, new reading, external sources, personal experience, professional experience, friends and colleagues) and where they will use these (summarize and narrate content, plot, and so on; cite evidence to support points made; narrate anecdotes and personal examples; and explore possible scenarios) to support positions they may only partially understand, through
- *Guided criticality*, where people may use evidence with more confidence but still largely within parameters recognized in the field. They can now search for and use evidence more actively and broadly, perhaps exploring relationships between domains and linking theory and practice or

personal experience (probably dynamically and iteratively). They may test evidence or argue with evidence in a limited way (e.g. finding and rejecting irrelevance, evaluating theory against data and consequences in action), but will mainly work within recognized principles of evidence use and the organizing principles of a field. They have more capacity to assess arguments on the basis of greater substantive knowledge, greater field-specific knowledge of key concepts, the logical structure, methods of enquiry, rules of representation, and greater understanding of values and ethical frameworks in the field. They may try, somewhat tentatively, to build explanatory frameworks.
- *Late criticality*, where people will have a broad and deep understanding of data and evidence across the domains and be willing and able to challenge principles and broad frameworks of evidence where appropriate.

Off the lower end of the continuum of criticality, people might not recognize that positions should be supported by evidence. Those who are instrumentally critical can only challenge and manipulate evidence within given parameters.

Such issues of engagement relate to discussions in Chapter 2 on field-specific aspects, critical thinking and intellectual resources and to discussions in Chapter 3 on texts as social exchanges in subjects such as history.

4. Making links between the domains of formal knowledge, the self or action

We propose a continuum ranging from:

- *Early criticality*, where there is limited scope for using linking strategies between domains, where the early critical being has only tenuous control over the processes of making links, and where theories and permitted links are defined by others, through
- *Guided criticality*, where other people still usually define the shape and extent of links, but there is more confident and skilful forging of links between domains and some pushing of the boundaries, to
- *Late criticality*, where people make links creatively and confidently between domains, especially oriented towards redefinition of understandings and actions.

Off the lower end of the continuum of criticality, people do not make meaningful links between domains. Those who are instrumentally critical will only reflect within terms set by others, although they may do this competently.

This element relates to discussions in Chapter 2 of Barnett's domains, of transfer in cognitive psychology and of emancipatory approaches to criticality.

5. Reflection on knowledge, self and actions

We propose a continuum ranging from:

- *Early criticality*, where people reflect in a limited way within bounds set by others on such matters as immediate competence, through
- *Guided criticality*, where people reflect more confidently on thoughts, self and action and where there is some reflection on underlying purposes, to
- *Late criticality*, where people reflect extensively on thoughts, actions and the self, including underlying direction and values.

Off the lower end of the continuum of criticality, people may not reflect with any degree of confidence or care. Those who are instrumentally critical will reflect only within terms set by others: that is, they will function largely at the early criticality level, although they may learn to do so confidently.

Such issues of reflection relate to discussions in Chapter 2 of metacognition and social emancipation. They also relate to discussions in Chapter 3 of super-expertise where people continue to develop in professional practice after initial training.

6. Constructing a case

This relates to gathering and processing knowledge and building a case with a view to representing it in speech, in writing or in the shape of actions. It may involve making generalizations, testing out values and evidence and thinking how to persuade. We propose a continuum from:

- *Early criticality*, where people may build a case only uncertainly and with limited skills and understanding of how to do so and why. They will make generalizations, state and test personal values, propose interpretations of theory and explanatory frameworks, seek to persuade or act with limited autonomy of thought or action and test propositions, through
- *Guided criticality*, where people will have more control over the process and where they will seek to persuade or act with some autonomy and have greater control over the process of case construction, to
- *Late criticality*, where people have mastery over the process of constructing a case and are able to challenge and shape rules, where appropriate.

A Proposed Framework for Criticality Development

Off the lower end of the continuum of criticality, people may not be able to construct a case with any degree of control or confidence. Those who are instrumentally critical may be able to build a case with confidence and competence, but be unable and unwilling to challenge the rules for doing so.

Such issues of constructing a case relate to discussions in Chapter 2 of creative thinking and criticality as embedded in specific fields.

Rationale building

This aspect includes one element: spoken or written representation of a case. We propose a continuum ranging from:

- *Early criticality*, where people will have tenuous and emerging control over acceptable forms of representation, through
- *Guided criticality*, where people know the rules for representation and are able to operate competently within them and there is some pushing at the existing boundaries of what is acceptable representation, to
- *Late criticality*, where people will be able to operate fully competently within existing representational rules and, where appropriate, be able to challenge those rules.

Off the lower end of the continuum of criticality, people will not know how to represent a case. Those who are instrumentally critical may be able to represent a case confidently, but be unable and/or unwilling to challenge the rules for doing so.

Such issues of constructing a case relate to discussions in Chapter 2 of criticality within specific fields and discussion of resources.

Understanding the nature of the territory

This aspect includes the elements of understanding power relationships and functioning effectively at an interpersonal and political level within the territory. We propose a continuum ranging from:

- *Early criticality*, where people are finding out where legitimacy and authority lie within a field and what the rules of action are, through
- *Guided criticality*, where there will be more confident working within established power relationships and perhaps some small attempts to challenge the status quo, to
- *Late criticality*, where people may engage as active protagonists and challenge and shape the rules of action where appropriate.

Off the lower end of the continuum, people will not recognize or be able to function within power relationships. In some cases, they may reject the power relationships from a principled point of view, which may constitute an alternative territorial position. Those who are instrumentally critical will merely work within existing power relations. Such issues of power relationships relate to Barnett (1997), to social emancipatory approaches and to discussions of context throughout Chapters 1, 2 and 3.

The nature of professional development in an applied subject

Given that one of the subject areas under special consideration in this book is a professional field, the nature of professional development needs brief consideration. Barnett (1997) presents a conceptualization of critical professionalism which incorporates the domains of formal knowledge, the self and the world. He argues that a professional should be able to:

- interpret the world through theory;
- handle theoretical frameworks effectively in action;
- understand the principles of different frameworks of action and how to act within these;
- act within ethical codes and values;
- speak out on public controversies relevant to the profession and their professional knowledge;
- show loyalty to their profession rather than wanton self-interest;
- deploy professional knowledge throughout society, and not only with clients;
- engage with multiple and perhaps competing discourses (e.g. a patient as consumer of expensive services and a patient in need of attention); and
- show personal qualities of fortitude, steadiness, integrity. (pp. 132–44)

We might wish to add commitment to inter-professional activity, an area which has grown in significance in the last decade.

We think that this conception is beyond what can be expected of undergraduate student practitioners, that is, of nascent professionals who are struggling to come to terms with the substantive practical and theoretical knowledge expected of them by external agencies. However, Barnett's conceptualization sets out a clear vision for advanced or transformative criticality in professional life, which agrees substantially with the goals that Social Work educators expressed to us in interviews.

How people develop criticality

In this section, we outline our understandings of how people learn to be critical, discussing first the process of acquiring resources and moving through the developmental levels proposed in 'Developmental Aspects', p. 81 in this chapter. Secondly, we discuss how the overall curriculum and assessment processes relate to critical development.

How people acquire the resources necessary for criticality

To develop criticality, people must acquire the resources discussed in this chapter (see 'Resources Aspects', p. 74). People will develop resources by various means, formal and informal, often operating in combination. Three approaches to learning, discussed in Chapter 3, are especially useful for understanding how people acquire the necessary resources for criticality. The first is social constructivism, especially the Vygotskyan tradition where language is viewed as a means whereby joint knowledge and understandings are created and by which people can teach one another, not necessarily in a formal environment. The social constructivist models of intellectual development offered by Perry and others add a metacognitive or reflective element, for example, the claim by Perry (1968/1999) that going through the process of working out whether a position is reasonable or not leads in itself to development. Secondly, communities of practice approaches (Wenger, 1998; Lave et al., 1991), also focus on social aspects of learning and are especially useful for developing understandings of how people learn social practices, although not so useful for developing understandings of how they develop beyond existing practices. Thirdly, cognitivist understandings of high- and low-road transfer, of cyclical alternation between abstractions and empirical presentations of cases, and of crisscrossing territory in diverse ways are likely to be useful practical strategies for teaching and learning.

How people develop through levels and across domains

People work through the developmental levels, learning basic concepts, principles and practices underlying the substantive material with which they are engaged before exercising advanced levels of criticality. They must develop the various types of knowledge and personal qualities necessary for critical processes.

People will reach fully effective criticality only after a prolonged and strenuous process, probably requiring experience of the world (at least in the fields we are investigating). Many intermediate levels of criticality exist, and these are sufficient for effective functioning in most everyday circumstances for most people. We are sceptical that it is reasonable or desirable to expect many undergraduate students to reach the higher transformative levels of criticality or to expect higher education to enable them to do so.

Progress from early to advanced criticality is unlikely to be smooth and uniform, given its complex nature. A more uneven process of development is likely with partial moves forward, unexpected returns, temporary and partial understandings, sideways moves and variable motivation. This accords with Vygotsky's views of the uneven, unpredictable nature of learning as discussed in Chapter 3. Students may be able to carry out the activities at each level with varying levels of competence and consistency, even within a single assignment. People may learn from going through a critical process, even if the associated critical product is unsuccessful. People may exercise criticality at variable levels in different domains. However, it would be highly unusual not to see any development in a student over the years of a degree programme. The speed of development also varies considerably according to individuals and context. As well as individual biographic context, there is always the uncertain contested element of genetically heritable aspects of ability (see 'Intelligence', Chapter 3, p. 56); our argument is that at least part of the practice of criticality can be learned.

The developmental process is filled with tension and complexity as priorities and agendas compete, as our analyses in the following chapters illustrate.

At times students may appear to develop critically, but the authentic nature of the development is uncertain as conformity to the requirement for 'independent thought' may hide underlying compliance rather than true independence, as described by Perry (1968/1999) in Chapter 3 (see 'Intellectual Development Approaches', p. 59). It is difficult to discriminate between students mimicking criticality as an external process and those undertaking criticality as a process they have internalized. We see both processes in our data, but we also see students struggling to take on the criticality process and being unable to do so effectively because of their lack of resources.

The complex developmental moves through the levels and across the domains will probably be accompanied by personal changes as we will see clearly in Chapter 8 in discussions of the year abroad, for example.

Curricular and assessment aspects

The overall arrangement of the curriculum will facilitate critical development to a greater or lesser degree. There are at least two aspects to consider: the formal, overt curriculum; and tacit, underlying aspects.

For undergraduates, the university is structured as a learning environment, and the curriculum planned overtly by individuals and committees, organized in time and space by timetabling procedures and described in documentation as explained in Chapter 5. Curriculum models reflect a learning ideal as envisioned by those who create the curriculum. This ideal should offer an appropriate environment to encourage criticality development, as envisioned by the arguments put forward in this chapter.

The formal curriculum model may or may not reflect reality on the ground and has a complex relationship with that reality. There are many tacit aspects underlying the overt, formal curriculum. Snyder (1970) provides a discussion of such aspects: lecturers' assumptions and values, student expectations, the social context of the institutions, and so on. Classroom relationships and student perceptions of lecturer expectations, for example, will affect the type of critical development encouraged. There may be formal assessment tasks, but the students will actively reinterpret their requirements.

Assessment has an important role in developing criticality; there are strong links between learning, feedback and assessment (see Black et al., 1998; Becker et al.1968; Brown et al., 1994; Elton et al., 1979; Snyder, 1970) and a strong backwash effect from assessment on learning. Therefore, the nature of criticality development will be influenced by the type of assessment to which a student is exposed. As well as the formal overt manifestation of assessment, its shadowy, unintended consequences have to be considered. For example, the formal description of a course may say that critical thinking is required, but the assessment format consists of an assignment which does not allow criticality, for instance, a descriptive task. Students may learn to play the assessment system, earning high grades while not undertaking critical thinking, as described by Miller et al. (1974).

In their review of how assessment can best support learning, Black and Wiliam highlight the importance of intrinsic motivation, confidence building, detailed and substantive feedback, collaboration rather than competition and the need to encourage students' metacognitive skills and thus their ability to monitor and direct their own learning. This aligns with social constructivist approaches to learning and assessment, described in Chapter 3, and contributes to a favourable context for criticality development.

In later chapters, we show how assessment practices within particular fields influence students' critical development.

Disciplinary assessment practices affect the shape of students' critical development, depending on the nature of the assessment. As we will see in Chapter 7, the assignments in each field in our study focus on different aspects of criticality, encouraging the development of different types of resources in the students.

Conclusion

In this chapter we have proposed a conceptual framework for understanding criticality and its development. In following chapters we explore how the conceptualization of criticality described above relates to official documentation on an international, national and institutional level (Chapter 5) and the reality of our data (Chapters 6 through 8). In Chapter 9 we continue this exploration, drawing together the conceptual implications arising from Chapters 5 through 8.

Chapter 5

Criticality Goals in the Undergraduate Curriculum

Introduction

In this chapter we explore in more detail the ways in which goals associated with criticality appear in written curriculum documentation. These documents are increasingly defined in terms of competency and 'learning outcomes', with potentially problematic implications for more open-ended and process-oriented visions (Barnett, 1994). In the context of the UK we examine documentation relevant for programmes in the Humanities (Languages) and the Social Sciences (Social Work), ranging from national documentation produced by the Quality Assurance Agency for Higher Education (2008 and preceding versions), to internal documentation produced by our case study institution, the University of Westford. But first we will briefly consider the international policy context and the treatment of criticality in a selection of strategic national documents.

International trends: declared goals for higher education

Governmental and employer policy statements on higher education in countries like the US, Australia and the UK are increasingly focused on the development of skills among graduates which will equip them for careers in a globalized and post-industrial environment, often conceptualized as the 'knowledge society'. Examples include the report of the US Department of Education, *A Test of Leadership* (2006); the Commonwealth of Australia's *Review of Australian Higher Education* (Bradley Report, 2008); the report of the UK National Committee of Inquiry into Higher Education, *Higher Education in the Learning Society* (Dearing Report, 1997); and the report of the UK Department for Business Innovation and Skills, titled *Higher Ambitions* (2009).

What is the place of criticality among the graduate qualities envisaged by these policy pronouncements? Both *A Test of Leadership* and *Higher Ambitions* are mostly concerned with financing, participation and access to higher education, and meeting the general needs of the 'knowledge economy' for a flexible and highly skilled workforce; they do not elaborate in detail on the skills to be developed. *A Test of Leadership* makes a brief reference to broader goals: 'We want a world-class higher-education system that creates new knowledge, contributes to economic prosperity and global competitiveness, and empowers citizens' (p. viii).

From our perspective, different types of criticality are essential for achieving such goals. However, *A Test of Leadership* refers only in passing to critical thinking as part of a necessary disposition for employment: 'Employers report repeatedly that many new graduates they hire are not prepared to work, lacking the critical thinking, writing and problem-solving skills needed in today's workplaces' (p. 3).

Higher Ambitions defines the broad social role of higher education in somewhat similar terms, minus the reference to citizenship:

> Alongside its social and cultural role, higher education is, and will continue to be, central to this country's economic performance in the twenty-first century. It is the key mechanism through which knowledge is generated, preserved and passed on. It equips people for the increasingly complex challenges of the modern workplace by teaching skills and instilling intellectual curiosity and self-confidence. (p. 12)

Higher Ambitions also refers specifically to aspects of criticality, although only in the context of employability. It mentions 'the skills that globalisation and a knowledge economy demand' (p. 3) and 'generic skills in teamworking, reasoning and communicating' (p. 40), while calling for increased employer input in defining skills and in developing appropriate curricula.

The earlier Dearing Report (NCIHE, 1997) and the Bradley Report (Commonwealth of Australia, 2008) deal in greater depth with the wider goals of higher education and consequently treat criticality issues more explicitly. The Dearing Report was produced during the rapid expansion of the UK higher education system. It, too, was concerned with funding issues, and promoted the introduction of substantial student fees to fund expansion. To justify this new funding stream, the report also advocated new and more transparent accountability systems, including much greater explicitness about the knowledge and skills to be acquired from higher education programmes.

Like *A Test of Leadership* and *Higher Ambitions*, the Dearing Report was concerned centrally with the preparation of graduates for employment. However, it took a more traditional liberal view of the broad purposes of higher education:

- to inspire and enable individuals to develop their capabilities to the highest potential levels throughout life, so that they grow intellectually, are well-equipped for work, can contribute effectively to society and achieve personal fulfilment;
- to increase knowledge and understanding for their own sake and to foster their application to the benefit of the economy and society;
- to serve the needs of an adaptable, sustainable, knowledge-based economy at local, regional and national levels;
- to play a major role in shaping a democratic, civilised, inclusive society. (NICHE, 1997, para 5.11)

An ambitious view of criticality is at least implicit in these objectives; the report also took the view that acquisition of the skills expected by employers must be underpinned by creativity, the ability to work across disciplinary boundaries and 'development of general powers of the mind' (para. 5.18).

The Dearing Report also distinguished between types of degree programmes in terms relevant to our study, reflecting to some extent the differing 'cognitive purposes' associated with 'soft pure' and 'soft applied' disciplines, discussed in Chapter 2 (Neumann et al., 2002). Considering applied or professional qualifications such as the Social Work degree discussed in this book, the report presented a definition of professionalism involving development of the self and capability for action in the world:

> The essence of professionalism is a thorough and up-to-date grasp of the fundamental knowledge base of an occupation; sufficient understanding of the underlying theoretical principles to be able to adapt to novel circumstances and to incorporate research findings into practice; and appropriate practical skills and professional values. (para. 5.19)

These were contrasted with 'programmes in higher education which give students the chance to pursue, in depth, an academic subject in which they have a great interest, but which is not likely to be used directly in subsequent employment' (para. 5.20). It was argued that, while such programmes 'develop high level intellectual skills in their students', they should also promote capabilities such as communication and IT skills, flexibility, teamwork and self-development, for employability reasons. Finally, the report commended interdisciplinary programmes for responding to: 'the need in society, and in work, for people who have a breadth of understanding and an educational basis from which they can build in a range of directions as life develops' (para. 5.21).

These distinctions among programmes point towards possible disciplinary differences in the development of criticality, which we explore later.

The recent Bradley Report (Commonwealth of Australia, 2008) is concerned with increasing student participation and investment, after a decade during which Australian public funding for higher education has fallen well below that of other members of the Organisation for Economic Cooperation and Development (OECD); it also deals with a perceived decline in educational quality. This report shares much of the broader Dearing vision of the purposes of higher education, showing considerable continuity with traditional liberal educational values. Thus, the 'educational' function of higher education is described as:

Developing and disseminating advanced-level knowledge and skills through teaching and scholarship:

- to provide for self-fulfilment, personal development and the pursuit of knowledge as an end in itself;
- to provide the skills of critical analysis and independent thought to support full participation in a civil society;
- to prepare leaders for diverse, global environments; and
- to support a highly productive and professional labour force. (p. 5)

However, the Bradley Report also favours strengthening audit processes and curriculum regulation, with increased emphasis on explicit definition of academic standards and intended learning outcomes. This interest is shared today by many higher education systems internationally (Harris, 2009). It calls into question whether and how far advanced criticality development is compatible with an outcomes-based philosophy of education; this book explores how the development of criticality is faring in practice in the UK system, where the curriculum is already framed substantially in 'outcomes' terms.

International trends: criticality in undergraduate 'standards'

The OECD is examining the feasibility of defining and measuring shared sets of learning outcomes across different national higher education systems through its 'Assessment of Higher Education Learning Outcomes' project (OECD, 2008). Various European countries are also attempting to develop shared standards in individual academic disciplines through the so-called 'tuning process' (Harris, 2009). This initiative has accompanied the Bologna process, which is reshaping European higher education into three administrative cycles, following a 3 + 2 + 3 model: Harris (2009) reports similar standard-setting and standard-measuring projects in a wide range of countries.

When examined from the perspective of criticality, however, these projects and initiatives are not altogether consistent in their expectations. For example, the official descriptors for the lowest-level Bologna award depict students who:

- have demonstrated knowledge and understanding in a field of study that builds upon their general secondary education, and . . . includes some aspects . . . informed by knowledge of the forefront of their field of study;
- can apply their knowledge and understanding in a manner that indicates a professional approach to their work or vocation and have competences typically demonstrated through devising and sustaining arguments and solving problems within their field of study;
- have the ability to gather and interpret relevant data (usually within their field of study) to inform judgements that include reflection on relevant social, scientific or ethical issues;
- can communicate information, ideas, problems and solutions to both specialist and non-specialist audiences; and
- have developed those learning skills that are necessary . . . to continue to undertake further study with a high degree of autonomy. (Bologna Working Group, 2005, pp. 194–5)

The word 'critical' does not appear in this definition, though references to 'arguments', 'problem solving' and 'judgements' imply some critical activity. Neither does the current *Australian Qualifications Framework Implementation Handbook* mention criticality in reference to Bachelors degrees; the notion of 'critical evaluation' first appears in the section on Masters degrees

(AQF Advisory Board, 2007, pp. 51 and 69). On the other hand, these definitions were criticized as outdated by the Bradley Report (2008); the 'graduate attributes' proposed by the University of Melbourne as part of its own curriculum reform project, for example, are much more ambitious. According to this framework, graduates should be:

- Academically excellent:
  o have a strong sense of intellectual integrity and the ethics of scholarship;
  o have in-depth knowledge of their specialist discipline(s);
  o reach a high level of achievement in writing, generic research activities, problem solving and communication;
  o be critical and creative thinkers, with an aptitude for continued self-directed learning;
  o be adept at learning in a range of ways, including through information and communication technologies.

- Knowledgeable across disciplines:
  o examine critically, synthesize and evaluate knowledge across a broad range of disciplines;
  o expand their analytical and cognitive skills through learning experiences in diverse subjects;
  o have the capacity to participate fully in collaborative learning and to confront unfamiliar problems;
  o have a set of flexible and transferable skills for different types of employment.

In addition, they should be 'leaders in communities', 'attuned to cultural diversity' and 'active global citizens' (University of Melbourne, 2007).

Thus it seems that, internationally, there is interest in finding an appropriate place for criticality within increasingly explicit definitions of the desired outcomes of higher education. However, there is still uncertainty about how much can be expected, and whether to frame criticality narrowly in terms of problem solving and employment skills or much more broadly in terms of the development of creative and independent actors in the world.

The national context

A national agency for curriculum oversight

Following the recommendations of the Dearing Report, universities in England, Wales and Northern Ireland adopted a national accountability framework for curricula and awards, regulated by the Quality Assurance Agency (QAA) for Higher Education. (Scotland has a separate though cognate system, the *Scottish Credit and Qualifications Framework*, 2001.) Established in 1997, the QAA 'safeguards quality and standards in UK higher education', checking how well universities and colleges meet their responsibilities and encouraging ongoing improvement (QAA, 2009).

Although the primary responsibility for standards and quality rests officially with individual institutions, the regular publication of detailed reports (Subject Reviews from 1995–2001, then Institutional Reviews) by QAA became a significant means of ensuring that degree programmes conformed to the agency's expectations.

In the field of curriculum design, the QAA carried through several proposals of the Dearing Report (1997) including:

- publishing the 'Framework for Higher Education Qualifications in England, Wales and Northern Ireland' (2008 and preceding versions);
- drawing up 'Benchmark Statements' for individual academic disciplines; and
- promoting 'Programme Specifications' as the main tool for designing individual higher education programmes.

Each of these initiatives has influenced both general and field specific perspectives on criticality in the UK undergraduate curriculum, as we show briefly below.

A national qualifications framework

The Framework for Higher Education Qualifications (FHEQ) was first issued in 2000 and revised subsequently to align it more closely to the European Bologna process (2008). However, the Framework descriptor most relevant to our interest in undergraduate criticality (BA Honours) has remained virtually unchanged over the period.

As in the European and Australian cases, the BA Honours descriptor is brief and schematic. It refers to the acquisition of knowledge, understanding and analysis techniques within a particular field of study. Critical thinking skills mentioned include the ability to frame questions, design and sustain arguments and take account of 'the uncertainty . . . of knowledge' (p. 19, para. 35), to evaluate arguments and concepts critically and to make judgements. There are expectations that 'analytic techniques and problem-solving skills' (p. 19, para. 36) acquired when studying can be transferred to employment, along with communication skills. The only personal qualities mentioned have to do with initiative and personal responsibility; there is no mention of self-reflection, and employment is the only social context mentioned. Neither values nor ethics are mentioned; overall, the prime focus is on defining the knowledge and cognitive skills to be acquired by the individual student, typically within an academic field, but employability is seen as the main rationale for degree level study.

In the next section, we examine how this short descriptor is complemented by the much longer 'subject benchmark statements' devised to guide curriculum development in individual academic disciplines.

Benchmark statements

According to the QAA, subject benchmark statements:

> set out broad expectations about degree standards in subjects . . . They describe what can be expected of a graduate in terms of broad subject coverage and the techniques and skills gained at first degree (and sometimes Master's) level in a subject. (2009)

Like the FHEQ, subject benchmark statements were introduced following the recommendations of the Dearing Report (1997); by 2010, over 60 statements had been written. The declared rationale was to make more transparent the content and standards of HE curricula, and accordingly to increase 'confidence' in the system. They were used as reference points for the Subject Reviews conducted by the QAA up to 2001, and the disciplinary programmes developed by individual institutions are still expected to take them into account.

The benchmark statements discussed here are those for 'Languages and Related Studies' (QAA, 2002, 2007) and 'Social Work' (QAA, 2000, 2008). In the following sections we explore their respective conceptualizations of criticality. During our empirical investigation of undergraduate teaching and learning from 2002 to 2004, the first editions of these statements were in force. The second editions have changed little in essence, however, and are the main focus of discussion below.

'Languages and related studies' benchmark statement

The 2007 benchmark statement argues that languages as an academic discipline are at the same time:

- a medium of understanding, expression and communication, described ... as the use of the target language;
- a means of access to other societies and cultures, described ... as intercultural awareness, understanding and competence;
- an object of study in their own right, described ... as the explicit knowledge of language; and
- a gateway to related thematic studies, ... described ... as knowledge of the cultures, communities and societies where the language is used. (QAA, 2007, p. 2)

The first of these dimensions, the acquisition of language proficiency, is presented at length in the document as a matter of skill development. The only allusion to any aspect of criticality involves the expectation that students will be self-aware as language learners, able to manage the learning process to suit their learning style and level (p. 8, para. 5.9); this may be interpreted as a type of knowledge of the self, though at a fairly basic instrumental level.

The second dimension (intercultural awareness) is presented in a variety of ways, first to do with the self (para. 5.7): as a disposition (e.g. 'ability and willingness to engage with other cultures') and as a value position (e.g. 'appreciation of the uniqueness of other culture(s)'). Secondly, intercultural awareness is viewed as a domain of knowledge and cognitive skill:

> the ability to compare the view of the world from their own languages and cultures with the view of the world from the languages and cultures they have studied ... comparing, contrasting and mediating between the two (or more) societies with which they are familiar. (p. 6, para. 4.4)

Finally, intercultural awareness is seen as involving instrumental problem solving ('an ability to function in another culture', para. 5.7).

The third dimension, explicit knowledge of language, is treated as an aspect of subject knowledge supporting the practical business of language acquisition and use, together with some instrumental skills ('make effective use of language reference materials ...', para. 5.8). 'Knowledge of language structure' (para. 4.5) is seen as supporting skill development but not in itself contributing to criticality development.

The final dimension, 'related thematic studies', acknowledges the multidisciplinary nature of language studies in higher education. Students are expected to encounter a range of disciplines in the humanities and social sciences, with reference to target cultures and societies (such as history, literature, politics), and acquire 'analytical, critical and specialist skills drawn from the relevant discipline areas' (para. 5.11, p. 8).

In terms of undergraduate criticality development, the most distinctive feature of the Languages benchmark is the emphasis placed on 'intercultural awareness'. This is discussed somewhat confusingly in different places as an attribute, a skill, and so on. However, this domain has evident potential for self-conscious development of relativist dispositions and values, and for comparative reflection on home and other cultures. There are clear expectations here for extended reflection on the self, and indeed an openness to possible self-development and change. Another feature of interest is the multidisciplinary content of languages. While this relatively 'free-ranging' content is characteristic of 'soft pure' subjects (Neumann et al., 2002), an obvious question relates to the extent to which relationships and links are developed across fields, and skills learned in one field are transferred to another (as outlined in Chapter 4, 'Solution-Searching Processes', p. 87).

Finally, the investment of time and effort in the development of language proficiency (including the common experience of residence abroad) has ambiguous implications for the development of criticality. As noted above, this is described in the benchmark statement as a matter of skill development and use, without direct reference to any aspect of criticality (para. 4.3, p. 6). However, language use has to be about something, and in this respect the statement could be argued to be leaving a semi-open space within which institutions and students can themselves define content and activities, perhaps promoting additional critical development in line with their own priorities. For example, institutions are free to decide whether the target language will be used as a sole or significant medium of instruction on units in culture, history, literature, and so on, and therefore serve as the discourse medium for the development of disciplinary criticality.

Social work benchmark statement

The benchmark statement for the applied professional field of social work was originally published in 2000, at a time when professional registration for social workers was a separate process from their academic studies. However, the first degree in social work subsequently became integrated with professional registration processes as the 'qualifying award' for future social workers.

This change led to a second (2008) edition of the benchmark statement, with input from a range of professional bodies as well as service users.

Here we focus on the 2008 version in interpreting the criticality expected of the newly qualified social work professional.

Social work is an example of a 'highly vocational' programme (see NCIHE, 1997, para. 5.19, quoted earlier). The benchmark statement itself presents social work as 'an applied academic subject . . . characterised by a distinctive focus on practice in complex social situations to promote and protect individual and collective wellbeing' (p. 6, para 4.1).

The underlying curriculum philosophy is summarized as follows:

> At honours level, the study of social work involves the integrated study of subject-specific knowledge, skills and values and the critical application of research knowledge from the social and human sciences, and from social work (and closely related domains) to inform understanding and to underpin action, reflection and evaluation. Honours degree programmes should be designed to help foster this integration of contextual, analytic, critical, explanatory and practical understanding. (p. 6, para. 4.2)

This paragraph links the acquisition of subject knowledge and understanding with professional practice, and this linkage is reiterated throughout later sections dealing with 'social work services', 'service delivery context', 'values and ethics', 'social work theory' and 'social work practice'. For example:

> [ETHICS] 'the moral concepts of rights, responsibility, freedom, authority and power *inherent in the practice of social workers* as moral and statutory agents . . .';
> [SOCIAL WORK THEORY] 'research-based concepts and critical explanations . . . that contribute to the knowledge base of social work, including their distinctive epistemological status *and application to practice* . . .'.

The contested nature of social work practice is explicitly acknowledged. Correspondingly, there are very high expectations of graduates' capacity to gather and evaluate both academic knowledge and 'real world' knowledge (relating to social work service users). There is an extended treatment of 'problem solving' encompassing information-gathering and analytic skills, as well as skills in the management of problems, including intervention in 'real world' situations, and evaluation of processes and outcomes.

The social work benchmark statement thus takes a distinctive view of the domain of 'subject knowledge and understanding', and associated 'critical thinking'. The statement also pays sustained attention to criticality within the domains of both the 'self' and the 'world'. There is an expectation of critical reflection:

> All social work honours graduates should show the ability to reflect on and learn from the exercise of their skills. They should understand the significance of the concepts of continuing professional development and lifelong learning, and accept responsibility for their own continuing development. (p. 10, para. 5.3)

More specifically, this includes the capacity to:

- reflect on and modify their behaviour in the light of experience;
- identify and keep under review their own personal and professional boundaries;
- manage uncertainty, change and stress in work situations;
- handle inter- and intrapersonal conflict constructively; and
- take responsibility for their own continuing acquisition and use of knowledge and skills. (p. 13, para. 5.8)

In Barnett's terms (1997), these expectations involve both regular self-reflection and a conscious commitment to development of the self. They are complemented by expectations concerning the world of action. These include skills of 'intervention and evaluation' when working with clients, community members and other professionals; 'communication skills' appropriate to working with a wide range of stakeholders and 'skills in working with others', including the capacity to 'challenge others when necessary'. These accounts move well beyond instrumental problem solving, to encompass reflective practice.

Unsurprisingly, the document does not explicitly address 'transformatory' levels of criticality; its core concern is with preparing new social workers to operate effectively within existing frameworks of social work legislation and practice, that is, 'guided' criticality in our terms. On the other hand, as we have seen, the 'contested' nature of social work practice is acknowledged, and graduates are expected to appraise critically the 'evidence base' for social work. The moral underpinning for social work is a consistent theme; for example, among 'skills in working with others' is included the call to act with others to increase social justice by identifying and responding to prejudice, institutional discrimination and structural inequality (p. 13, para. 5.7).

Thus, a foundation is laid in terms of reflective habits and commitment to moral and ethical judgement, which could lead over a lifetime's career to a more 'transformational' form of critical engagement.

Benchmark statements: conclusion

When compared with the generic BA Honours Descriptors of the *HE Qualifications Framework*, discussed above, the two benchmark statements seem considerably more ambitious in terms of criticality development. Both statements involve engagement with disciplinary knowledge and associated skills, though in languages these associated skills are more clearly related to selected 'knowledge' domains, while in social work there is considerable concern with transfer of disciplinary knowledge and integration with practice in the world. Both statements include considerable expectations regarding development of the self, one through intercultural encounter and exploration, the other through engagement with action and the evaluation of action. Areas of the languages experience are left relatively 'open' and undefined (in particular, residence abroad). Social work, on the other hand, expects its graduates to develop a portfolio of skills to do with critical action in the world, within the defined parameters of social work practice. A final difference is the strong emphasis on moral choices and judgements to be found in the social work statement, which is largely absent from the languages statement, but overall these documents make strong and positive statements about the types of criticality to be expected of graduates.

Institutional documents and statements

In this section we move from the national level to our case study institution, the University of Westford, and we examine the 'programme specifications' (or defined curricula) produced for selected individual BA/BSc programmes. We explore these documents for the view presented of criticality and criticality development, within the constraints of a discourse focused substantially on competencies and 'intended learning outcomes'. Where these documents provide an abbreviated account we briefly explore other complementary documentation.

The nature of programme specifications

Programme specifications were adopted as a tool for curriculum design in the early 2000s, in the interests of greater transparency and accountability.

The QAA states: 'A programme specification is a concise description of the intended learning outcomes of an HE programme, and the means by which the outcomes are achieved and demonstrated' (QAA, 2006).

The Dearing Committee anticipated that programme specifications could explain to prospective students what the 'intended outcomes' would be for their chosen programme. In practice, programme specifications have primarily supported audit and accountability, describing programme content for an audience of quality managers. They typically deal with:

- the knowledge and understanding that a student will be expected to have upon [programme] completion;
- key skills: communication, numeracy, the use of information technology and learning how to learn;
- cognitive skills, such as understanding of methodologies or ability in critical analysis; and
- subject-specific skills, such as laboratory skills. (Dearing, 1997)

Under these or related headings, lists of behavioural statements are normally provided, summarizing the intended learning outcomes for each. An account is also included of teaching, learning and assessment processes leading to achievement of the intended learning outcomes.

This outcomes-based approach to curriculum design was pioneered in higher education in the USA, UK, Australia and New Zealand (Nusche, 2008). Programme specifications can be seen as part of the apparatus for developing what Barnett (1994) terms 'operational competence', that is, the equipping of a mass labour force with predetermined knowledge and skills. We have commented already on the problematic relationship in principle between the shift towards mass higher education focusing on employability, and the older 'liberal' legacy. However, we have also noted in the benchmark statements just examined an evident commitment to the development of various dimensions of criticality. It is not evident that all aspects of criticality as defined in this book can easily be captured within a discourse of 'intended learning outcomes'. As Nusche notes, the outcomes of higher education are not limited to those which can be formally defined (she cites the disposition of 'civic engagement' as an example: Nusche, 2008, p. 8). Here we examine actual examples of programme specifications from the case study institution to explore how far 'criticality' is captured formally within statements of intended outcomes or is otherwise embedded as a focus of attention.

A sample programme specification in languages

The University of Westford offers a range of BA programmes, including languages taught singly, in combination, or in combination with other disciplines. The programme specification selected here for analysis to represent the disciplinary area is that of Single Honours degrees in Modern Languages (2007 version).

The document begins with an extended prose preamble which explains the aims of the languages curriculum in broad terms. The development of target language proficiency is conceptualized with reference to the Common European Framework of Reference for Languages (CEFR). This is a 'ladder' model of foreign language proficiency produced by the Council of Europe (2001), which serves as an influential point of reference in outcomes-focused language curriculum planning internationally. While the university organizes language teaching in terms of its own set of seven 'stages', these are related to the six-level CEFR, with Stage 6 (in between C1 'Effective Operational Proficiency' and C2 'Mastery' on the CEFR) as the minimum declared target for single honours graduates, and Stage 7 a clear C2 equivalent. The preamble describes the intended learning outcomes for languages at the various stages as encompassing:

- linguistic competence;
- knowledge and understanding of language form, use and cultural context; and
- language learning strategies.

The preamble also describes in broad terms the aims for 'knowledge and understanding' in languages, including the following:

- major social, political and cultural developments within Europe and the other countries where our languages have been spoken during their recent history;
- one or more cultures and societies, other than their own, and the similarities and dissimilarities between those cultures and societies in comparison with their own;
- aspects of the cultures, linguistic contexts, history, politics, geography, social and economic structures of the countries studied;
- significant, and sometime competing, methodologies, theories and issues relating to Social and Political Studies, Linguistic Studies or Literary and Cultural Studies within the context of the curriculum;

- the interaction of language, text, image and sociocultural context;
- social, political and/or gender aspects of the cultures they have chosen to study;
- the culture and society of a particular country where they have spent their residence abroad.

'Residence Abroad' is briefly referred to; this normally comprises the third year of a four-year languages programme, which may be spent at a foreign university, working as a foreign language assistant in a school, or working in business. This experience is designed 'to contribute to students' language development, their knowledge of the country concerned, their intercultural skills, and their ability to conduct an independent study project'.

Finally, the preamble deals with the 'key skills' addressed across the languages curriculum:

- communicate effectively and confidently in English and in one or more foreign languages (including English), both orally and in writing, including being able to engage an audience in discussion and sustaining a long and complex piece of writing;
- demonstrate intercultural competence;
- demonstrate effective learning and research skills, including the use of ICT.

This broad characterization of the curriculum does not include any explicit reference to criticality or critical thinking, but presents the field largely in terms of knowledge resources and instrumental skills, including linguistic skills. However, there is acknowledgement of the need to problematize aspects of multidisciplinary knowledge, with the reference to 'sometimes competing' theories and to interrelate different areas of knowledge ('language . . . and sociocultural context'). There is mention of 'independent study' undertaken during residence abroad; all these presuppose some elements of criticality development, at least in the knowledge domain. The concept of 'intercultural competence/skills', potentially highly relevant to critical development of the self, is not elaborated upon at this point. Finally, it is not made clear whether the target foreign language will be used as a study medium for substantive content (and related development of critical thinking), though it is implied to be a substantially separate 'skill' strand.

The sample programme specification amplifies the preamble in some relevant respects, mainly through the specification of 'thinking skills' to be acquired through both language development activities and content courses:

- define, present and exemplify concepts;
- identify concepts and data relevant to the task in hand;
- select, synthesize and focus information from a range of sources in both English and your target language;
- analyse and discuss theoretical questions;
- apply knowledge, understanding and analysis critically to different topics;
- formulate and defend personal judgements clearly and persuasively on the basis of evidence;
- engage with subject matter and opinion in both breadth and depth;
- understand, apply and evaluate different methodologies;
- formulate and clarify critical questions;
- collect, analyse and present empirical data (where appropriate);
- analyse and question assumptions and received opinions and propose alternatives.

This list is essentially an elaboration of the 'knowledge' domain within what we have characterized in Chapter 4 as 'guided criticality'; how the development of these skills relates to the different programme elements (language and content) is not further clarified at this point, apart from the reference to use of multilingual sources.

Concerning the domain of the self, the programme specification makes reference in the 'key skills' section to the development of confidence, independence and initiative, and to the ability to manage one's own learning ('setting and monitoring goals, reflecting on your own learning, and learning from feedback'). However, the concept of 'intercultural competence' is not further elaborated. The contribution of residence abroad to development of the self is described primarily in terms of 'independence and initiative', along with further contributions to critical thinking ability: 'the emphasis is on enhancing independence and initiative in studying a foreign language and culture, developing empirical research skills and producing a long project'. Finally, there are no substantive mentions of 'real world' critical action nor of moral dimensions of academic criticality. Here, of course, the document matches the Languages benchmark statement presented earlier, and fits the broader positioning of non-vocational academic subjects. (See, for example, the Dearing Report's sketch of such subjects:

paras. 5.20, 5.21, quoted in this chapter, 'International Trends, Declared Goals for Higher Education'.)

A Sample Programme Specification in Social Work

The University of Westford ran a BSc in Social Work throughout the period of our empirical investigation. In 2003, as noted earlier, following policy changes in England the degree became an integrated professional qualification leading to award of the Diploma in Social Work alongside the three-year BSc degree, and regulated by the General Social Care Council.

The programme specification developed at Westford in the early 2000s for the BSc in Social Work remained in place with only minor changes throughout the 2000s. Here we draw primarily upon the 2007 version.

The Westford document is closely aligned to the social work benchmark statement as far as criticality development is concerned. The overall aims of the programme were described in 2007 as:

- to provide you with a thorough generic grounding in the academic and professional discipline of Social Work; and
- to produce graduates who are both intellectually well-equipped and professionally competent to embark on careers in several aspects of Social Work.

In 2008 an additional general aim was added, dealing with development of knowledge resources:

- to incorporate relevant foundational study in sociology, social policy and social statistics as well as in social work itself.

Distinctive features of social work graduates from Westford were said to be

- the ability to adopt an approach to social work practice, knowledge and values that is both critical and evaluative; and
- a commitment to become a reflective professional.

Finally, the aims also include a strong focus on values-driven action in the world, mentioning commitment to 'forms of practice that are intolerant of oppression and discrimination'.

The statements of intended learning outcomes for knowledge and understanding relate systematically to the benchmark statement. They include the nature of social work theory and practice; theory for social work (referring to 'models' from sociology, social policy and psychology which are deemed relevant to social work); social, legislative and organizational contexts for social work; values and ethics. A strong concern for relating knowledge and understanding to social work practice pervades these statements.

The statements of intended learning outcomes for skills are divided by Level according to the National Qualifications Framework. 'Critical appraisal', 'evaluation' and 'analysis in relation to academic writing' are mentioned as Level 1 cognitive/intellectual skills; otherwise, references to criticality are concentrated at Levels 2 and 3. Level 2/3 cognitive/intellectual skills are limited to 'synthesising research material' and 'skills required to produce a dissertation'; other listed skills relate extensively to action in the world (planning, implementing and evaluating real world problem solving, working with others, providing leadership and challenge, making theory–practice connections) and to the self (independent learning, reflection, self-management, monitoring own performance). Finally the document lists the expected 'Professional Standards' deriving from the National Occupational Standards for Social Work.

In terms of the Barnett framework (see Chapter 2) and our own (Chapter 4), the social work intended learning outcomes deal centrally with self-monitoring, self-reflection, problem solving and reflective practice, in addition to critical thinking. They arguably provide a platform for the development of self, and eventually a more ambitious transformatory engagement with the world, but these are not their main concerns. Like the stated outcomes for languages, they provide a 'floor' for criticality development rather than a set of maximum aspirations, but they also capture the different domains of criticality more explicitly, due to their focus on professional preparation.

Key concepts: digging deeper

In this section we examine further institutional documentation relevant to domains of criticality which are significant for the subject disciplines in which we are interested.

For languages, we pursue two issues: expectations concerning the contribution of courses and activities promoting language proficiency development to student criticality; and the institution's conception of 'intercultural competence/intercultural skill'. (These issues have been discussed more briefly in Brumfit et al., 2005, and will be pursued further in Chapters 6 and 8.)

For social work, we examine selected documentation dealing in more detail with expectations concerning transfer of cognitive/intellectual knowledge and skill to problem-solving domains, and reflection and action in the world. (These issues have previously been discussed in Ford et al., 2006, and will be revisited in later chapters.)

Language proficiency development and criticality

As explained earlier, the development of language proficiency was conceptualized at Westford in terms of seven language 'stages', from beginner to near-native-speaker level (roughly C2 'Mastery' on the CEFR). The descriptors for Stages 6 and 7 are of most interest here. With regard to the cognitive domain, Stage 6 referred to the ability to understand and to read, with 'relative ease', texts in most registers, including 'specialist areas within the aims of the course' (presumably the reference is to authentic academic texts); Stage 6 students were expected to speak and interact orally on a range of complex, abstract and unfamiliar topics. In writing, they should write clearly on complex topics; they should also 'be aware of' differing rhetorical traditions in different languages. Stage 7 students were expected to understand and to read 'virtually everything', and to 'interpret critically virtually all forms of the written language', including 'abstract, structurally complex, highly colloquial literary or non-literary writings'; they were expected to develop these skills to the level expected of a 'general, educated target language audience'. In speaking they were expected to manage 'linguistically complex interactions, including . . . presenting and defending arguments and analysing concepts'. An important limiting consideration, however, was that 'content' courses were mostly taught and assessed in English (though readings included target language sources). This means that there was no sustained practice in writing critically in the target language in the academic genres associated with the various content fields.

The most substantial piece of target language writing was a 5,000 word project report produced during residence abroad. This project was an empirical investigation of the student's own choice; it was supposed to give students an opportunity to draw together previously learned research skills and employ them in the target language setting. The intended learning outcomes for this project included the following:

- learned how to choose a viable and focused topic . . .;
- adopted a method of investigation appropriate to your topic;

- adopted an analytical approach to your sources . . .;
- organized your material into a structured discussion and drawn appropriate conclusions. (2004 version)

The marking scheme for this project allocated 65 per cent of the marks to content-related areas ('data', 30 per cent; 'analysis of topic', 35 per cent), leaving 35 per cent for quality of language and of presentation. The content-related band descriptors for the highest level of achievement in the investigative project report read as follows (2003 version):

Data	Thoroughly researched, clear evidence of extensive background knowledge, excellent overall understanding of issue; data used effectively to support argument
Analysis of topic	Excellent understanding of issues and highly effective application of methodology, original/independent thinking

This investigative project completed during the third year might be undertaken by students at Stages 5 or 6 on the university's language proficiency scale. The assessment scheme used during the final year for target language compositions by Stage 7 students distributed marks similarly (55 per cent for content, 45 per cent for language). The descriptor for the top band of language performance at Stage 7 read as follows: 'Thoroughly researched and argued piece; challenging received views or suggesting new and worthwhile ways of considering material or approaching material from an unorthodox point of view, when appropriate'.

It is interesting to compare these descriptors stressing originality and independence of thinking with the criteria used for assessment of essays in 'content' courses taught through English. These latter criteria were more elaborate, referring to critical evaluation and use of sources as well as to argumentation. Value continued to be placed on 'originality', but there was a stronger focus on cognitive and disciplinary understanding (2003 version):

- originality of ideas, aims and approach;
- relevance of the answer to the question set;
- accuracy of information;
- the appropriateness of the facts and ideas expressed;
- use of secondary literature;
- quality of analysis, argumentation and critical evaluation;
- argumentation and understanding of topic-related and critical issues;

- structure and organization of argument;
- quality of expression;
- presentation (including referencing).

Overall, it seemed that the fostering of critical thinking skills was not absent from language-related activities, and increased steadily from one language level to the next, but that general communicative proficiency, confidence and initiative, and elements of creativity were most prized. However, during the 2000s, staff continued to review the residence abroad project, and later documentation placed stronger emphasis on cognitive skills, with explicit references to the need for a theoretical framework, research questions and argumentation.

The second distinctive theme of interest in languages documentation is that of intercultural competence. We saw earlier that the benchmark statement for languages stressed this theme, while the institutional programme specification paid it less attention. Here we examine briefly some other relevant institutional documentation.

First, documentation describing the language 'stages' made consistent reference to cultural dimensions of language use. The Stage 6 outline stated that learners should possess 'a confirmed knowledge of most aspects of the target language culture', be aware of how language use varies between social groups, and be aware of 'situational and cultural constraints on language use' (e.g. politeness forms and norms of conversation). In terms of their interpersonal skills, learners should understand underlying 'implications and intentions' of spoken and written language, and be able to manage 'culturally complex interactions'. The Stage 7 outline took this further, referring to a 'thorough, in-depth knowledge of several aspects of the target culture . . .' and the ability to 'handle all situations likely to be encountered in social and professional situations in an acceptable and professional manner'. Stage 7 also emphasized translation skills, expecting that learners would translate material in a range of genres from English to the target language, transferring both content and style.

Thus far, these expectations were concerned with self-monitoring against given norms and expectations, those of the so-called 'target language culture'. However, other activities within the programme could also be expected to provide opportunities for criticality development in the domain of the self: in particular, those associated with study abroad.

There is a large and growing international research and conceptual literature on the nature of intercultural competence or intercultural understanding, its teaching and assessment (e.g. Byram, 1997; Council of Europe, 2001). There is also a growing literature dealing with study abroad and its consequences for intercultural awareness and the development of the self (e.g., Roberts et al., 2001; Murphy-Lejeune, 2002; Pellegrino Aveni, 2005; Jackson, 2008; Kinginger, 2008). This work offers a range of conceptualizations of intercultural competence and its development. These include not only knowledge about cultural difference and the skills to adapt and navigate communication in line with others' norms and expectations, but expectations for identity change and in particular the development of what we have called 'dispositions', but what the Council of Europe call 'existential' competence (or *savoir-être*), that is:

- openness towards, and interest in, new experiences, other persons, ideas, peoples, societies and cultures;
- willingness to relativize one's own cultural viewpoint and cultural value-system; and
- willingness and ability to distance oneself from conventional attitudes to cultural difference. (Council of Europe, 2001, p. 105)

However, at the time of our empirical research, the residence abroad documentation at Westford made rather limited reference to intercultural competence in this broader sense. The general student handbook stressed that how to spend residence abroad was 'one of the most important decisions' for students but did not present any explicit rationale for the various options (study at university, working as a foreign language assistant, or other approved work experience).

Actual preparation for residence abroad took the form of a second-year course, optional during the period of our research but subsequently made compulsory for all students. This course was described as having dual objectives (2006 version):

> You will be prepared both for managing your language learning and acculturation (and keeping a reflective log) and for writing an investigative project during residence abroad, which is separately assessed. The research skills that you acquire will not only be directly relevant to the successful completion of your investigative project but they will also be essential for any other research project you may carry out in your final year as an undergraduate and at postgraduate level.

Thus, the course was partly designed to develop the thinking and research skills needed for the investigative project discussed earlier, and partly to develop elements of self-reflection ('managing language learning and acculturation'), including the tool of a reflective log (later changed to an electronic discussion board). There were references to intercultural issues in the course aims: 'make you aware of cultural differences and help you develop strategies to enhance your personal development'.

The intended learning outcomes for the course also included brief statements of 'skills' such as 'think about cultural differences as an asset', 'cope with the demands of cultural differences', which touched on the development of the self, and formulation of intercultural dispositions or *savoir-être*. The references were brief and undeveloped, however, and it is necessary to examine data from students and lecturers to explore how such statements were interpreted (see Chapter 8).

The documentary guidance offered to students for the investigative project encouraged them to engage meaningfully during the stay abroad with the local community, including, for example, conducting interviews with community members. However, the intended learning outcomes did not contain any reference to dispositions or *savoir-être*, or to self-reflection, and referred to the local community somewhat narrowly as an information source. Similarly, the assessment criteria for the project report focused essentially on thinking skills and did not explicitly require evidence of self reflection or *savoir-être* or the development of intercultural awareness.

In later interviews, the Westford staff showed full awareness of the potential of residence abroad for self-reflection and identity change (see Chapter 8), but overall these aspects of the overall languages experience were not captured clearly within curriculum documentation.

Development of the self, action and reflection in the social work curriculum

For social work, we examine some further documents in order to explore formal expectations concerning a) the development of the self, and b) transfer of cognitive/intellectual knowledge and skill to problem-solving domains, including reflection and action in the world.

During the period of our fieldwork, the first-year social work curriculum included three compulsory social work courses alongside other social science courses. Here we title these courses 'Social Work: An Introduction'; 'Introducing Values and Ethics'; and 'Developing Professionally in Social Work'. The first course prioritized developing students' knowledge and understanding of contemporary social work in national and international settings. The stated aims of the second, however, were to present the 'specific values and ethics' held by contemporary social work professionals, plus a number of key 'moral concepts': 'oppression, participation, power relations and empowerment, and social justice'. The intended learning outcomes included:

- an appreciation of the role of the social worker in reproducing or countering oppressive and discriminatory relations in and through social work practice;
- an understanding of how social workers can work in empowering ways with others.

The key skills identified for this course included:

- the ability to reflect on the interaction in practice between professional and personal values;
- the ability to respect and learn from the expression of a diverse range of viewpoints.

Overall, these goals imply concern from the start that students should adopt a key set of professional values and the disposition to act in support of them.

Finally, the third course, Developing Professionally in Social Work, set out to introduce social work practice, its underpinnings in theory and research, and the skills needed. The intended learning outcomes were phrased largely in terms of knowledge and understanding; however, some dealt with an awareness of the self in terms of readiness for practical social work activity. (This course preceded the first practice placement of the programme, and a significant assessment item was a 'learning portfolio' where students reflected on their own existing skills and those they would need to develop during the placement.) Thus, from the first year onwards, there was commitment to self-reflection in relation to the development of skills as well as values and dispositions.

In later years, alongside further academic courses, students undertook two 'practice placements' with local social work providers, supported by elaborate documentation. We write in more detail about this experience in Chapter 8. Here we note that assessment of the practice placement was carried out with reference to 'core competences' laid down by the General Social Care Council, that is:

- communicate and engage;
- promote and enable;
- assess and plan;
- intervene and provide services;
- work in organisations; and
- develop professional competence.

These 'competences' were interpreted somewhat differently for the first and second practice placements, partly in terms of the amount of initiative and personal responsibility expected of the student. For the first placement, the descriptors detailed in the Student Handbook made consistent references to processes of self-reflection, for example:

- Communicate and Engage: . . . You will be expected to demonstrate your awareness of your own interpersonal skills and how these might impact upon others . . .
- Promote and Enable: . . . Identify and question your own values and prejudices and their implications for practice . . .
- Intervene and Provide: . . . You must demonstrate your use of self awareness and your ability to recognize the impact of self on others . . .

. . . and, most strikingly:

- Work in Organizations: . . . you must identify and question your own values and prejudices and their implications for practice and respect and value uniqueness and diversity, recognizing and building upon strengths, including being able to identify issues within teams. You must identify the potential for conflict within teams and your own role within this . . .

For the second placement, an externally derived and much more behavioural wording was used so that, for example, the descriptors for Work in Organisations became:

- demonstrate capacity to work as an accountable and effective member of the organisation in which placed;
- contribute to the planning, monitoring and control of resources; and
- contribute to the evaluation of the effectiveness, efficiency and economy of services.

The final assessment also included the expectation that the assessor would 'make explicit reference to how the student has demonstrated own values', however, thus acknowledging some interaction between the self and the expected professional standards.

The two practice placements were supported by university-based teaching intended to develop students' practice skills, their self-reflective abilities and their ability to relate social work theory to their developing experience of practice. During the final year, for example, practice placement occupied between three and five days each week. On other days, the students attended university classes, including workshops supporting the final-year dissertation (see Chapter 7), and a non-assessed course titled 'Social Work Theory and Practice'.

Students' actual learning experience on this course is discussed in Chapter 6. Here we note its intended contribution to their criticality development. First, the students attended so-called 'skills development' workshops, practical sessions targeting the development of four interactional skills, deriving from counselling theory: 'authenticity', 'empathy', 'respect' and 'reframing'. In these sessions, a group member (described as the 'talker') presented some genuine personal problem or issue and discussed this with another group member (the 'listener'). The paired discussion was observed and evaluated by the rest of the group. The overall aims as stated in the course handbook were to:

- develop participants' ability to listen attentively;
- demonstrate the importance of a speaker's awareness of the effect on those listening;
- highlight the importance of the listener's role . . . illustrate the value of listening without judging; and
- understand the impact of non-verbal communication.

Here we can see another example of how consistently this programme tried to help students not only to develop professionally needed skills but to reflect on the self and on relations with others, and to develop a relativized and non-judgemental perspective on other people.

The other strand of the 'Social Work Theory and Practice' course was a seminar series titled 'theorising practice', described in the handbook as follows:

> These seminars are a forum in which students can learn how to learn to address the question of what social work 'means' to them as individuals (p. 12) . . . a context where students can learn how to go on learning through taking responsibility for multilevel reflection on their personal and professional experience (p. 14).

The handbook acknowledged that most discussion would derive from ongoing placement experiences. However, it is clear that these open-ended seminars were again intended to promote critical self-reflection and development of the self.

The practice placement was in principle a major opportunity for the development of varied aspects of criticality: critical action in the world, in particular. As noted above, this was accompanied by elaborate forms of documentation to structure and regulate the experience, some locally produced and some deriving from external professional regulatory bodies.

This included a range of formal opportunities for students to evaluate their own practice and also to evaluate the quality of the placement experience in terms of their own development.

One key assignment was known as the 'placement project'. This project centred on a 'piece of work' undertaken during the second work placement. In a 3,000-word report, students were expected to give an account of the context and of relevant legal frameworks; a 'full analytical description' of the piece of work and of the skills the student tried to apply, and 'a discussion' of relevant theory. From the perspective of criticality development, this task can be seen as an opportunity to document reflective practice and to integrate certain knowledge resources (social work theory and legal information) in an 'analytical' discussion of practice. However, the expectations for the task were described in quite open terms and it seemed they might be satisfied by relatively descriptive interconnections between these different domains. In Chapter 7, we examine actual examples.

Conclusion

In this chapter we have examined various curriculum documents from the perspective of criticality development. We have noticed tensions in international policies and policy debates, where discourses of competence, outcomes-based education and employability regularly imply a fairly narrow focus on the lower levels of criticality development. On the other hand, both national and international policy declarations also acknowledge roles for universities and higher education in the creation of knowledge, in the promotion of social cohesion and ethical behaviour and in cultural development, which imply a continuing concern for more open-ended development of individuals as creative and critical beings.

At the level of individual fields, our examination of benchmark statements and programme specifications has shown considerable disciplinary differences with respect to criticality and the extent to which it is captured explicitly within curriculum frameworks. Our sample 'pure' academic subject, Modern Languages, spells out in considerable detail expected gains in the domain of knowledge and critical thinking; development in terms of the 'intercultural' self is clearly viewed as also of great significance, but is spelled out less explicitly and is hardly captured at all in terms of 'intended learning outcomes' within institutional documentation. Our sample 'applied professional' subject, Social Work, also pays attention to the development of knowledge and critical thinking. However, it also pays sustained attention to the development of the 'professional' self, and capacity for action in the real world, including the adoption of an appropriate set of values as well as a range of interpersonal and problem-solving skills, and captures much of this in terms of defined competences and learning outcomes.

In later chapters we explore how key elements of these curricula were actually experienced by students at our case study institution.

Chapter 6

Becoming Critical: Teaching and Learning Processes

Introduction

In this chapter we explore how teachers at Westford understood what it meant to be 'critical'. We trace the promotion of criticality through successive years of study and in different types of classrooms. Overall we explore the lecturers' goals for the development of criticality in their discipline, how far the students shared these goals and how far they progressed in achieving them.

Criticality in modern languages learning and teaching

The Modern Languages curriculum at Westford was divided into two strands known informally as 'content' and 'language'. As explained in Chapter 5, the 'content' courses dealt with history, literature, culture, society and linguistics relating to target language contexts. Most content courses were taught predominantly in English, though they also drew on resources in the target language. The 'language' classes also aimed to develop students' knowledge resources and their critical abilities through discussion of cultural and social themes, and by promoting reflection on language use and on language learning strategies.

Perceptions of criticality among Modern Languages content lecturers

This section is based on interviews with several Modern Languages 'content' lecturers, all with considerable teaching experience gained both at Westford and elsewhere.

Lecturers' definitions of criticality

The lecturers all mentioned aspects of 'critical reasoning' as central to their thinking; that is, being able to define a researchable problem or question, to analyse and compare a range of theoretical positions, and to develop a sustained argument using theory and appropriate exemplification. Criticality within literary and film studies involved analysing underlying messages of written and visual texts, thinking critically about both content and technique, examining how texts are structured to influence the reader, and being aware of personal response to literature and film:

> the approach [to literature] that I'm interested in is the one which forces people to think about how works are put together to communicate their message, and work on the reader . . . so it's a question of providing students with an awareness and analytical tools to be able to do that. (John Hall)

Criticality within social and political studies involved analysing historical and sociolinguistic phenomena, theoretical arguments and political debates, and interpreting processes of social change. A questioning attitude was expected:

> I always start my final year course by saying 'this is going to be a course that's going to raise a whole range of questions . . . what I want you to learn to do is ask, ask, ask and think about how you would set about answering, but it's actually not the answer that we're interested in'. (Sue Rivas)

Students needed to understand the dynamic nature of theory:

> I'd like them to . . . come to an understanding that the work is never done, the solution is never arrived at, it's just a case of building on what's gone before, and that their own critical insights and feelings can contribute to that whole process of moving things forward. (Shirley Hunt)

Individual lecturers also mentioned various dispositions they hoped to develop among students: the ability to handle complexity, to enjoy uncertainty, to reflect on learning processes, and to use feedback and criticism constructively. Some argued that higher education should lead to greater social engagement and 'a general questioning attitude towards life' (Kath Meyer).

Echoing the Languages benchmark statement, literature lecturer John Hall saw the development of a critical perspective on one's own culture as a distinctive feature of Modern Languages. History lecturer Joan Wright stressed multi-disciplinarity as an outcome:

> Many of our students come in thinking that they're just coming to study language, but by the end we've turned them into people who are at an interesting cutting edge between the Humanities and the Social Sciences, where they [are] able to draw on different language abilities, different language cultures, to analyse sociolinguistic and historical phenomena.

Lecturers' accounts of student development

The lecturers' views of entry level students were mixed. John Hall noted that some students attending his first-year course were already good at academic writing and discussion, and Joan Wright commented that some of those entering her (second year) course were already familiar with concepts such as gender or ethnicity. Most believed, however, that first-year students generally lacked confidence and were not used to taking initiatives for learning: 'Well in my experience, it's quite routine for first year students to be really rather reticent and need a great deal of encouragement to speak' (Shirley Hunt).

According to John Hall, many students were critically naïve, that is, they did not realize that what they experience as a personal response to novels or films is actually the product of 'manipulation' by authors, and they did not recognize irony or cross-genre references. New students were still finding their feet socially and might be distracted by this: 'First years . . . most of them anyway, are not totally good at doing the work that they're asked to do, so they often come unprepared, or they don't do a paper they said they were going to do' (Shirley Hunt).

Lecturers described various precursors to criticality as important in the first year. First, building shared knowledge resources was seen as essential. Students needed a basic framework of twentieth-century intellectual and cultural history (such as to know what is meant by 'Marxism', 'surrealism', 'psychoanalysis'), and a general historical framework (such as to know who Franco was, or what happened in 1492). First-year courses met this need: 'I try and give them an overview of some of the major issues . . . , the huge historical sweep of Latin America' (Joan Wright).

The development of target language fluency was another obvious requirement. The first-year course 'French Culture Today' was taught in French and contributed to fluency development through rapid study of several novels, plays and films. According to lecturer John Hall, this developed students' grasp of specialist academic discourse and terminology, which they would need when engaging more deeply with the secondary literature, much of it written in the target language.

Lecturers also spoke about developing students' analytical skills in working with texts and films. John Hall described how he broke down the process of textual analysis into very small tasks, for instance, asking students to comment on the use of 'colour' or 'water' metaphors in a literary text. He also gave students required readings from secondary sources with contrasting viewpoints. Kath Meyer described how she wove intensive analysis of very short film clips into her second-year course, 'Studying Spanish Film'.

Thirdly, first-year lecturers were committed to development of academic literacy. They spoke at length about the value of academic writing in learning how to construct an argument and articulate a personal response. They described a variety of first-year coursework tasks (e.g. reviews and textual commentaries, alongside more conventional essays), plus guidance on structure and conventions. Lecturers also believed that most students paid serious attention to feedback and that the quality of writing improved as a result.

Sue Rivas saw second-year students as more confident and independent, more willing to take risks and more able to apply concepts and skills introduced in the curriculum. Kath Meyer commented that they were also becoming aware that multiple viewpoints, contradictions and uncertainties are normal. Joan Wright pointed out that second-year courses were more focused on theory; she expected second-year students to undertake substantial 'case study' investigations and present them in seminars.

Kath Meyer described some difficulties that students may encounter when attempting to be critical. Insufficient background knowledge may lead to flawed interpretations and over-generalizations; she gave the example of students who had only a superficial knowledge of the role of totalitarianism in twentieth-century Spain and consequently overestimated its influence on Spanish intellectual life. Students may interpret films directly as sociological evidence about daily life, without appreciating that film is an art medium, not a medium of realistic representation. Finally, she pointed to limits on skill transfer and the need for field-specific skills: for example, students may have good general essay writing skills, but if they lack cinematographic training they cannot write effectively about film.

Lecturers also debated how target language use may influence criticality development. John Hall noted tensions between learning to read fast in the target language and learning to read analytically. Despite his commitment to target language lectures in first year, he thought that students might also have later difficulties in expressing their own critical viewpoint in the target language, and the lecturers' majority view was that students' critical writing and oral presentations on 'content' topics should be in English.

Final-year students were described as more intellectually independent. Following residence abroad they were more mature, and their intrinsic motivation, confidence and language skills had all developed (Shirley Hunt). They had developed a critical perspective on what they read, could think more abstractly and handle complex theories (John Hall). They could define their own projects and investigative questions, find out necessary information and present arguments effectively (Kath Meyer).

Some lecturers mentioned factors still limiting students' critical development. These included possible instrumental motivation – students who mainly wanted to get a qualification were not predisposed towards intellectual flexibility. Some mature students had acquired rigid knowledge structures though their previous education and life experience which they were unwilling or unable to question. Kath Meyer commented on some young students' problems with extending critical expertise beyond the classroom:

> they can become really sophisticated in producing an argument around a particular academic corpus of material, but when it comes to how that translates into general attitudes, to how the world works, it doesn't seem to have produced an ability to make connections and think critically.

Criticality in Modern Languages lectures and seminars

Here, we explore the development of criticality in a small number of content classes observed in first, second and final year (the third year was spent abroad and is discussed in Chapter 8).

The first-year course 'French Culture Today' introduced students to a variety of novels, plays and films. Every week students attended one lecture and one seminar, sometimes including student presentations. Assessment consisted of a literary commentary written part way through the course and a final essay. The sociolinguistics course 'Language in Spain and Latin America' ran on similar lines with a weekly lecture and seminar.

The second-year course 'Latin America: Nation, Race and Gender' was a modern history course with a weekly lecture and seminar. A seminar presentation and a related essay were the bases for assessment.

The final-year course 'Narratives of Desire' was a French cultural studies class. Weekly double sessions consisted of class discussion based on novels, articles and films, with regular student presentations. There was a final examination preceded by an optional practice essay.

The first-year classes

All of the first-year lectures centred on building up students' knowledge resources and establishing relevant analytical frameworks.

For example, in an early lecture for 'Language in Spain and Latin America', Sue Rivas gave a historical overview of the colonization process indicating the diverse contributions of Spanish colonists, the Church and the major administrative centres. She explained some major factors affecting relations among languages today: national identity, schooling and literacy, urbanization, language academies, and finally the status of both Spanish and English as world languages. In this way, students encountered a number of core sociolinguistic concepts. In an introductory lecture for 'French Culture Today', film lecturer Clare Harper set out some key contrasts: popular versus arts and *auteur* cinema, cinema as art form versus cinema as industry, Hollywood cinema versus French cinema. She also outlined a number of 'codes' relevant for the analysis of film: *mise en scène,* costumes, actors and camera work. In a lecture on the Simone de Beauvoir novel *Les Belles Images* (1966), Shirley Hunt drew attention to 'narrative technique':

> Let's move on now to the narrative techniques used in *Les Belles Images.* These techniques . . . are closely linked to the theme of the novel . . . First of all we need to examine the point of view adopted in the representation of the characters and especially of Laurence. These characters, are they shown from the inside or the outside? Do we have the feeling we are invited to slip inside the skin of the characters, or to keep them at a distance? Secondly, it is necessary to focus on the use of dialogue, which will lead us to examine the clichéd language which dominates in the book. Thirdly, I will talk about some quite diverse techniques which function to shed light on the defensive manner of Laurence . . . (translated from French original)

However, these lecturers did not only provide an apparatus of facts and concepts. They integrated elements of criticality, for example, problematizing concepts such as 'national identity'; highlighting the dynamic nature of theory; emphasizing the historically and socially conditioned nature of response to literature and film; evaluating theoretical claims and points of view (e.g. concerning the status of 'standard' languages); making comparisons and posing questions. Overall, the lectures modelled key aspects of disciplinary critical reasoning.

In later seminars, however, 'critical reasoning' was not always so evident. When asked to discuss in groups, first-year students commonly started by checking on each other's basic progress: 'How far did you get with the book?' 'What did we have to do?' 'Have you done it?' and so on. These preliminaries sometimes expressed struggle and difficulty with, for example, understanding set texts. Seminar preparation and attendance were uneven.

In a seminar attached to 'French Culture Today', Shirley Hunt explored students' knowledge of French film. One student could refer to some typical features and was just beginning to use terminology modelled in lectures:

Isobel: There's not such a fast pace compared to American movies.

Shirley H: No, very often there isn't, occasionally there is, that's right.

Isobel: It depends on the film but, I remember I began watching French films to revise at GCSE, various ones my Mum had on video, they were so slow and boring, they were just sort of quiet people sitting in a room, just not much happening, an observation of life, [since then] I've seen more commercial ones.

Shirley H: What about cinematic styles in respect of plots and things like that? I mean you say that they're slow, that says something about the plot.

Isobel: Plots are really different to what you see in American cinema, they are also really different from each other as well, every film I have seen seems to be completely different.

Shirley H: Right, yes, that's an interesting point.

Isobel: And also in a lot of films I have seen they tend not to use, ehh, many different ehm what's the word, different scenes ehm —

Shirley H: Not too many, you mean they tend to be all in one place?

Isobel: Yes.

However, most of the critical activity in the seminar (e.g. problematizing 'point of view' in film) was initiated by Shirley Hunt herself. Just one anonymous student made a more sophisticated contribution, apparently drawing on analytic resources acquired in school:

> I think a lot of people just assume the camera never lies, so what you see is what you get. I remember when I was in school [we were told] that's one of the most manipulative forms of propaganda or media. But . . . I think a lot of people realize you can't just take what you see as reality, and as long as you study it in conjunction with testimonies, or you know, autobiographical accounts, or things like that . . . It's the most accessible form of history.

In another 'French Culture Today' seminar, Isobel gave a well-prepared presentation about the view of marriage expressed in the Maupassant novel *Une Vie* (A Life: 1883), in which she supported her points with selected quotations:

> First of all the marriage. It is a bit of a disaster for Jeanne. There is a complete contrast between her hopes and reality. Her dreams are shattered. It demonstrates Maupassant's cynical outlook on the marriage of the time. He says in chapter 4: [She quotes in French from the novel]. The obvious difference between Jeanne and Julien is in the physical relationship. Jeanne is shocked at first.

Shirley Hunt commented intermittently throughout, and Isobel interacted with her confidently. However, the presentation was based largely on personal interpretation of the text and lacked reference to secondary literature.

The second-year classes

For Joan Wright, the aims of her second-year course 'Latin America: Nation, Race and Gender' went well beyond 'knowledge building':

> I've assumed that . . . they have that broad historical sweep type knowledge, and then in Year Two it's focusing on some themes and the themes in this course are race, gender, ethnicity . . . And I definitely introduce ideas of theoretical analysis, what is race, what is gender, some students are fairly sophisticated already and have good ideas about that, others are

completely innocent of these ideas . . . And what I attempt to do is in my lectures, try and treat the more theoretical abstract ideas to a degree, I mean this is only Year Two, and hope then in their seminar presentations that . . . they'll make an effort to apply some of these more theoretical ideas to the particular case they are studying.

One of her lectures described the Zapatista movement in Mexico, and analysed its stance on gender and ethnicity. In a following seminar, two students gave related presentations. Sarah's presentation was well informed though descriptive, detailing the poverty of the Chiapas region. Amy continued the historical narrative from 1994 until the present, and contrasted military repression in Chiapas with wider ideological changes arising from the movement, including greater pressure on the government to respect human rights. She also tried to relate this particular movement to longer term struggles for indigenous rights. Overall, she successfully developed an extended argument and supported it with evidence.

In discussion, both of these students developed their ideas further; Sarah tried to explain how relations with the US might influence government policy, and Amy commented on the wider impact of Zapatista ideology on gender in Mexican society. Both students cited material, including Zapatista posters and documents as well as secondary sources. During the discussion Joan Wright limited herself to asking information questions and encouraging the students to make predictions about the likely future for Chiapas; feedback was reserved for a separate occasion.

This second-year seminar included much more evidence of critical reason coming from the students themselves than seen in first year. This seemed to arise from genuine interest in the topic, a good understanding of the lecturer's expectations and a good knowledge base enhanced through students' personal reading and research.

The final-year classes

The final-year classes are represented here by two sessions from 'Narratives of Desire', whose aims were described by the lecturer (Shirley Hunt):

I try to get the students operating both on a body of theoretical knowledge to do with the construction of sexuality and the representation of sexuality and to use that theoretical knowledge in looking at imaginative texts, both written and filmic, and also, as part of the same exercise, to get them thinking about their own experience and ideas and weaving the three areas together.

The first example is a student presentation on the Cyril Collard film, *Les Nuits Fauves* (Savage Nights, 1992). The student knew the film well and had also read several critical commentaries in French, showing good control of the needed language resources. Her presentation developed close interpretations of characters and relationships (the hero and his two lovers), with apt quotation (in French). She introduced some psychoanalytical constructs (death wish and sadomasochism) to elaborate on her chosen theme of 'transgression':

> I think the theme of transgression actually takes a multiplicity of forms . . . first there is a continuing link between love and death as a theme within the film, and one of the most powerful scenes within the film is when Jean tells Laura that he's HIV positive after he's slept with her. And then when they next sleep together, when he goes to use a condom, she tells him that she doesn't want to, and she wants him to come inside her. And I was asking myself, 'Why does she do this?', and I think the idea that Collard is trying to bring up in the film is that this is the ultimate form of transgression, seeking death through making love.

In much of her presentation this student used evidence from the film together with background reading to construct a reasoned argument. Her analysis focused on plot and character, however – only Shirley Hunt had much to say about more technical aspects.

This seminar moved on to discuss further questions posed by the lecturer. In this more spontaneous phase the students contributed much less analytically. For example, Shirley Hunt wanted to explore connections among different kinds of prejudice, starting with the AIDS prejudice and racism addressed in the film; students responded with relatively undeveloped opinions and anecdotes.

The last seminar for the same course was a revision session which included several prepared student presentations. The first concerned the novel *Passion Simple* (Simple Passion, 1991) by Annie Ernaux. The presenter (Pam) was again very familiar with the text and with a number of critical writings about it. She drew on various psychoanalytical constructs as the basis for her interpretation (obsession, masochism) and contrasted this with a possible alternative religious interpretation; both were well developed with reference to the text. Pam also made some comments on technical aspects of the novel. However, later student presentations in this seminar were briefer, and presented arguments and interpretations in a tightly compressed form, often without any examples or textual analysis. One student commented: 'This is the point of a revision session'. Presumably, in the final examination the students expected to elaborate these schematic arguments into fully developed academic essays.

Finally, as we have seen above, some lecturers hoped that their courses might impact students' personal development and value systems, but also acknowledged that this did not always happen. Resistance could occasionally be glimpsed, as in the *Les Nuits Fauves* seminar, where Shirley Hunt invited students to compare the film with a comedy of lesbian sexuality, *Gazon Maudit* (*French Twist*, 1995):

> In terms of the two films *Le Gazon Maudit* and *Les Nuits Fauves,* they both deal with alternative sexualities, and look at the very general question of how we make alternative sexualities more acceptable in society at large. Which of those two films do you think is more likely to serve that purpose, to bring more understanding about the different forms of sexuality and acceptance of them into the general public?

After some response from the group to her actual question, an anonymous student made a more personal comment: '*Gazon Maudit,* I don't think it could ever, it hasn't changed my views about anything you know it hasn't made me think, "Oh it would be all right for a lesbian to have babies", I mean, I don't think.'

Rather than contributing to the more general discussion, this particular student seemed to be resisting the possibility that studying such films might influence her own attitudes.

Criticality in language skills classes

In Chapter 5, we considered the expectations for criticality development of the 'language' curriculum strand and saw that these were less ambitious than those of content classes. Nonetheless, the language curriculum expected the more advanced students to focus on the target language culture, to read texts in a variety of genres, to write on complex topics with an awareness of genre, and to develop arguments and analyse concepts orally in target-language presentations and discussions.

Several language tutors elaborated on these themes. French tutor David Newby spoke about the development of target language writing skills, leading by final year to essays on topics such as 'globalization' and also to creative writing. In addition, the Stage 7 language course gave practice in translation and promoted analysis of target language texts in terms of genre and style:

I think that's reflected in the way of looking at the text, always thinking about what the author was trying to do, why they've chosen particular turns of phrase . . . why *Le Monde* will quite happily cram an article full of slang expressions when this isn't the way that most of its readers speak, what are they trying to achieve?

His expectation was that this 'language awareness' would transfer eventually to students' own writing in French. Study of academic modes of expression, in particular, would help students to use authentic target language resources confidently in content classes. He attached great importance to students' language-learning strategies and ability to evaluate their own linguistic strengths and weaknesses and described activities intended to develop these. His colleague Sam Ledkes talked about the teaching of translation and the development of students' awareness of style and register through this means. Overall, this awareness-raising work could be understood as contributing to criticality development within the domain of the self, though at a fairly instrumental level.

The Spanish language tutor Lucia Baxter also spoke about developing learners' awareness and control of register and style. She argued further that language classes should develop students' awareness of the world, and perhaps influence their social values:

> it's important that as a human being you're well informed about what is happening around the world, that it's not just a perfect beautiful world. And . . . it is important that you attach the language to the cultures and dynamics of those societies, . . . and not only different cultures but different socio-political settings . . . Perhaps I'm being ambitious, I'm just trying to make people more conscious, more aware, about our responsibilities as human beings.

Accordingly, her Stage 5 Spanish classes were organized around social topics including immigration in Spain, human rights in Latin America and poverty and hunger internationally. The texts studied in this class came mostly from contemporary media, and written exercises involved genres such as journalism. Her hoped-for outcome was that 'they should be able to handle the subject and be able to express in Spanish an informed opinion about the dynamics of a particular problem or subject'.

A number of language classes were observed for the research project. Students were generally well engaged with ongoing activities, which often involved close work on texts, including reading and listening comprehension, and translation. Although some students responded in English, tutors led discussion in the target language and spent much time working on texts at a fairly micro level (that is, clarifying and discussing individual words and expressions, the best way to translate them, and so on). Texts were varied and contemporary; however, sustained discussion of the social and cultural issues raised was relatively uncommon. In one observed example, students gave their opinions about changes in French language legislation, stimulated by a French newspaper text.

Criticality in social work learning and teaching

Perceptions of criticality among Social Work lecturers

This section is based on interviews with a number of Social Work and Sociology lecturers contributing to the Social Work degree programme.

Lecturers' definitions of criticality

The Sociology lecturers taught the Social Work students in their first year only. They thought of criticality essentially in terms of critical reason within their discipline, including awareness of the power of discourse: 'it's certainly a sense of the way in which discourses including theoretical discourses enable us to think and say some things and entirely exclude the possibility of thinking and saying others (Elizabeth Price).

The Social Work lecturers also acknowledged the importance of 'academic' critical thinking, but their outlook was considerably broader, centring on the ability to relate theory and practice, to engage in independent professional action in the world and to understand the self when working in challenging circumstances:

> Often Social Work students come on programmes . . . to learn how to do it, they don't come on programmes to learn how to think about it. By the time they get their degrees . . . that's my ultimate goal, that a student at the end of the three years can say 'yes, I have learned how to *think and do* Social Work' (Nancy Barron, our emphasis).
>
> [It is] reflecting about how other people may experience a problem, what the impact is of self on the situation, those sorts of dimensions (Ruth Thomas).

Becoming Critical: Teaching and Learning Processes

> What is criticality in Social Work? . . . something to do with doing it and reflecting about it. And I think it's something to do with an independence of position, knowing that organisations and distressed people can so easily reduce you to helplessness, confusion, misery, therefore it's crucial that you are developing a strong sense of independent thought and emotional strength to manage all that (Jake Alby).

Nancy Barron spoke of the creative nature of criticality:

> It's critical reflection on abstract ideas, on experience, on different sorts of sources of knowledge, and bringing them together, and thereby generating new ways of thinking and doing.

Lecturers' accounts of student development

The Social Work programme had a diverse intake (illustrated in Chapter 7), which meant that some non-traditional students had not previously practised 'critical reason' activities such as writing academic essays, despite being well motivated and hard working. Social Work lecturer Nancy Barron thought that students' personal dispositions might determine how 'critical' they eventually became, especially in domains of self-reflection and critical action:

> Some . . ., in the first year you can pick up and you think they're a natural, they're going to turn out to be one of these really good people who've got the interpersonal skills, who can make sense of their world and their contribution to it . . . and you've got others who are really going to have to work terribly hard, and you don't know how far you can get with them.

As in Modern Languages, lecturers mentioned various precursors to criticality as relevant for first-year students. First, knowledge resources were developed through several formal lecture courses. The courses called 'Introduction to Sociology' and 'Introduction to Social Work 1' were compulsory for first-year Social Work students, who attended them alongside students from other social science disciplines. (Several lecturers expressed a preference for small group learning, but blamed lack of resources for the reliance on lecture courses in the first year.)

Lecturers expected such courses to provide a shared foundation of knowledge and academic skills, but also some modelling of disciplinary criticality.

One challenge was the students' very different entry level knowledge. Sociology lecturer Elizabeth Price commented that 'about half of the Sociology first-year cohort had done A Level Sociology, which she described as contributing 'a packaged kind of knowledge'; her personal 'first year agenda' was to destabilize this knowledge. She described the overall goals of 'Introduction to Sociology':

> It's a compulsory course for all our degree programmes, social policy as well as sociology. It's intended to teach them basic skills in [academic] reading and writing, as well as basic skills in reading and writing sociology. It's meant to introduce them at least briefly to different theoretical frameworks and different methods, although I don't labour either of them in this course.

Nancy Barron also believed that early teaching should 'destabilize' commonsense understandings. She described 'Introduction to Social Work 1':

> it's to provide a sound knowledge and critical understanding of the discipline of Social Work, and . . . introduce students to some of the major contemporary intellectual and practice issues . . . to gain a better understanding of the nature of Social Work as a complex activity which can be understood as both a profession and discipline, . . . to get beyond the rather simplistic 'Social Work is helping people' position.

She also described the related Semester 2 course (here called 'Introduction to Social Work 2'):

> a unit which is quite specific for the Social Work students, which is much more practice-focused, and we have practitioners and service users who come in to talk about their work and experience. Running through that unit is the notion of critical reflection and also research, so students are introduced more specifically to notions of critically reflecting on Social Work.

These lecturers thought it was important to locate both Sociology and Social Work in their social, historical and international context. Some also tried to relate social issues to students' personal experience: 'so that's one of my ways of trying to get people to think, I work more on that experiential level, trying to get people to think about themselves and their life worlds and make those connections' (Leslie Bennett). Other lecturers were more concerned to ensure that particular domains of knowledge (e.g. working with disabled adults, family and community) were 'flagged up' in first-year courses.

All lecturers believed that students needed to learn to write 'a traditional academic essay' (Ruth Thomas); the department of Sociology ran a compulsory first-year course in academic study skills, including writing. Essays remained of central importance for critical development in Sociology at all levels:

> I'm thinking of my current third years, some of them are fantastic in the way that they can write, so what I would expect is a marked improvement year on year in terms of ability to construct coherent argument and to use secondary resources towards that argument, and I would expect their writing style to improve substantially. (Judith Matthews)

Within Social Work, however, while essays continued to be set, other types of writing became increasingly important from second year onwards. As Jake Alby explained to his first-year tutorial group:

> If you look at Year 2, there will be a number of assignments at the end of the semester . . . It is very much connected to the workplace. It is a portfolio of practical experience. It is broken down into competencies. It is about the ordinary things of doing Social Work. You have to do evidence sheets. There is a move from classical academic essays to an emerging account of your practice. (Field notes, first-year tutorial meeting, October)

However, the continuing difficulties of some students with core academic literacy skills were remarked on by some lecturers:

> I often feel that the ability to write about social policy is about being able to take in, not necessarily from the lectures but from associated reading. . . . The reading is very important as well, the ability to be appropriately critical about social policy developments depends on this kind of ability to think about quite big pictures, about complex policy developments, and I think quite a lot of our students find that rather difficult. (Ruth Thomas)

From the second year, Social Work classes centred mainly on professional issues. Some courses deepened students' knowledge resources in particular domains (e.g. Social Work with adults or with children). Lecturer Ruth

Thomas underlined the ongoing importance of classroom teaching for critical reason: 'They have a lot of teaching on Social Work values in Semester 1, and so I notice that they find it easier to articulate criticisms about values than they do criticisms in other areas'. But, overall, the balance had shifted:

> In Year 2 one is focusing much more on how to do Social Work . . . and the notion of critical reflection on practice, on some of the methodologies of Social Work, is introduced there, but hopefully in the context of having encouraged students to think critically [in first year] about the nature of Social Work, the nature of Social Work values and the role of research. (Nancy Barron)

> Second year, we're talking about people who have joined the club of practice, they've moved from the general talk about sociological principles to doing Social Work, and they hear the stories, and I think they're very engaged by it all. (Jake Alby)

Criticality in Social Work lectures and seminars

We observed several courses attended by Social Work students in the first, second and final year. In this section we consider the first-year lecture-based courses 'Introduction to Sociology' and 'Introduction to Social Work 1' and the second-year course 'Adult Social Work'.

First-year classes

'Introduction to Sociology' was taught to a very large cohort of a hundred students from different disciplines, with lectures twice a week and fortnightly small group seminars. The course outline included lecture overviews, suggested readings including a recommended textbook, and a list of essay topics. (The course was assessed by essay and examination.)

The lectures were formal occasions with little student participation. Lecturers were well prepared and fluent, using visual aids and videos to enhance their presentations. Topics ranged from home, food and personal relations to life in the workplace and the notion of 'community'. The lecturers explained current sociological theories on these topics and their intellectual origins. They evaluated the empirical evidence supporting different theories and the research methods used. For example, a lecture on the nature of 'community' explored the idea that:

Time is an important element that people have to have in common alongside shared place, interests and identities. The thesis that it is increasingly difficult in the modern world to synchronize activities is examined, along with the idea that the pace of life is speeding up. The lecture concludes by considering what sort of evidence would provide convincing support for the argument that a trend towards more 'individualized' and less community-minded patterns are emerging. (Course outline, Lecture 15)

During the lecture itself, Keith Lee explained the contrasting views of two sociologists, Ulrich Beck and Robert Putnam, and evaluated the evidence base on which they rested. He discussed how far their analyses might apply beyond the communities they were writing about, that is, Germany and the US, and summed up their positions:

Now, as I say, Putnam is taking it as given that community is a good thing and that we should be worried about the decline of community. Beck is not. Beck is of the view that actually community, or at least traditional patterns of community, are quite stifling and are quite oppressive, they impose particular limits on our ability to be who we want to be and to do what we want to do, so Beck has a much less positive assessment of community.

Keith Lee's own views remained unstated. However, he did try to relate the debate to students' personal experience, with a suggestion for seminar discussion of a recent public event:

One of the things you may talk about in your seminars is, did the Jubilee mean anything in terms of your involvement in community, what did you do on that weekend? Was it an opportunity for you to say 'we've now got a common tie, we've now got the opportunity to come together and to celebrate what we have in common'? Because that's the analysis of the royal family . . . the idea of this common commitment to the values that are held to be embedded in the monarchy. Whether people did that on their Jubilee weekends, I'd be interested to know.

Seminars usually centred on a set reading, with discussion questions encouraging students to draw on their own experience (e.g. of the nature of 'community' among university students). In the observed seminars, the students were active and had done the reading. However, much time was needed to clarify concepts and arguments, and attempts to relate these to students' life experience were somewhat haphazard and inconclusive. In the final seminar, students opted for a briefing about the course examination in place of the suggested synthetic discussion of themes from the course.

'Introduction to Social Work 1' was shared by two lecturers, Nancy Barron and Celia Aventuro. The course outline presented Social Work as a contested profession and/or vocation, introduced the 'care–control dilemma', and promised an introduction to both 'historic and contemporary' discourses on these issues. The course surveyed the historical, social and legal origins of Social Work, its recent development, and the challenges of globalization, marketization and internationalization. The last few lectures introduced Social Work with particular groups: the socially excluded, asylum seekers and refugees, sexually abused children and others.

Again, these lectures were well planned and lively. They aimed to develop students' understandings of intellectual and practice traditions and changing legislative frameworks. Nancy Barron also problematized concepts consistently, using rhetorical questioning. This discussion of 'objectivity' comes from an early lecture:

> Nancy B: Objective, subjective, what do we mean by that? Do you think professionals are objective? In professional practice are we objective? You'd like to think so. . . . What do we mean by objective? We say professionals are objective, what do we invest in that, professionals being objective?
> Student: Not emotionally involved.
> Nancy B: Yes, they can stand outside of the situation, they can stand sufficiently outside of it in order to understand better and therefore if you like offer their professional expertise. That's an important part certainly of the development of professional activity, and not least the development of the scientific method that's been sufficiently called the 'objective'. 'Subjective' suggests being involved, perhaps even suggests over-involved, if one thinks of the professional.
>
> It is always that interesting question that's posed, you know, like can a social worker actually work with members of their family? Should a medic actually become involved in providing medical treatment for members of his or her family? Can you actually be both involved and inside and outside? That's an interesting debate. (Lecture 6)

Celia Aventuro made many references to her own career, expounding her personal value system and critiquing her own past positions and arguments. For example, she had participated in the 'radical Social Work' movement of the 1970s, which had reacted against an earlier tradition of casework with individuals and focused on structural inequality. She commented in her lecture:

> I think we forgot about the person, because people focused too much in the early days on the structural, because what we said was 'Oh we have to organize collectively to gain control over decisions affecting one's life', and the minute we started focusing on collective organisation, of course the individual and the personal . . . went out of the window. There wasn't a deliberate kind of decision made to say 'Well we're not going to deal with individuals' . . . and certainly for someone like me, the link between the personal and the structural [was not raised], until I got involved in organising women and black people. (Lecture 9)

Sometimes Celia Aventuro appealed very directly to her audience, telling anecdotes and advising as if students were about to engage immediately with similar situations:

> So, social workers I think ignore the significance of domestic violence in family dynamics generally, except as a child protection issue . . . Well what are the things that you can use as a social worker in terms of trying to help women and children in these situations? Well, there are a number of things. You can go for injunctions . . . But these are very limited. The resources given to these are limited. The impact on perpetrators is limited, I mean I had a case of an injunction where this guy was ordered not to be anywhere near the matrimonial home, so he disappeared and he got his friend to drive his pickup truck and leave it on the drive, so that every time the woman looked out of the window she would be reminded who was boss in the relationship. (Lecture 18)

In such episodes, a discourse of transformatory professional action and engagement with the world was modelled, along with some rehearsal of alternative types of action and evaluations of these.

Students also attended fortnightly seminars for 'Introduction to Social Work 1'. In those we observed, students' understanding of lecture material was reviewed and checked. However, there was usually time for more open discussion as well. For example, following a lecture on child abuse, two students used seminar time to describe cases of family violence which had personally affected them. The students were mainly preoccupied with narrating events, with limited reference to the professional context: 'As a social worker, how do you build up trust? My friend would not trust social workers'. Lecturer Leslie Bennett listened supportively, while also suggesting further reflection: 'This was a cycle of terror, a cycle of power . . . to bring this away from the personal, use what you have learned, and think about how people get caught in these cycles'.

Second-year classes

In the second year, students attended further Social Work courses, alongside their first practice placements (discussed in Chapter 8). The example discussed here is 'Adult Social Work', also being attended at the time by third-year students from the old four-year programme. The coordinator, Ruth Thomas, had recruited several outside speakers, including both Social Work practitioners and service users. The classes were double sessions, sometimes including small group discussion. Even the 'lecturing' style in this course was highly dialogic, with extended question and answer sessions.

Ruth Thomas introduced the course in the first session as challenging any 'pathology model' of adults with disabilities. She also quizzed the students on their own past experience of working with adults, highlighting the range of knowledge already available within the group.

The sessions run by university lecturers introduced theoretical concepts and empirical research, and critically evaluated these. Students with relevant placement experience were encouraged to provide examples. In a lecture on ageing, Ruth Thomas spoke about reduced lifestyle choices in residential care, picking the example of personal care and bathing:

Ruth T: . . . so if you like, cleanliness becomes not an option as it is for the rest of us, but it suddenly becomes mandatory. Anybody here experienced that or been through that sort of situation?

Student: I have actually, I worked on an elderly unit and there was this old chap and he always wore this woolly hat, and one day one of the care assistants was desperately trying to get it off him because she felt it was dirty, it was disgusting, and eventually when he actually spoke to her about it, his wife had made him this woolly hat and he just wore it always because it was something she made, and he just didn't want to take it off. Eventually we were

able to just let him wear the hat, and it was very dirty, but it was his choice.
Ruth T: So it offended the standards?
Student: Yes, and a lot of the nurses were very angry but it was what he wanted to do.
Ruth T: It's an example of somebody who's made a choice, a positive choice. (Lecture 4)

Some guest speakers were adults with disabilities, for example, a wheelchair user who spoke about independent living. These were lively sessions which were extremely well received by students. Again, these sessions could be seen as building up students' knowledge resources, but this time in domains of practice and including direct familiarization with service users' perspectives.

Criticality in Social Work skills classes and tutorials

A variety of university-based activities were intended to complement Social Work practice placements. The research team observed a final-year course titled 'Social Work Theory and Practice' which ran alongside the final practice placement and offered both video workshops and seminars. These activities are described briefly here and more fully in Ford et al. (2006).

Video workshops: learning to listen

In each video workshop a student presented an authentic personal experience or dilemma to a fellow student in the role of listener; the episode was both video-recorded and observed by the rest of the group. The interaction was then reviewed and discussed with reference to counselling concepts such as 'authenticity', 'empathy', 'respect' and 'reframing' (elaborated in course readings). These workshops thus promoted critical reflection on a professionally important skill – the ability to relate to an interlocutor who may be disclosing sensitive personal information.

In one such workshop, for example, a student described her feelings about her father's new partner (her mother had died some time before):

June: They are going to buy a place together. It's just about feeling odd about it. This lady is really nice. She is fairly similar to my Mum.
Sandra: She has taken the role of your Mum?
June: Not really. I am grown up. But I want just to be able to ring her up and talk about anything. Like with my Mum. Talking about

	painting rooms which colour. But I still have feelings about it. My Dad has no idea. As far as he knows it is all great.
Sandra:	Do you have any brothers or sisters?
June:	A brother. He is a bit of a worrier. He would probably be happier if they still had single houses. One thing that worried me – will I have a room to go back to if I need to? I felt really comfortable in the old house. But now it is someone else's house.
Sandra:	You feel like a guest.
June:	Yes, no one has made me feel like that. But I still do have these feelings.

The lecturer leading this group (Philip Brown) described his feedback style: 'I try to aim to leave them puzzled and reflective, rather than totally demoralized or thinking that they're wonderful'. The following extract illustrates his approach:

Philip B:	Was that [the decision to ask about siblings] conscious?
Sandra:	I felt it was time to say something. I was also just interested to know.
Philip B:	How did you [June] experience it when Sandra invited you to reflect on your brother?
June:	It made me feel she was listening.
Philip B:	It was very interesting. I was trying to focus on the feelings you were expressing. At the beginning, it was quite simple, but it really was quite complex. The question about the brother was an opportunity to reflect feelings on to someone else.

In response, the students often adopted the terminology used by the tutor and the course handbook. For example, they talked of 'empathy' and 'mirroring', and tried to use these behaviours in the sessions.

One student reported a resulting growth in self-awareness:

I can look back at a performance of mine and by the end of it I could be thinking 'Well you did that very well, and you said that really well, and I like the way you re-framed that, but why didn't you then follow up what was said, at that point, or why have you gone from that point to that point?' Seeing the video, seeing how you absolutely are, makes it easy to be critical . . . or makes it easier. Or impossible not to be critical, might be a more accurate way of putting it. (Ian, Interview 2)

There was, however, no real debate around the theoretical concepts introduced during these sessions; students did not question the values underlying the skills being promoted and concentrated on mastering them. That is, students' responses to these workshops reflected an overall focus on learning to practice confidently within existing parameters.

'Theorizing practice' seminars

The 'Social Work Theory and Practice' course also included 'theoretical discussion and analysis of issues arising from the concurrent placement experience' (Course Handbook). The agenda for these seminars was self-directed, and the overall aim was 'an integration or synthesis of the diverse personal, intellectual, behavioural and emotional dimensions of their professional development' (Course Handbook).

Students on practice placements were keen to share problems and seek moral support. As Jayne put it: 'Just general airing of problems and discussing what's going on in our placements and things like that really . . . the different ways of going round different problems and how you would tackle them.'

Tutors, however, wanted to relate theory and practice in these sessions:

> It's easy for them to turn into an unfocused discussion about all sorts of things, and I think we did keep on track, and I think we did systematically encourage the students to reflect, as the rubric says, on the full range of their learning . . . we made a point of discussing the relevant law each week. (Philip Brown interview)

In the observed seminars with Philip Brown, students presented problems from their practice placements. Fellow students typically probed facts and suggested practical courses of action, while the lecturer tried to encourage more analytical discussion. For example, June spoke about a client who she felt was being pressured to move to residential care. Other students checked on details:

Joan: He wants to go home and why can't he?
June: The main problem is, it's a second floor flat and he's not at all mobile.
Joan: Is there a lift?
Jim: Could you not get him private care? I mean you might have to fight for it but –

June: We could probably, we could get him care, but it is getting him into his flat and once he was there he'd need complete care, bedridden care.
Jim: Oh right yeah.
June: And because he abuses alcohol, I mean that's his choice obviously . . .
Joan: Does he own the flat?
June: Yes.
Joan: Can he not sell it and buy a ground floor one? (etc.)

After this exploration of practical options, Philip Brown intervened:

Philip B: Any elements of Social Work practice theories that you could bring to bear in this understanding and making sense of this?
Student: Sorry, say that again.
Philip B: Well you've looked at Social Work practice theorists, is there anything in these books which is going to help to cast new light on referral?

The students responded to some extent to this question, showing they could relate the case to relevant legal and methodological frameworks, and discussing the possible role of different stakeholders. However, when not prompted in this way, their orientation was typically very instrumental, sharing knowledge about care options and resource limitations.

The role of tutorial groups

Lastly, we observed a number of tutorial groups led by lecturer Jake Alby. The first-year meetings largely involved people getting to know one another, and practical guidance about assessment. From the beginning, however, Jake Alby stressed the strategic purpose of the groups:

> This is a vehicle for learning. It is also for supporting one another. It is essential for managing stress in Social Work. . . . Keep talking. Keep talking about assignments. You have to write your own essays. But help one another as much as you can. (Field notes, first-year tutorial, October)

However, in a November tutorial, some first-year students expressed frustration with the 'academic' nature of their programme. Among other issues, they were struggling to see the relevance of the historical and global context setting of 'Introduction to Social Work 1': 'It is difficult to understand and relate to it'. The lecturer again promoted a strategic view:

> Try and project yourselves past this year. People in Year 2 will have a very concentrated term of looking at issues of practice. For example, children and families, psychology. The idea is that you get the broad stuff – sociology for a year, and then the contrast in the second year.
>
> I suspect this is a problem for all formal learning. You get chunks, later you put things together. (Field notes, first-year tutorial, November)

However, it seemed the most helpful thing he could do on this particular occasion was to explain and allay anxiety about upcoming examinations, and this was the main function of an observed second-year tutorial as well.

Jake Alby's final-year tutorial group had a distinctively informal and supportive atmosphere. Each session began with brief reports from individuals on their current practice placement. There was also continuing intermittent discussion of assessment requirements. However, the sessions centred on student-led presentations or discussions. For example, one student made an ambitious presentation on his dissertation topic, the relationship between Social Work and human rights, drawing on the ideas of Paolo Freire and Jim Ife. This led to a well-informed discussion of the potentially conflicting rights of the individual and of society, in cases of mental illness, and of resulting dilemmas for social workers for example about disclosure of information. Later in the tutorial, however, discussion drifted to a much more anecdotal level. This kind of untidy hybrid discussion seemed to reflect the need of final-year students both to 'let their hair down' and make sense of events by narrating them and also to deepen their understanding of their professional values and roles.

Conclusion

This chapter has looked for evidence of criticality development in university classrooms. We have seen lecturers' efforts to develop common knowledge resources and academic literacy among students. In Modern Languages 'content' courses, in Sociology and in some Social Work courses, we have seen the use of lectures to model disciplinary criticality, largely in terms of critical reasoning. We have seen students learning to articulate disciplinary arguments in class, especially in prepared oral presentations.

In the 'soft pure' discipline of Modern Languages, lecturers' interest in the domain of the self has been apparent in the classroom, with encouragement to students to evaluate their own learning and to reflect critically on their own identities and values. However, it will be seen in Chapter 8 that in terms of critical self-reflection within Modern Languages, the Year Abroad was a more powerful influence.

In the 'applied' discipline of Social Work, we have seen sustained attention to self-reflection in skills workshops, seminars and tutorials. We have also seen lecturers' commitment to debate around Social Work values and to the integration of theory and practice; as the programme progressed, it seemed that students did become more able to relate their 'academic' learning and their professional practice. As Jayne put it in an interview:

> Its [theoretical background has] made me more knowledgeable, more aware of practice, I've been out on placement and I'm learning much more being out on placement, there's been a lot of theory that's been useful especially the psychology, child development, attachment theories, all that is very relevant to what I'm doing now on the placement I'm in . . . you understand the different theorists, the views they put forward on maternal deprivation and attachment, and you see it in cycles with your clients . . . And understanding the different theories that have been put forward, helps you to understand where [clients] are coming from and also what might be the next step forward.

This level of critical thought about the real world was common among the emergent professionals of final-year Social Work. However, they showed only limited interest in critiquing current theoretical frameworks, that is, in a more transformatory orientation.

In the next chapter, we move from exploring classroom communities to the criticality development of individual case study students.

Chapter 7

Student Writing and Criticality Development

Introduction

In this chapter we focus on criticality development in student writing. We start from the assumption that the extent and nature of student criticality depends partly on the intellectual and personal resources that students bring to university, but that these can be influenced by the new context. The learning context itself is not fixed, but takes the form of a dynamic community of practice. We show that there are clear differences between the writing development of individual students as well as patterns in common. We relate these individual differences to (often interconnected) factors such as educational background, motivation, field-specific background and the nature of the particular assignment. The shared patterns are related to year group, developmental level and field.

We examine both the students' writing processes and their products. With *writing processes*, we focus on types and amounts of preparation for assignments as well as students' motivations and feelings about their writing. This reveals the nature of student engagement with their writing assignments in terms of knowledge and skill as well as effect. With *written products* we focus on two major interrelated areas: student engagement with ideas and other voices in their fields, including engagement with the secondary literature; and their ability to construct an appropriate academic argument. In this way we explore interaction between the views and knowledge of the student and ongoing dialogues in the field as represented by themes and theoretical orientations presented in the courses; primary and secondary sources; and, in the case of Social Work, the processes of professional practice. Engagement in academic writing involves learning the rules of particular genres and sub-genres, and at the same time involves the writer in a variety of complex ongoing dialogues. In Social Work, participation in these dialogues is also an integral part of professional practice. Entry into these dialogues is a key means of practising and expressing criticality.

In what follows, we explore students' personal qualities, the contextual factors in play and how the students relate to the fields in which they are operating. We examine the kinds of knowledge they need in order to construct their written arguments, and the kinds of knowledge they actually display. We ask how students' resources develop over successive years of the degree programme and how far they are able to transfer skills and knowledge from one domain or field to another.

In this chapter we draw mainly on student interviews; student writing in the shape of notes, drafts and final written products; and lecturer feedback. Typically, writing assignments were set at the beginning of the semester. For each course, the students usually had to complete one or two writing assignments, often essays, although Social Work students had a wider variety of tasks. Assignments had strict word limits, and the students had to plan their time over the semester in order to complete all required work. Usually, feedback on written work took the form of summative assessment provided on a written comment sheet. The feedback was usually balanced and sometimes insightful, but first-year assignments were marked anonymously and thus feedback could not be personalized.

As we saw in Chapter 6, in Modern Languages, the priority was to develop students' ability to critique and to relate theories to literature, film, history and so on. The written work discussed in this chapter was produced in English. (Written work in the target language arising out of similar language courses has been analysed from the perspective of criticality in another research study; see Romero de Mills, 2008.) In Social Work, from the second year onwards, assignments were increasingly focused on professional practice. In both fields, assignments became longer as the degree programme progressed.

Modern languages students

This section discusses the writing of ten case study students: three from the first year (Harriet, Jane and Isobel); three from the second year (Jessica, Amy and Olivia) and four from the final year (Kate, Rebecca, Susie and Henry). The students were following different Modern Languages undergraduate programmes including both single and combined honours. Each programme comprised a mix of optional and compulsory courses. The students took both language and content courses, as described in Chapter 6. The range of options was sufficiently wide for students to be able to specialize to some extent in a particular 'content' field, such as literature or linguistics.

The Modern Languages case study students

The Modern Languages students all had traditional academic school-leaving qualifications and had gone straight to university after school, apart from Rebecca, a mature student in her thirties. Isobel and Henry had very high A level grades, Susie a mixture, and Harriet and Jane relatively low grades. The three second-year students had moderate grades, as did Kate. We do not know Rebecca's grades. The students had studied a variety of subjects at A level, often arts but sometimes sciences. Some students had a background mainly in languages, where they had not been required to write extended essays in English (Harriet, Jane and Olivia).

The students' parents typically had middle-class occupations, and often they were graduates, had some connection with languages, or both. Two of the UK-educated students had been to private, fee-paying schools (Harriet and Amy), and the rest came from state-funded, selective grammar schools (Jane and Jessica) or state-funded, non-selective comprehensive schools (Isobel, Olivia, Susie, Henry and Kate). Amy and Rebecca had been educated abroad.

The students often had previous, non-academic connections with the languages they were studying. Amy had lived abroad all her life and had a Spanish mother. For the rest, school exchanges had been popular, and the cultural background at home might include second language contact. Isobel mentioned watching her mother's French videos and seeing French films at a local cinema.

As reported in Chapter 6, the first-year students were still settling into university life while the second-year students were well integrated. The final-year students, apart from Rebecca who had been exempted, had all spent the third year of their degree programmes abroad.

First-year writing

The first-year Modern Languages assignments were 1,500-word essays on a topic chosen from a list of pre-set questions, plus literary commentaries.

All students had to read in English and at least one foreign language. In general, the first-year students had difficulties reading for seminars, even in English. All the students studying 'French Culture Today' faced difficulties reading the required novels and plays. At A level, they reported reading a maximum of three books a year, whereas at university they had to read at least two novels and two plays, as well as watch two films, in one semester. Jane described her laborious French reading process:

> in this course we have to read a book every three weeks for nine weeks and I find that really difficult because they're thick novels . . ., and they are in French as well, so you spend a lot of time looking words up in the dictionary and they said that you just had to get the gist of it but I find it difficult to get the gist when I don't know many of the words, so it takes me a while. (Interview 2)

Even Isobel, a stronger student, reported feeling pressured by these demands. As we saw in Chapter 6, lecturers acknowledged the problem and saw this course as key in promoting reading fluency.

These students also had basic difficulties using the paper and electronic resources of the library. Harriet talked about visiting the main university library, but only succeeding in finding an article because she had a friend who helped her (Interview 1). Isobel said she could find books in the library, but not articles (Interview 2).

The students wrote with varying degrees of seriousness and effectiveness. Isobel worked hard and thoughtfully on all her assignments. In contrast, Harriet wrote a respectable first assignment, a commentary, while her second assignment was weaker and rushed. This may indicate the distraction experienced by first-year students as they tried to find their feet socially, a factor commonly mentioned in interviews, or an inability to allocate time effectively over a range of assignments. Some students seemed far more engaged with study than others. Jane declared that 'I don't really like reading books, it makes me tired' (Interview 2).

The students had widely varying writing strategies. Isobel reported a complex process:

> Because I work on my computer, I write ideas . . . I write my introduction and then I write in note form all the different things I want to include. And then I sort of cut and paste and edit bits, and write it in chunks, and when I get bored of a paragraph I skip to the next one and get back to it. (Interview 1)

In contrast, Harriet had a rather simplistic view of the nature of writing: 'I'm quite confident in my English writing, I've always been quite good at spelling and stuff like that, and grammar, and so I think I'm quite good at English writing' (Harriet, Interview 1).

However, few students reported writing an essay at the last minute; Jane was an exception, reporting writing one only the day before the deadline.

First-year students usually did not engage actively with abstract ideas. Their literature commentaries and essays for 'French Culture Today' consisted of personal responses to literary texts. These were sometimes sensitive and perceptive as in Isobel's exploration of the 'lost cat' metaphor in the Klapisch film, *Chacun Cherche son Chat* (1996):

> Literally, the film title means, 'Everyone is looking for his cat', which suggests that the cat represents more than just a lost animal in the film. If the search for the cat is a metaphor for love, the film title highlights the idea that ultimately everybody is looking for their own companionship and love. This can be seen through characters such as . . . .

Sometimes, however, responses were naive and superficial. Harriet commented in her essay on the Sartre novel, *Huis Clos* (1944): 'Personally, I find the whole plot humorous and do not look too deeply into any of the ideas associated with it.'

This reliance on personal response as distinct from the 'analysis' which was required was commented on in lecturer feedback. Limited experience of literary analysis at A level, lack of secondary reading and difficulties with reading and decoding the primary texts probably contributed to students' difficulties in developing appropriate responses.

For the sociolinguistics course 'Language in Spain and Latin America', Jane and Harriet produced essays reflecting ideas introduced in lectures. In her German history essay, Isobel produced a smooth, explanatory narrative to answer the set question but did not acknowledge possible contradictions in interpretation. However, she had selected ideas of her own to include.

Students' use of secondary sources was limited. Harriet only referenced one external source in her French literature essay, a direct quotation describing the function of the literary text she was discussing. Neither Harriet nor Jane made any references at all to external literature within their sociolinguistics essays, although each had short bibliographies dominated by website references and articles written by their lecturer. Isobel attached a bibliography of six sources to her French literature essay, but only one, a direct quotation from a film critic, was referenced within the text, though the interpretation of the film relied substantially on her sources. However, in her German history course, Isobel wrote an essay with a bibliography of nine sources and 18 internal citations. She used these sources to provide historical analysis to back her case, as well as factual or statistical information.

It is unclear whether students lacked the skills to use secondary literature *or* did not realize that this was expected, although this requirement was sometimes highlighted in course documentation, which also provided relevant bibliographies.

The students sometimes had difficulties constructing appropriate academic arguments and might include irrelevant material. For example, in an essay on the ideas and dramatic potential of *Huis Clos*, Harriet included extended biographical information about the author. Usually, the students used appropriate, if not sophisticated, formal academic language, but Harriet sometimes used colloquial expressions.

Previous educational background affected first-year students' ability to write effectively. Harriet and Jane commented in interviews that as A level languages students, they had not needed to write extended essays in English:

> I didn't enjoy 'Reading Culture' [a first semester course] very much. I think mainly because a lot of people had done English Literature for A level and the course was essay based and I hadn't written an essay in English since GCSE, so I found it quite difficult to get to grips with. (Jane, Interview 1)

In contrast, Isobel had written similar essays for her English literature A level. However, she found it harder to write history essays: 'I found it [introductory history course] really interesting, but extremely hard to write a history essay for the first time . . . like the one on imperialism and history in the first semester, I was just really swamped by that' (Interview 1).

Second-year writing

The second-year essays were longer (2,000 and 2,500 words). For 'Latin America: Nation, Race and Gender', discussed in Chapter 6, an assessed presentation on a related topic preceded the essay, where students could either answer a set question or create their own. In 'Studying Spanish Film', the students had to write a cinematographical analysis of a clip and answer a given essay question. None of the students had previous academic experience of film.

All three second-year students worked hard on their assignments, showing more consistent motivation than the first-year students. They had settled into university, were usually finding second-year work more interesting and were conscious that their second-year marks would count towards their final degree classification. Amy described this change:

> At the end of last year, I felt I could have done better and I think this year, I have really made the effort . . . since my interest developed over the first year through reading, I thought 'Well you know now in the second year I can really carry on with this' . . . I'm working harder definitely and they have also given us more work to do . . . I'm trying to be much more organized and doing more of the readings and things like that. (Interview 1)

The students were able to use the library and on-line resources more effectively than the first-year students. They usually did the required reading for seminars and tried to participate in discussion. However, they were still uncertain how to process challenging theoretical readings. Jessica described the difficulties she faced with particular readings for 'Latin America: Nation, Race and Gender':

> it's such a big topic that, I don't know, they do every single viewpoint and then they get to their own and then I don't agree with all these things they've said. You don't know whether to write down all these things, all the bits along the way, or whether just to get to the main point and write that down . . . it's quite heavy going really. (Interview 2)

In their writing, the students only engaged with conceptual frameworks in limited ways, usually in line with the views of their lecturer or those of the authors they were reading, if they engaged conceptually at all.

For example, the Latin American history course was Olivia's first-ever history course (her A levels were in Sociology, Spanish and English Literature). For the presentation she chose her own topic and, despite copious reading and preparation, Olivia could not devise an appropriate focused question. In the event, she produced a narrative account of a period of Mexican history rather than an analytical presentation. This was a positive achievement for a student new to the study of history, but one which only earned a poor grade. Lecturer Joan Wright explained in interview that:

> I didn't just want some kind of pot-boiled history of the Mexican Revolution but I wanted them to take a problem, an analytical problem within that sort of historical time period, and analyse what the political debate is, what the theoretical debate is, how different authors treated it.

Before writing the related essay, Olivia asked for lecturer advice and produced a theoretically based essay using ideas from an article recommended by Joan Wright. Olivia's essay achieved a far higher mark than her presentation, but was not based on independent reading and evaluation of the literature, unlike her presentation. Olivia could not cope independently in the world of theories and concepts without considerable support at this stage.

For the same course, Jessica wrote about the situation of women in a particular Latin American country, adapting a topic suggested on the course outline. She made a clear case in her essay, but her degree of engagement with the main concepts promoted in the course was ambiguous. The essay did not draw on theoretical notions of gender and class discussed in class and referenced in the course outline. Instead, it tacitly adopted an alternative 'rights and needs' approach to the situation of women in this country. There were some mentions of theory such as a reference to a 'practical' and a 'strategic' approach to women's interests (Molyneux, 2000), but this was confined to a single paragraph and not pursued further. Similarly, the possible influence of feminism and of US imperialism on the position of women was mentioned, but not developed.

From the evidence, it is not clear whether Jessica was consciously rejecting theoretical perspectives on gender presented in the course, or had not appreciated their relevance. The lectures on gender, class and patriarchy had been presented at an abstract level, and it is entirely possible that Jessica had not made the connections Joan Wright had hoped for. In interview, Jessica explained that she found the lectures somewhat 'bitty' and had difficulty in working out themes, which implies limited engagement with concepts.

In 'Studying Spanish Film', students' responses included both cultural and formal analysis, unlike the personal responses of the first-year students. Jessica was clear that the film she discussed in her essay was a constructed text, and she analysed it in terms of plot and *mise-en-scène*. She blended analytical ideas from lectures, interpretations from the secondary literature and her own interpretations. She provided further examples from British television advertisements to illustrate points. The essay was a creditable effort for a newcomer to filmic analysis.

Such performances do not mean that the students had necessarily internalized the ideas of their lecturers. Olivia explained that with analysis of literature and film:

> I don't search for these things [underlying meanings and constructions in texts]. I don't think I would like to do it in any more depth, because it does reach a point when I do start saying 'Oh come on, this is getting silly'

... But I am like that with ... literature and poetry ... I think sometimes lecturers look very ... precisely at minute details that seem meaningless.

Olivia also said that she would sometimes put points in her essay to please lecturers:

> I would rather not dispute the lecturers, I will just go along with them. I mean, [the lecturer] did say that she liked people to raise different opinions but ... I don't know how easily she would take to different opinions. Through erm ... knowing the lecturers now I think you have got to really write the way they want you to write. (Interview 6)

Olivia, however, also said that some lecturers did want different opinions from their own: 'Some would like lots of different arguments and opinions ... and I guess you have just got to change the style of the essays to suit them' (Interview 6).

The second-year students all engaged with secondary literature in their writing. Essays that included extensive lists of references and citations were usually well integrated. Amy, especially, used an impressive range of both primary and secondary sources for her history essay on the Zapatista movement (academic books, journal articles, websites and a personal interview with a human rights observer). She used these to provide statistics and other background information, specific examples of atrocities, illustration of government policy, information about the rebel movement's aims and activities, and analysis of events.

Olivia wrote her Latin American history essay based on one major article, but was aware she had to include various other references:

> I didn't want to seem like I was just taking his ideas, and I hope that it doesn't look that way. But we will see about that, and ... I did use some of my old notes from the presentation ... oh, I took some notes from [author recommended by the lecturer], his book ... and another [author recommended by the lecturer] article ... and I selected a few other books that I thought were relevant. I used the notes from the lectures ... but other than that, I think I only had five books in the bibliography, because I thought there was no point having an enormous amount if they are not particularly relevant. (Interview 6)

Within her essay, Olivia had 13 references to the key article and 6 to a single book from the class reading list, plus 3 individual references to other texts. She used her sources to provide analysis of developments and evidence of events, explore the nature of ethnicity and race, give statistics, and highlight a difference of interpretation among historians which she did not attempt to resolve. Her main conceptual framework was also adapted from the recommended article.

This extensive use of secondary sources was a significant advance on the first-year students. All students, however, continued to have problems with adequate acknowledgement of sources and matching references in running text with their bibliographies.

Final-year writing

The available final-year written work consisted of two timed examination essays and a practice essay of up to 2,000 words from the observed course 'Narratives of Desire', a literary commentary from an unobserved poetry course and dissertations. The dissertation was an optional extended writing task of 8,000 words, equivalent to two taught courses and requiring the students to do primary analysis of documentary data as well as using secondary literature.

The final-year students all worked hard. Rebecca, a high-achieving mature student of French, was strongly committed to her subject. She had many domestic problems and often worked through the night on assignments. She described the care she took with her dissertation:

> I had certain . . . elements that I wanted to include in each of the chapters. And then having read already to get an idea of what those things were going to be, I then had to re-read all the stuff to get all the finer detail of what I was going to pack into those different elements in each chapter. So that was very, very time consuming, and I do work in a way that I like to check and double check . . . and to get an idea of which historian or which theorist said something, that I have got a very clear picture before I write that next paragraph . . . in the end it was really like getting blood out of a stone to get a sentence out of me, because I was . . . wanting to be so sure that what I was saying was right and it wasn't going to be construed in any other way . . . I found the writing of it almost like a torture. (Interview 3)

However, feelings were complex. A practically oriented person, Susie found the theoretical focus of some of her courses challenging. As a devout Catholic, she also had difficulty in engaging with certain theoretical perspectives relating to feminism and sexuality:

> I get a bit fed up with having them [prevalent ideas] forced down my throat and having to think the same way as the lecturer, if you know what I mean. . . . With some arguments it's very much, if you disagree or don't come from exactly the same angle as the lecturer then you're not going to do well, and I don't think that's on. (Susie, Interview 1)

The students gave ample evidence in their written work and interviews of extensive literature searches. By now, they knew how to use both the library and online information sources.

The course 'Narratives of Desire' was challenging in its content (sexuality and related taboo areas) in both the primary and secondary texts. Students were expected to discuss highly personal issues, in class and in writing, and to relate these to theory and the primary texts they had studied.

Rebecca achieved a high mark in the examination for this course. In her responses, she took on the course themes and articulated ideas clearly within this framework. She referred to six primary texts in her first essay and five secondary sources. Lecturer Shirley Hunt was particularly impressed as Rebecca included references to literature not on the course syllabus, an indication of student independence and motivation. Rebecca used the secondary sources to introduce and support her own interpretation, and as stimuli for a new section of the essay. She used the primary sources to provide extended examples and, in the case of a non-course text, to provide a parallel with a character in the class text. On the first page of the essay, a clear plan was set out. She constructed a clear and well elaborated argument using appropriate language, even under examination conditions. Primary texts, secondary sources and her own interpretation were seamlessly blended. In her written comments on this paper Shirley Hunt was largely approving, and criticism was limited to pointing out potential issues not addressed in the essay.

Kate had a long plan in note and sentence form of more than two and a half pages at the beginning of her examination paper. She summarized the concepts of the French psychoanalyst Jacques Lacan and applied them to an extended example from a primary text. She then moved back to Lacan to provide a more general explanation for events and emotions in the primary text. She referred to two primary texts and one secondary source. However, she did not apply any theoretical framework to her second primary text, instead explaining and interpreting it according to her own understandings, a strategy more typical of first-year students. In her second examination essay, she only addressed half of the question in any depth and some colloquial language crept in. Kate's basic ideas were more difficult to follow than Rebecca's, indicating perhaps examination pressure or perhaps that she thought less clearly about the underlying issues.

In her practice essay, although not under exam pressure, Kate constructed an introduction where the thesis statement did not follow smoothly from earlier text, again a problem more typical of first-year writing. She lost marks because of limited reference to secondary literature. Overall, Kate never achieved strong control over an academic argument, unlike Rebecca.

In a literary commentary written for the poetry course, Rebecca included significant amounts of secondary literature, wrote about technically sophisticated issues and used appropriate academic language. This commentary contrasted strikingly with the simpler commentaries written by the first-year students.

All the students who chose to write dissertations constructed capable and thoughtful arguments. They found the process of choosing their own topic highly engaging, as was clear from the quality of the dissertations produced and how they talked in interview. For example, Susie's topic was the global 'drug gap' between developed and developing nations, with particular reference to a Latin American country in which she had spent her year abroad. This was a topic close to her heart and one, moreover, where she did not have to use theoretical perspectives which sat uneasily with her Catholic beliefs and practical trends in her character.

The dissertation students used secondary sources in a sophisticated way. For example, Henry was analysing French media and government discourses on the first and second Gulf Wars. He used a variety of secondary sources in both English and French: books, book chapters and journal articles. He also used a range of primary sources, largely French media articles from the web. He used the secondary sources to build an argument and the primary sources to exemplify it, adapting discourse analysis frameworks from the literature to analyse his data.

There were only a limited number of books and journal articles for Susie to draw on, a source of some concern for her and her supervisor. However, she also used a number of primary sources taken from websites, organizational reports and official and non-governmental organization publications. Her argument was constructed on the basis of a limited number of secondary sources, but supported by factual evidence and charts gleaned from multiple sources.

Rebecca's dissertation topic was the inclusion of West African people as exhibits at the 1931 *Exposition Coloniale Internationale* in Paris. She produced a meticulously constructed analysis of aspects of cultural politics in the colonial era, engaging with secondary sources with her usual sophistication and erudition.

The dissertation students received considerable amounts of usable formative feedback. Their supervisors assisted with topic choice, the structure of the argument, issues of style and academic conventions. The students could ask questions during supervisory meetings, and their supervisors commented on draft chapters and generally guided the process.

Conclusions

There were clear differences among the first-year students in the amount and quality of their written work. The students were able to articulate their own point of view in assignments, but most encountered difficulties when they had to engage with secondary literature. (Isobel was a partial exception, especially in her German history course.) They also usually gave personal responses to literature and film, rather than engaging with critical literature.

First-year students, especially Harriet and Jane, often struggled with basic academic skills such as referencing as well as reading and decoding texts. Engaging with the ideas of others in the complex moves required in their particular fields was challenging.

None of the second-year students formed their own independent theoretical question for their history essay. It seems they preferred at this stage to follow through a question proposed by the lecturer; in our terms, practising early criticality. In the film essays, understandably the students were more focused on constructing essays in a new field than in challenging existing interpretations.

By the final year, the students were more sophisticated, in line with lecturers' accounts (see Chapter 6). In writing for 'Narratives of Desire', Rebecca and Kate attempted to engage with theory and the secondary literature. Both showed advanced abilities to interpret complex texts. The variation in ability to cope with theory, mentioned by the lecturers, was borne out to some extent by the written work. However, both students made serious attempts to locate their examination responses within a theoretical framework.

The final-year students were much more able to cope with academic conventions than students in the earlier years; they did not report field-specific difficulties any more. Presumably, they had caught up in the relevant areas and anyway only chose options where they felt comfortable. By this time they had had considerable practice and academic training in their chosen fields.

As we saw in Chapter 6, the lecturers invested considerable effort in written feedback on students' work. However, our observations suggested that this type of feedback was a less important learning mechanism for students than lecturers believed. During the research period, because of an upcoming quality assurance inspection in Languages, students had to return all corrected work and feedback sheets to the department after a one week 'loan' period. Often, the students chose only to check the grade, and returned the work without carefully reading the written comments. If students' written work nonetheless improved from year to year, it seems that modelling and discussion of appropriate argumentation styles in classes, supervision sessions and readings were influencing student development more strongly than formal feedback.

Social work students

This section discusses nine case study students: three first years (Margaret, Janet and Rita), three second years (Katy, Sarah and Mark), and three final-year students (Ian, Jayne and Emma, all completing the old-style four-year programme). All courses were compulsory, so as to meet the professional requirements of the concurrent Diploma in Social Work.

The Social Work case study students

The Social Work students were often mature students with past experience relevant to social work.

Three students (Rita, Sarah, Emma), had A levels in subjects not necessarily directly relevant to Social Work and with widely varying grades. Rita, for example, had studied Art, Theatre and English Literature while Sarah had A levels in Psychology, Sociology and Religious Studies. The remaining students had left school at age 16 and re-entered higher education many years later with non-traditional entry qualifications.

Margaret had gained secretarial qualifications after leaving school and had worked for her husband's small business while raising two children. Before starting the Social Work programme age 50, she had completed two-thirds of a part-time MBA course. Janet, 30, had been a Somalian refugee. Katy, 34, had been a dancer, a hotel worker and a book-keeper. Mark had been self-employed as a printer for 20 years until deciding for personal reasons to become a social worker. Ian, 34, had returned to education after traumatic family circumstances. Jayne, 32, had decided to return to education after looking after her children and working as a hairdresser. Apart from those with A levels and Jayne, the students came from working-class backgrounds. Only Jayne had attended a private school.

The first-year students experienced various social and academic problems. Janet felt socially isolated as the only black student and former refugee. Rita had difficulties managing a health problem in her hall of residence, and Margaret had various domestic problems. Their academic problems included, for example, not yet knowing how to use the library. The second-year students were more established socially and academically and usually had part-time jobs to earn money and to gain relevant work experience. The final-year students were close to becoming qualified social workers, spending much of their final year on placement. They were juggling the formidable demands of the course in addition to family commitments (Jayne), two part-time jobs (Ian), and a part-time voluntary job (Emma).

First-year writing

The first-year Social Work assignments consisted largely of 1,500- to 2,000-word essays which the students had to select from a given list of questions, apart from one assignment where each student had to reflect on their potential to become a critical social work practitioner. There were also some timed examinations. The Social Work essay topics included some practical aspects while the Sociology assignments usually had a conceptual orientation.

The two mature non-traditional students, Janet and Margaret, both worked hard. Janet talked about the considerable amount of preparation she did for her essays – speaking to lecturers and available PhD students, reading, making an essay plan, making notes and writing multiple handwritten drafts before typing up a final version. Although both Janet and Margaret read considerable amounts, they had problems in locating relevant information and coping with journal articles.

Rita invested much less effort in reading and writing, instead focusing mainly on her social life. In her final interview, she described her approach to essay writing: 'Well every essay I've done this year I've crammed in the last week or something, so I'd say most of them have been written within a week, if not less.' Because she had often missed lectures, she started writing essays with a low level of knowledge.

Perhaps reflecting their non-traditional background, Janet and Margaret had considerable difficulties in building clear arguments in writing. Often, points were taken from the literature to make a claim, provide a definition, or present a fact, but the point itself was not clearly introduced or elaborated on. Instead, Margaret and Janet moved on to the next paragraph with another referenced point on a somewhat different topic. Both students referenced secondary sources in their essays in a non-standard way.

Margaret would regularly put her main connecting idea in the conclusion, after presenting an array of ideas earlier in the essay. In one essay on social security and its role in reducing poverty, she started with some definitions and a clarification of the significance of the essay title, all well referenced. This was a positive start, but was not followed by any overview of the essay and its argument. Instead, Margaret moved into an unreferenced, but sub-titled, discussion of 'the Underclass'; then in another sub-titled section, she embarked on a well-referenced background history of the social security system in the UK. After this, Margaret moved to her conclusion, where she presented her main argument.

Janet often wrote very short paragraphs which did not connect easily with the text, before or after. One lecturer gave critical feedback:

> The essay could have been *much* better than it actually was if it had been written more carefully and structured more efficiently. You may have far more ability in terms of analysis, for example, than is demonstrated here – the style of writing and lack of planning weaken your argument.

In addition, both Margaret and Janet had problems with language and sentence structure. Margaret used sentence fragments and colloquial expressions. Janet, for whom English was a second language, had even greater problems. A lecturer rather bluntly commented on one essay: 'This is a very poorly organized and presented paper. As a result the good points that are made are lost in a mass of rhetoric, poor spelling, poor grammar and badly referenced writing.'

Rita entered the Social Work course with good A level grades, and was able to structure essays appropriately, construct coherent arguments and use appropriate language. However, she struggled at times to make theoretical linkages. One lecturer commented on a Sociology essay about the social significance of clothes that 'You make some good points and include lots of material. Your work would be improved with more detailed reading, especially of more theoretical accounts of the social meaning of clothes, so that fashion could be linked with broader social issues.'

While smarting from negative feedback, Rita pointed to her lack of the field-specific background in A level Sociology, possessed by many of her classmates:

> I've only ever written English essays and perhaps one History essay when I was in Year 9 or something, but it seems to be quite a different way of

writing ... obviously the people that are doing Sociology as a degree have most likely done A level Sociology ... if you've done two years of Sociology already then you're already miles ahead of anyone else ... maybe a few people have a head start in that sense. (Interview 4)

This is a somewhat different perspective from that of the Sociology lecturer described in Chapter 6 who sought to 'destabilize' knowledge gained from A level Sociology.

Even Rita had problems integrating information from secondary sources and technical difficulties with the referencing required in Sociology. Sometimes she omitted references or left them incomplete. However, she did refer to secondary sources in a more sophisticated way than the other two students, using these to support her argument with quotations, paraphrases and summaries, and to present arguments which she then commented on.

Apart from Rita, the students engaged seriously with their writing. They drew on personal experiences and tried to make sense of them. For example, in Margaret's essay on relations of power and romance, she drew on her troubled relationship with her husband and her history of providing support to him.

At times, the students' backgrounds engendered conflict. The first-year course 'Introduction to Social Work 2' included discussion of values, and Janet found that reconciling her personal values with those expected of a social worker was challenging:

> To me they [Social Work values] are rules, they're not values, there is so much regulation in there, so I find I have to compromise some of my values ... to me I'm somebody who takes faith seriously and I believe in God and doing what I think is right ... and as a social worker you tend to work with people [who are homosexual] ... it's this issue of respecting them and I found it really difficult ... but when I'm a social worker I'll come across these people, how am I expected to treat them, how am I supposed to deal with them without being biased ... that is quite difficult. (Interview 2)

In a positive sense, such conflicts can be a driver for personal change. However, they can also limit development of criticality if a student is obliged to compromise and hide personal values.

Even Rita drew on personal experience in the essays where possible. For example, in writing about the social significance of clothing, she discussed the meaning of her own dress style. She reflected on how diabetes had affected her:

> The emotional stages of development that I have experienced through the seven years of having the condition have given me a good insight into what it is like for someone to have to accept change in their life, and how to go about actively changing in order to suit their new lifestyle. (Reflective essay)

The students took their feedback seriously, but sometimes misunderstood what was intended. For example, Janet understood that she should 'analyse' more as her assignment feedback indicated. However, she thought that meant she had to put both sides of an argument clearly, rather than develop her own opinion and connect this to the literature: 'My opinion? Does it matter? . . . I don't think you write down what you think – I don't think your opinion matters, as a person' (Interview 3).

Second-year writing

By the second year, Social Work students had a variety of writing assignments: (1) 3,000 word essays; (2) evidence sheets (which required students to take an element of their practice and relate it to social work theories, relevant legislation and relevant agencies); (3) law case studies (2,500 words); and (4) a personal piece where the students reflected on their professional practice learning goals (3,000 words).

The assignments had a practical and reflective direction as well as asking the students about social work theories. For example, in the law case study students had to go through a short documented 'case' line by line, explaining in detail how current legislation would apply. One sample case concerned a young, recently widowed mother with two young children who was living in impoverished circumstances and finding it hard to cope for various reasons. This was a carefully guided assignment, supported by a lecture on how to complete it successfully.

The second-year students read extensively for their essays. Katy, for example, reported having read ten books for her essay on grief and loss and some specialized articles. Some were library books, some were her own and some a friend and colleague lent her. In addition, she ordered materials from voluntary agencies. She estimated (Interview 3) that she had already spent three to four hours in the library finding the books and an hour and a half on the essay plan.

The second-year students were enjoying their written work more than in their first year, saying they could see its direct relevance to social work. Perhaps for this reason, they all worked hard. For example, Sarah produced successive drafts of the law case study as she thought carefully around all aspects of a particular case. Sentence by sentence, she considered the implications of the case, pointing out relevant legal clauses, especially in the Children Act (1989).

The second-year Social Work students had very different writing profiles from one another. One non-traditional student (Mark) achieved good grades, while another (Katy) achieved less highly. The student who entered with relevant A levels (Sarah) achieved well.

All three students made connections with other voices in the field as well as reflecting on themselves and their practice, although Katy did so less expertly than the others. All referred extensively to secondary sources, knitting together references to theory and their practice experience.

Mark and Sarah constructed arguments appropriately. For example, in a reflective essay on his practice placement in a Youth Offending Team, Mark made extensive connections between theory and the practice he confronted in a challenging setting. He also connected the ethical and practical dilemmas that he faced with published literature:

> My initial dilemma centred on issues of care vs. control. As a Youth Worker young people have a choice on whether they wish to engage or work with me. This was not an option for many of the young people that I worked with on placement. I was aware of the complex ethical dilemma that presents around the notion of young people's right to self-determination (Biestek, 1961). As a Youth Offending Officer I had to recognize that I not only had a duty to the young person but also to the courts and to the community. Therefore, the challenge for me was to manage these tensions while acknowledging that practice can become oppressive. Therefore, in many situations on my placement I had to acknowledge that control was part of care. (Thompson, 2000, p. 3)

Sarah also wrote coherently, providing appropriate exemplification and links to theory and research. She engaged extensively with secondary sources, citing, summarizing and critiquing research and theory. She usually used other secondary sources for her points of criticism, rather than making original criticism. Where required, she related secondary sources to practice issues, and she displayed considerable personal insight in the professional practice reflective piece, where the students were asked:

'What do you see as your professional practice learning goals at this point in time?'

Sarah was a young, relatively shy student who was aware that she needed to become more assertive (Interview 5). In her writing, she developed this point: 'Although I am understanding and a good listener, I never challenge people in a constructive way, as I do not want to upset them. This is something which I will need to learn so that I can enable service users to become empowered' (Professional practice reflection).

In feedback on her written work, Sarah was often scolded for not using adequate referencing. She may have thought that only direct quotations needed to be referenced, but this point was never made specifically by those giving feedback.

In an essay for 'Adult Social Work', Katy was asked: 'Working with experiences of grief and loss is common in social work with adults. What skills and resources might the social worker need?' Katy evaluated her secondary sources in her essay, according to ideas presented in the lectures, but moved beyond these to draw on personal experiences. Several people in her family and a close friend had died of cancer, and she also worked with a man, C, who had traumatic brain injuries. She used these experiences to evaluate theories of grief and loss. We see this in the following quotation:

> One of the main problems with Kübler Ross theory (1969) is that the stages are unlikely to happen sequentially and some people may never experience some of the reactions at all or may stay in one stage indefinitely as C's father who is still in the anger stage after four years post-injury. (para. 9)

Katy's evaluations, although somewhat crude, were often her own. As well as discussing theorists mentioned in her lectures (Kübler-Ross, 1969; Murray Parkes, 1986), she examined the claims of Douglas (1990) about family response to traumatic brain injury, a source she had found for herself, but forgot to reference it at the end of her essay.

In all of Katy's essays, however, she had difficulty in developing a clear argument. Although most elements were present (a point of view, mention of secondary sources and links between domains), the paragraphs were often internally jumbled and the links between them were unclear. For example, the second paragraph of the essay just mentioned is about the importance of environmental factors in grief and loss processes. This is an important point, but does not easily connect to the introductory paragraph or the following paragraph on theories of grief and loss. A considerable part of her essay consisted of retelling lecture content. It was unclear whether Katy agreed with 'staged' theories of grief and loss or not. Katy's lecturer gave feedback as follows: 'Lots of semi-digested theory needs much more critical unpacking and explaining'.

Katy had most of the raw ingredients for answering the question in her essay – theory, practical information, personal experience related to theory – but these elements had not been sufficiently blended together. She had difficulty with manipulation of theories as distinct from retelling, expressing ideas logically, addressing the question fully and conforming to academic rules of presentation.

At times, even when students understood comments, it was not clear that they benefited. For example, Katy was told on one essay that she lost several marks by failing to check through her work after writing. However, on the next essay this pattern was repeated because, as Katy explained, she sometimes just ran out of time to check.

There was also evidence of developmental responses to feedback. After receiving feedback on one essay that her reading was too limited, Janet reported that she did read more widely for the next (Interview 4).

Students were sometimes upset after receiving poor marks, as seen in Mark's reaction:

> It was the Adults one. . . . it was the one about grief and loss and I did it regarding parents who have young people with disabilities, so like the grief process they go through, and I thought that was a great title, brilliant essay, it was the worst mark I've ever got for anything and I couldn't believe it, I got 53 for that, I was gutted. . . . It was a great essay, I should have got far more for that . . . I was in trauma for weeks after that! (Interview 5)

Katy, on the other hand, was delighted to receive both positive and negative feedback on her essays, feeling she could learn from the guidance given and gain confidence from positive comments.

Final-year writing

Final-year Social Work students had to produce further evidence sheets and a placement project (5,000 words), all requiring extensive reflection on practice. A dissertation (10,000–12,000 words) provided an extended opportunity to make yet more connections between theory and practice.

The final-year students all read widely for their dissertations and also referred extensively to literature in their evidence sheets and placement projects. All of them located information with ease from multiple sources.

For example, Jayne described the information search processes she employed for her dissertation on adoption. In addition to web and library searching, and speaking to friends who had been adopted, Jayne's practice placement gave her access to colleagues with relevant knowledge (Interview 3). The students spoke about the role of reading in consolidating and extending theoretical understandings which would be useful in practice. As in Modern Languages, the final-year students were far more able to cope with theoretical complexity.

In the final year, the students worked hard; even Jayne, with her young family, managed to spend four to five hours on each evidence sheet (Jayne, Interview 2). Ian described how he had spent three hours on each of four separate days on one evidence sheet of 1,200 words (Ian, Interview 3).

The final-year students had somewhat different writing profiles from one another. Emma, a young student with A levels, wrote well as did Ian, a mature student with non-traditional entry qualifications. Jayne prioritized her children and fitted in her assignments around their needs.

All the students could make fluent connections between Social Work theories and their own practice. In her placement project, for example, Jayne wrote about her client, P, who had missed school for a long period and been referred to the Education Welfare Service where Jayne spent her first placement. P had a difficult relationship with his step-father. Jayne made theory–practice connections as follows:

> A good relationship with a step-parent can act as a moderating factor in terms of positive development into young adulthood, conversely a bad relationship could amplify already existing vulnerabilities, increase low self-esteem and lead to reactive, rather than thought-out behaviour, on the young person's part (Barnes, G et al., 1998). (Jayne, Placement project, p. 4)

Jayne then described the theoretical foundation for her approach to P's case. She decided to use task-centred practice 'even though the basis for task-centred practice is the client's own willingness to change the situation/problem identified and P was at first hostile to any social work intervention' (pp. 4–6). She mentioned research by Goldberg et al. which 'found that task-centred practice was most successful when working with clients who have requested help as opposed to involuntary/unwilling clients or those who had chronic, complex problems were less amenable' (Placement project, pp. 4–5). Jayne then justified using task-centred practice, despite these findings, drawing finally on Coulshed et al. (1998) for support. Jayne made further connections with the literature when discussing the difficult relationship P has with his step-father (p. 10); she drew connections between Rutter's Family Adversity Index (Rutter et al., 1977), with its exploration of the link between family stressors and disorder in the child, and her client. Jayne also related P's behaviour to the literature on depression. She made further connections between theory and her own practice when dealing with P's mother, referring to Reid et al. (1972).

In her placement project, Emma also made many connections between the academic literature and her case, including 28 references. She described the nature, extent and effects of child abuse, according to the literature, and related this to the behaviours and feelings of her case study child; she then discussed the theoretical background to 'direct work', which was her contact style with the child. Additionally, Emma made many connections between her case study clients and the relevant legal framework.

In all assignments, Ian expressed clear connections between Social Work theories of action (e.g. task-centred practice, psychosocial models) and his own practice. For example, in an evidence sheet from Ian's second placement we see him reflecting on a challenging client situation, probing the nature of the problem, displaying awareness of and ability to use different kinds of listening and response skills. He related these to Social Work literature, and described employing basic social work values in his interactions, practical activities and strategies with his client.

All three dissertations dealt with the practice interests of the students. They each reported a thorough investigation of a particular aspect of social work (dual diagnosis, open adoption and direct work with children) rather than presenting any theoretical critique. The underlying aim was to work out what might constitute good practice by taking the evidence into consideration. For example, Ian's dissertation was a sophisticated and detailed synthesis of existing theories and treatment models used in dual diagnosis (of co-existing mental health and substance abuse) and was set in the context of community mental health teams. He chose this topic because he wanted to integrate what he had learned on placement while writing about a topic which was attracting increasing interest in social work (Interview 5). However, Ian did not attempt to critique the various theories of dual diagnosis or argue for any one of these. His markers did not comment on this aspect, dealing instead with descriptive matters such as the sequencing of chapters and the relationship between them.

Two students engaged in a limited way with primary data in their dissertations. For example, Jayne mentioned interviewing social workers, although this did not seem to be very extensive or systematic.

Overall, the final-year students varied in their effectiveness as academic writers. Ian constructed arguments appropriately, used formal written English and engaged with secondary sources to support his case. Even in some essays from previous years, he showed a similar command. In later final-year work, he made links between his own actions on placement, supporting theories of action and, where appropriate, the law.

Emma was also a strong writer, making fluent theory–practice connections and writing in an appropriate academic format. Her dissertation was somewhat more argumentative than the other two, claiming that 'direct work' is structured and useful, and pointing out its limitations.

In her placement assignments, Jayne wrote appropriately. For example, in the conclusion to her placement project Jayne summarized her thoughts on a child guidance case, demonstrating the connections she made between theory, ethical commitment and her practice. However, in her dissertation, Jayne put her potential arguments in the conclusion of her dissertation in the shape of somewhat contradictory recommendations.

For the final-year students, the experience of theory and practice at last became more integrated, as the lecturers quoted in Chapter 6 had hoped. For example, in the final year, after the practice placement spent engaging with real people, Ian found his academic work to be more meaningful than in the early parts of his degree course when he had been writing about theories from textbooks (Ian, Interview 1). He spoke about how the care he took with his work had increased over time, as his confidence and knowledge had developed and pride in his work had grown (Interview 4). He also spoke about trying to make this written work relevant to his practice so that he could gain knowledge that would be useful to him (Interview 4).

Jayne operated under extreme time pressure, and viewed her written assignments much more instrumentally. She preferred doing her placement project to her dissertation as she could complete it more easily (Interview 3). Jayne spoke about the evidence sheets and placement project as time-consuming hoops to be jumped through and downplayed their developmental potential (Interview 2).

Conclusions

In the first year, we see inconsistency in writing performance which could mainly be explained in terms of personal and academic history. Personal difficulties, past and present, health problems and age all played a role in how students engaged with their writing. All the students struggled with academic writing conventions and building appropriate arguments.

In the second year, we see more consistent effort from all the students, as first-year uncertainties diminished. The students experienced their first practice placement, and this motivated them to grasp theory and its relationship to practice. One of the 'non-traditional' students had developed effective writing strategies, although the other still struggled with conventions.

By the final year the increasing focus on making connections between theory, practice and the self in assignments ensured that the students developed and applied understandings and linkages they had made. Their main focus was to make these horizontal connections, rather than to challenge theory. All had reached an acceptable level of writing effectiveness, though Jayne lagged behind somewhat, perhaps because she was the least engaged with her writing.

Chapter 8

Experiential Learning and Criticality Development

This chapter explores student criticality development through the special, out-of-class experiences provided in our two fields: the Year Abroad (Modern Languages) and practice placements (Social Work).

The chapter first analyses the Modern Languages Year Abroad experience before turning to Social Work placements, and for each (1) describes the specific context and expectations of various stakeholders; (2) analyses critical development in terms of different levels and domains, along with associated development of relevant knowledge resources; (3) takes account of individual variation in terms of dispositions and personalities and (4) theorizes the special contribution of this experiential learning to criticality development.

The Year Abroad

The analysis of criticality development during the Year Abroad in Modern Languages is based on interviews with Westford lecturers and case study students before and after the stay abroad, documentation and reports of preparatory meetings for students and student projects.

Expectations of the Year Abroad

Institutional preparation and expectations

Modern Languages students at Westford had to spend the third year of their four-year programme abroad. They might go as an exchange or visiting student to a foreign university, teach as an English Language Assistant in a school or undertake a work placement.

While abroad, the students had to carry out an investigative project and write a 5,000-word report on this in the target language; at the beginning of the final year, they also made an assessed oral presentation on this project. The report and presentation combined were worth around 10 per cent of the final degree mark for students working or teaching abroad. For university-based students, half the mark for the year came from the project and half from courses followed at the host university. No other aspect of their activities abroad was formally assessed.

The academic aims of the Year Abroad were described in the *Guidelines for Third Year Investigative Project:*

> [The Year Abroad] constitutes an important part of your progression towards BA/BSc level work. It offers an opportunity to improve not just your linguistic and cultural proficiency in your chosen language, but also your ability to work independently over a sustained period. The Investigative Project provides you with an opportunity to consolidate and apply some of the analytical and conceptual tools acquired in Years One and Two, in an extended piece of work based largely on primary source material. You will develop the basic research and data handling skills introduced to you during Year Two, as well as enhancing your ability to synthesize findings in to a clearly structured discussion. In doing so, you will also be developing your proficiency in reading and writing in your target language. (Guidelines, p. 1)

Further guidance specified the schedule for handing in drafts and explained expectations further. The focus of the documentation was on gaining independence, not only through working away from the supportive context of the home university but also academically; students were expected to define their own research topic linked to a particular local context and carry out an empirical study on the ground. Thus, the Year Abroad project seemed to propose a considerable step forward in terms of critical thinking ability compared with the second-year tasks described in Chapter 7: taking control of the topic, locating and managing information in an unfamiliar environment and writing an extended piece in the target language. In terms of the criticality framework presented in Chapter 4, students were being asked to make a substantial leap towards some of the ways of working associated with late criticality.

Apart from explaining these academic goals, the preparation sessions for the Year Abroad paid some attention to intercultural issues, familiarizing students with potential cultural differences and 'culture shock'. Language tutor David Newbury also explained how second-year language classes dealt with topical cultural content: 'so that when they go to France . . . they'll hopefully know what young people are talking about'. Nonetheless, students who were interviewed did not feel fully prepared for many aspects of the new experience, confirming the view of many commentators (e.g. Coleman, 1996) that intercultural development requires authentic experience and encounters for significant learning to take place.

Lecturer expectations

The lecturers saw the Year Abroad as essential to develop both fluency and confidence in the foreign language and firsthand acquaintance with the target culture. However, they felt that achievement of these aims depended partly on factors beyond the control of the home institution. These included the student's personality and how much effort they made to engage with native speakers, as well as features of the local context. It could be difficult for students in a university abroad to avoid socializing with friends from Westford, and language assistants were teaching in English for much of the day. Even when socializing with locals and with other international students, the widespread currency of English as a *lingua franca* was a potential obstacle to target language use. The Year Abroad coordinator Beate Schmidt believed that of the two aims, 'immersion in the culture and understanding of the culture' was actually more reliably achieved, though this also depended on individual student effort and engagement.

Like other staff, Beate Schmidt believed that students benefited 'not just linguistically and academically, but also as people . . . as individuals'. All agreed that students gained in confidence and independence, at least in terms of problem solving capability: '. . . they all take these rather rough situations, as something that makes them stronger, that makes them into more assertive people' (Beate Schmidt).

Several lecturers commented that the combination of improved knowledge resources and greater maturity achieved during the Year Abroad led to greater commitment and academic achievement in final-year courses: 'I think the year abroad does open up their horizons tremendously . . . and they're just much more mature when they come back' (Shirley Hunt).

One language tutor reported a staff discussion about students' development in terms of intercultural awareness:

by discovering a new language and culture you're then reassessing your own culture . . . the students are saying that at the beginning of their year abroad they were very critical, that in France they couldn't do things like here and 'I miss England' and so on, then along the year, they slightly change their mind, they think 'all right, OK, so they do that ... so maybe what we do in England is not that great on that particular aspect', and so [this involves] reassessing or being critical of what you thought before, and discovering new things. (Sam Ledkes)

To sum up, the lecturers' focus was primarily on the acquisition of linguistic and cultural resources. However, they also commented more broadly on the independence and maturity gained by students and made links between these and greater academic sophistication in the final year. In contrast to much more structured expectations in the applied professional field of Social Work, the lecturers' expectations were expressed throughout in relatively open terms, and there was considerable tolerance of diversity both of student experience and student response to that experience.

Student expectations

The second-year students we interviewed were all looking forward to their Year Abroad, a feature which had encouraged them to study languages at university.

Olivia was going to Mexico as a language assistant. Her expectations focused not only on language but also on gaining confidence and personal independence, having to live on her own and experience new challenges such as teaching.

Jessica was going to Spain as a language assistant. She was hoping primarily to develop her linguistic resources, which she felt were quite weak, but also saw the experience of living abroad as a kind of personal test as she did not think she would be living in Britain in a few years time.

Amy's expectations were somewhat different. Though her mother was Spanish, she had never lived in Spain; she viewed the chance to spend a year there as a personal quest for part of her identity.

To conclude, it is clear that all parties saw the Year Abroad primarily as a way of improving linguistic and cultural knowledge resources and skills, and these were the main dimensions captured in the assessed Year Abroad project. Reference was regularly made to independence and the development of the self as major benefits for individuals, and the possibility of growth in intercultural awareness and empathy was acknowledged. However, these were not captured in the formal academic agenda and assessment systems of Modern Languages.

Development of criticality through residence abroad

In this section we analyse the actual Year Abroad experience reported after the event by our three final-year case study students. All of them had been living in a foreign language environment for the first time. Kate had been a secondary school language assistant in a small town in France, Susie had worked as a volunteer with a Christian organization in South America, and Henry had been a visiting student in a Spanish university. In spite of these quite diverse settings, many common themes emerge from their experiences, reflecting those found in other larger scale studies (e.g. Murphy-Lejeune, 2002; Pellegrino Aveni, 2005).

We begin by investigating the experience in terms of its impact on the self, before examining the case study students' engagement with the world and its impact on their critical thinking skills and knowledge base, including development of linguistic resources. The significance of personal dispositions and resources for development during the Year Abroad are then explored before analysing any links that students establish between the domains of knowledge, the self and the world. Finally, the role of the Year Abroad in the overall development of criticality is assessed.

Development of the self: critical reflection

In our data, the students' experience abroad was a source of reflection, both while abroad and in retrospect. Barnett (1997) suggests two kinds of reflection related to criticality which seem especially relevant here. These are social formation and self-realization. In *reflection as social formation*, personal self-reflection engages with the 'language and perspectives' of those encountered in new real world settings. Barnett elaborates:

> This is no pure cognitive exercise, for the students have to invest themselves in these activities and so develop themselves by becoming accepted in communities . . . it is a self-reflection that springs out of the inner disturbance that unfamiliar social interactions can bring. (p. 99)

This is an advanced form of reflection, requiring personal change. It has clear affinities with the intercultural awareness and empathy referred to by some Westford lecturers and discussed for many years in the literature on intercultural competence:

> Each acquisition of a foreign language opens a new way of life. The individual who penetrates deeply enough into a foreign culture becomes a richer personality. He shifts readily from one language to another; from

one set of habits, attitudes and values to another. Thus he is in a position to look at problems from more than one viewpoint, and to see the essential ethnocentrism of each. (Stonequist, 1937, p. 178, cited in Murphy-Lejeune, 2005, p. 30)

As for *personal self-realization*, Barnett describes this as the enactment of personal projects: 'We define ourselves through our personal projects. More than that, projects hitherto classified as attempts to understand the world are reconstituted as projects of self-discovery' (Barnett, 1997, p. 98).

The Year Abroad students provided considerable evidence that they were engaging in both these types of critical self-reflection. Kate had spent many family holidays in France and expected to fit in easily, but found the first few weeks of her stay very difficult: 'I stuck out like a sore thumb . . . I don't think British people really understand how different the French are from us'. She struggled with unfamiliar bureaucracy and was missing home, while the challenge of living in a monolingual French environment was very tough:

> I was literally thrown in at the deep end . . . you start sort of doubting yourself, 'I can't do this, I can't speak French, why have I just wasted three years of my life doing a degree that I blatantly can't do?', but you know, you kind of get through it . . . (Interview 1)

This difficult beginning forced her to reassess her relationship to other cultures:

> I think the whole experience made me appreciate my own culture, but then also made me aware that you can't be so judgemental towards other cultures. . . . you just have to accept that this is the way they do things, and it might be different from what you were used to and you can't really judge that, you've just got to go with it really. (Interview 1)

Kate thus showed the kind of inner disturbance and reappraisal of her ethno-centricism characteristic of reflection as social formation.

Susie described her arrival at night in a small town in South America as 'the scariest thing I have ever done'. She undertook voluntary work for a Christian organization in youth camps and schools, and with street children. This work caused her to reassess her own values:

> I was seeing people who have nothing and seeing what's important to them, you know, very much 'if I can provide for my family, if I can love my

children even if I can't educate them, even if I can't feed them, you know if I can love them then that's what I'm going to do', rather than 'I've got to go and get a nice suit'. I don't know, just different priorities and stuff. (Interview 1)

Susie reflected at length on her experience of culture shock, going beyond the impact of shanty towns, street kids and child prostitutes, to describe that of fundamentally different values. For example, there was a very macho culture within her workplace, where men would never admit to not knowing something in front of a woman and frequently lied openly. This went against Susie's own Christian values, which she had assumed were shared by the organization. But nonetheless she came home with altered personal priorities, offering an example of reflection as self-realization.

Henry found it difficult to adapt to a new university system. He repeatedly commented on how disorganized the university was and how different the expectations were from those of Westford. For example, he reported on the workload being heavier, but also being demotivated by exams which were 'memory tests' rather than 'encouraging you to think for yourself'. Throughout his interviews, Henry analysed his Year Abroad experience through British lenses. When faced with problems due to cultural differences in his new environment, as well as linguistic difficulties, Henry's reaction was to return to the UK at every opportunity and to e-mail his tutor at Westford to ask for help; he was rather upset when his tutor told him to enjoy himself and not worry about things. Henry did claim he came back changed, but only in having become a more sociable person, because of having had to work harder at making friends through a foreign language.

Development in the world: growth of independence, confidence and maturity

All three students reported gains in confidence, largely due to the range of challenges they had met and overcome when abroad. For them this was the most important outcome, alongside development of language resources.

Kate said that having to function in a foreign country gave her much increased confidence in her ability to deal with problems and made her less shy. The alien nature of the Year Abroad context made her reassess how she viewed 'not understanding things', from a weakness to be hidden in her first year, to a natural phenomenon she could do something about in her final year. This confidence had transferred to the classroom where she felt much more willing to ask questions and state her point of view than she had in the past.

Susie was proud of having spent the whole year in Latin America without coming back to the UK; now, nothing 'fazes' her, she just 'gets on with things'. This increased confidence had transferred to her relationship with lecturers: 'if you need help you have got to pester until you get it' (Interview 2).

The three students spoke of feeling more mature and focused as well as of thinking differently about future career and life choices. For example, Susie stressed the need for fulfilment from one's job rather than earning a great deal of money.

Overall, our data again supports the conclusion of Coleman (1996): '. . . students grow while abroad, their L2 and experience evidenced by greater maturity, independence, self-reliance, self-awareness and confidence' (p. 66).

This increased maturity and confidence, together with the additional linguistic and knowledge resources gained, fed back into academic work on return to Westford. All the students felt more ready to tackle the final year; they also felt closer to the lecturers, who seemed to take their views and critical abilities more seriously.

As we have seen, lecturers also commented on students coming back 'more mature and more interested in the subject' (Lucia Baxter) with the Year Abroad 'opening up their horizons considerably' and enabling them to 'deal with the kind of issues I ask them to discuss' (Shirley Hunt). However, this stronger academic orientation seems to have developed through integration of a range of cultural and linguistic resources, personal reflective abilities and a revised sense of self gained through the Year Abroad, rather than being a direct outcome of any sustained academic study during it. This view is supported by consideration of the main academic project undertaken during the Year Abroad.

Development of knowledge resources and critical thinking skills

As described earlier, students were expected to carry out an independent investigative project while abroad. Several lecturers elaborated that the project was intended to promote students' engagement with the community where they were living. In practice, none of the students found the project easy to do, and all felt rather disconnected from academic work.

Susie often lacked internet access and found it difficult to keep in touch with Westford. She complained that her supervisor did not reply to her e-mails, but it is also clear from her interviews that she missed some deadlines for submitting drafts. Markers commented on the high standard of language in her project, but criticized its descriptive and non-analytical nature.

Henry also found the project difficult and did not invest very much time in it. He had trouble finding secondary material and also produced a rather descriptive piece of work.

The lecturers commented on students' problems with this project. Several observed that the resulting reports often lacked 'academic rigour'; one lecturer remarked that some students were 'too busy having a good time to answer e-mails' and did not fully grasp that an academic piece of work was required, rather than an anecdotal report. These comments on poor motivation gained some support from the student interviews. On the other hand, as we have seen in Chapter 7, some of the academic expectations built into the project were intrinsically challenging for students even when provided with considerably more support in the home academic context.

Overall, while the projects did lead to substantial pieces of writing in the target language and reflected acquisition of some cultural resources, it is not clear how far they led to other types of development; lecturers' comments and assessments indicate that critical thinking in these pieces was limited. This tension between the highly experiential nature of the Year Abroad and its academic goals in terms of the development of critical thinking skills remained essentially unresolved for the case study students.

Development of linguistic resources

Both students and lecturers saw the Year Abroad as key to improvement of linguistic skills, and in turn, linguistic development was seen as key to accessing cultural resources and intercultural development, as well as for problem- solving and social integration. As acknowledged in other research (e.g. Doble et al., 1985, in Coleman, 1996), however, a reasonable level of language resources at the start of residence abroad greatly facilitates further development.

The student who found it hardest to integrate within Spanish society was Henry, and he blamed this on his initially low level of Spanish (he had only been learning the language for two years). He commented that Spanish people do not make it easy for foreigners, either speaking English to them if their Spanish is not good or speaking Spanish at normal speed, which he could not cope with. Nonetheless, his Spanish did improve, catching up with his level in French, which he had studied to A level standard at school: no mean achievement. But even this was not enough to overcome his initial lack of social integration.

Susie, on the other hand, felt well prepared: 'we had done so much grammar before we went that when we went out there we were all ready to go. . . . I felt confident enough when I got out there' (Interview 2). She came back with near-native level Spanish, having developed the richest social network of all three students when abroad.

Although Kate had difficulties initially, her French improved quickly. She was very pleased that, after working really hard at 'getting her accent right', people mistook her for a native speaker (Interview 1). In her final year, the extra language resources were helping her 'to tackle different areas and different readings'.

Lecturers accepted that the linguistic benefits of the Year Abroad were variable, depending on the student's personality and motivation and on contextual factors. But students were nonetheless assumed to have progressed a full language 'Stage' and were placed accordingly in final-year language classes. The language teachers commented on being able to use more sophisticated materials with students who had been abroad, not only because their language was generally better, but also because they had had to deal with large quantities of linguistic input while abroad and could relate what they read to their increased cultural knowledge and experiences.

Personal dispositions in criticality development in Modern Languages

The students brought different personal dispositions to their Year Abroad experience. Henry was expecting a university in Spain to be the same as in England and turned to his home tutors for help whenever he experienced a minor problem, whereas Susie had opted to work with underprivileged communities in Latin America, knowing she could not keep in close contact with Westford. Through this choice of placement, Susie already demonstrated *greater independence and organizational skills* at the outset than the other two students.

Social skills were important as an enabling resource, and in turn developed during residence abroad. Henry struggled to make friends, partly because of language difficulties, but also because of lack of sociability. He commented that the Year Abroad had shown him that you have to work at making friends, and he came back more willing to do so. Kate socialized primarily with two other English girls when in France; it was difficult to assess whether this was due to the small-town setting she found herself in as she claimed, or to her rather introverted personality. Whatever the reasons, neither of these students became fully immersed in the culture in which they were living, though both also made clear gains in terms of personal confidence and social skills. Susie, on the other hand, made many lasting friendships while abroad.

The three students also varied in terms of *flexibility and adaptability*. Susie thrived on the challenges of her working life, in contexts varying from an orphanage for street children to the rainforest. Henry did not fully embrace the different ways of doing things, going back home whenever he could. Kate found teaching English challenging and remained rather reserved in her attempts to adapt to her new context. However, she acknowledged that her teaching experience had helped her to see things from other people's perspective, for instance, when communication in English was difficult for her pupils.

Lecturers also commented that the resourcefulness of students was variable, and our data suggests that their personal dispositions could play a significant intermediary role, in terms of the kind of learning and critical development which took place during the relatively flexible experience of the Year Abroad.

(Lack of) Connections between domains

We have seen major developments taking place in the students as a direct result of the Year Abroad in terms of the development of linguistic (and cultural) resources and also in the domain of the self. Here we consider how far the students related this development to other types of knowledge resources, and to critical reason in particular.

Our data show that students resented having to think about academic work while abroad. They felt disconnected from the world of Westford and were somewhat torn between wanting help with their project and being left alone to enjoy their new experience. A striking feature of the student interviews was their failure to connect their experience abroad with previous academic learning.

For example, Susie showed much evidence of reflecting on her 'life-changing experience' in a very different culture, and was able to be analytical about some incidents which were clearly gender related. However, she was adamant that gender theory studied at university could not possibly help her make sense of them. When asked explicitly about this, she said:

> To be honest I don't think they're relevant at all. . . . Well when you get out there in the nitty gritty of it, it's like 'oh who really cares about all these [arguments]', you know . . . does that really matter when

somebody's just been bitten by this like poisonous snake and is going to die if they don't get to the hospital, you know? . . . if I was to be working with languages, it's how I'd want to do it, you know, be very active, very hands on, very just 'get stuck in and do it', rather than spend hours analysing everything (laughs). Sorry, that's just me. (Interview 1)

Neither of the others reported connections between their Year Abroad experience and prior academic knowledge. The only links acknowledged in the interview data were between the world and the self. Having to solve real life problems and reflecting on intercultural differences forced them to re-evaluate not only their own self, but their understanding of others. For example, Kate's teaching experience gave her a better understanding of the Westford classroom, and she was less shy about intervening; and Henry came back more sociable, more aware of cultural differences and somewhat keener to learn.

Lecturers also agreed that students have difficulties at the time in making connections between academic content and the Year Abroad experience. Given the wealth of immediate challenges that students were coping with, this is unsurprising. However, all participants agreed about students' increased maturity, cultural resources and linguistic resources in the final year, and finalists' higher levels of critical reasoning have also been documented in Chapters 6 and 7. Thus it seems that linking the various kinds of personal and reflective development experienced during the Year Abroad and critical reasoning deriving from content courses is most likely to take place retrospectively rather than concurrently, that is, during the final year of the overall degree programme.

Conclusion: the role of the Year Abroad in criticality development

Stern wrote that the Year Abroad was seen historically as necessary for the student to 'pick up' the language, but that 'It is usually regarded as academically rather a waste of time' (Stern, 1964, in Coleman, 1996, p. 69). Today it is more usual to acknowledge that the Year Abroad changes the students in various, often interconnected, ways, and our data supports this view. These changes impinge on the final year of study and the criticality students practice there, as well as on the identity and related critical capacities which they take forward to their future lives.

The changes in the self are threefold. First, students need to develop problem-solving skills and to draw on personal resources to deal with a range of unforeseen real world problems. As a result, they become more confident about coping with difficulties and more willing to take risks. These are characteristics needed for criticality, especially at the higher levels. Secondly, students are exposed to a different culture which challenges their existing views of the world, sometimes in uncomfortable ways. Capacity to challenge existing formulations and to be aware of, understand and evaluate alternative viewpoints is required at higher levels of criticality. Thirdly, the students' language resources develop. This is more than a technical issue, given the close relationship between language and cultural awareness, the links between language and the ability to access and process information, and the role of language in mediating experience. The enhanced language facility in turn enables the students to engage with a wider range of sources and issues in their final year at university.

The process described above works more or less effectively for different students according to their individual starting points in terms of resources, knowledge and skills, individual effort and disposition, and the opportunities offered by the local context. Moreover, the developmental successes of the Year Abroad should not prevent us from probing limitations and missed opportunities. One important limitation to the Year Abroad experience seems to be lack of linkage between the different domains of criticality; however, the demands on the students at the level of the self are so great that it may be impossible to make such links concurrently.

Overall, we have shown how the Year Abroad has the potential to play a major role in criticality development by offering the students the opportunity to engage with the world and problematize their own perceptions and experiences. Our case study students did not make equal use of this opportunity, with much greater variation than, for example, in the professional field of Social Work practice discussed below, but all nonetheless became changed social beings as a result.

Social work practice placements

The analysis of criticality development during Social Work practice placements is based on the following data: interviews with lecturers and with final-year case study students before, during and after their Social Work practice placements; scrutiny of students' placement coursework, including evidence sheets and placement projects; observations of relevant courses, tutorials and workshops; and of student meetings with their practice teachers during their practice placements; and programme documentation.

The Social Work degree programme and its practice placements

The four-year Social Work degree programme being completed by these particular students combined an academic award with the General Social Care Council's national Diploma in Social Work. (The successor three-year programme similarly leads to a dual award; we have described elsewhere the programme changes which were taking place during our fieldwork, see Chapters 1 and 5.) To meet the professional qualifying requirements of the Diploma, students undertook two practice placements in which their skills, knowledge and demonstration of professional values were developed and formally assessed. The case study students had completed their first placement in the summer term of the third year. At the time of the research, they were engaged in their second placement, which ran concurrently with university study from October to March in the final year. The Diploma in Social Work required that these placements were supervised by a suitably trained 'practice teacher', normally a social worker based at the placement site.

At least one of the two placements had to be with statutory local authority social services; the other might be with a voluntary organization. In practice students had little choice, because of constraints to do with the availability of practice teachers and travel distances, although the university tried to arrange placements matching their interests.

Ian's placements were with a voluntary organization promoting youth inclusion and a Community Mental Health Team. Jayne's first placement was with the local authority's Education Welfare Service (doing social work in schools), and her second was in a Social Services Family Support Unit. Emma worked first in a hospital-based Social Services team with older people and then with a Social Services Children and Family Support team.

Academic work related to the Social Work practice placement

Academic courses and assessment tasks before, during and after these placements invited students to acquire knowledge, develop skills and demonstrate values relevant to future professional practice. Placement learning was supplemented in the university by workshops, seminars and tutorials, as described in Chapter 6.

As described in Chapter 7, written assignments undertaken during and after the placements included a series of 1,000-word evidence sheets analysing pieces of practical work, a 5,000-word placement project detailing students' ability to link theory and practice, and a final year 10,000- to 12,000-word dissertation on a topic of the student's choice relevant to

Social Work. Reports on practical work were prepared by practice teachers, with contributions by the student. This comprehensive assessment framework was very different from the Modern Languages Year Abroad with its single investigative project.

Expectations of the Social Work Practice placement

The national Diploma in Social Work was built on a set of six professional competences, mainly concerned with the planning, implementation and evaluation of Social Work interventions, that is, with the development of professional skills. Even the acquisition of knowledge was contextualized in terms of professional need: 'the professional competence to critically evaluate [their] own knowledge, skills and values'. Clearly, successful performance on the practice placements was central to the demonstration of all of these competencies.

In Chapter 5, we reviewed the expectations for the academic BSc in Social Work, taken concurrently with the diploma. These paid greater attention to the mastery of relevant knowledge resources and critical thinking skills; again however, these were justified as underpinning successful practice. This is clear from one of the main stated aims, cited in Chapter 5: 'To produce graduates who are both intellectually well-equipped and professionally competent to embark on careers in several aspects of Social Work' (Programme Specification).

The expected linkage between intellectual and professional capability is striking, and raises the question as to how this was to be forged. This is partly answered in some of the formal statements of intended learning outcomes, which include:

- knowledge and understanding of . . . evaluation and reflection in Social Work theory and practice,
- skills in taking responsibility for personal and professional development including independent learning, reflection and self-management,
- the cognitive/intellectual skills of critical appraisal, and
- the skills of monitoring your own performance in one-to-one and group situations.

These requirements make it clear that students were expected to reflect critically not only on their theoretical knowledge, but also on their own interactions with others in the practice context. Overall, the practice experience was expected to produce critically reflective practitioners (Schön, 1991).

Experiential Learning and Criticality Development 193

But how fit for purpose was the actual practice experience? Lecturers on the Social Work programme expressed variable views. One lecturer engaged in the redesign of the degree to meet new national standards was hoping for a profession offering continuous learning opportunity:

> the national professional standards can be used in ways that will ensure that employers have to create learning opportunities, learning organisations and opportunities for continuing professional development... that's my vision. (Nancy Barron interview)

Other lecturers and students spoke about the varying quality of actual practice placements, despite the university's efforts. Several students described how their idealized picture of Social Work practice was far removed from the overstressed, under-resourced agencies they found themselves in; we termed this experience 'grim reality'.

Development of criticality through the Social work practice placement

This section analyses the Social Work practice placement, using a similar framework to that developed above for Modern Languages, but paying greater attention to self-reflection and the development of procedural knowledge and the extent to which a reflective practice ethos is conducive to criticality development.

Development of the self: critical reflection and reflective practice

As noted earlier, Barnett (1997) suggested several kinds of reflection which may be related to criticality. Of these, *reflective practice* is especially relevant to discourses about the placement experience:

> [From this perspective] self-reflection is seen as residing in the concrete practices of professional life. Indeed, it is constitutive of professionalism, as Schön's notion of reflection-in-action indicates: a continual interrogation and imaginative reconstruction of one's actions as they are unfolding . . . The professional world is a multiple world, full of alternative possibilities of strategy, action and communication. It is reflection-in-action that brings order into this potential chaos and determines the course of action. (p. 98)

Barnett also comments, however, on possible tensions between reflective practice, as conceptualized by Schön, and criticality:

Reflective practice offers a space for a critical thinking wider than competence, but the sense of critical thinking made available by reflective practice is still limited. First reflective practice gives priority to practice: the critical frames that the professional uses to interrogate her professional practice are somehow generated by the practice itself. Unfortunately, Schön does not tell us how the critical frames are derived. His notion of reflection-in-action implies that the critical frames are just supplied by the action itself, the deposition of the professional's accumulated experiences that have been subjected to continuous evaluation by the professional. Secondly, it imports and implicitly celebrates a pragmatic definition of truth. Truth is what works. There can be no extra-professional validation of the professional's truth claims on Schön's account, for that could – on his story – let in pure theory; and that would never do, since that would open the door to an overly rational view of professional life . . . we need a larger account that that offered by Schön. (Barnett, 1997, pp. 138–9)

There was clear evidence of the case-study students engaging in some kinds of reflective practice. In the middle of his final placement, Ian described ongoing reflection on his engagement with clients:

It's me thinking as I'm going along, having to constantly think on my feet and be aware of the importance of my language and my attitude, and make sure that I espouse the basic Social Work values like confidentiality, empathy, client self-determination, enabling the client to help themselves as opposed to me coming along and saying 'I will help you' kind of thing. (Ian, Interview 3)

In this extract we can see both Ian's 'continual interrogation' of his own actions, but also a reference to the 'critical frame' of Social Work values, which are external to the practice itself.

Several other kinds of reflection suggested by Barnett are also relevant at this point. The Social Work students commonly spoke about the fulfilment of personal projects through Social Work training, thus demonstrating reflection as *self-realization*: 'I thought of doing French A level and using languages, and it came to me while I was doing the access course really, and I felt my skills were more people skills orientated and I thought that [Social Work] was the direction I wanted to go' (mature student Jayne, Interview 1).

Educational reflection involves notions of tolerance and empathy (Barnett, 1997, p. 96), as in Ian's account of someone he worked with:

> He was kept in a secure unit against his will, roughed up considerably because he was thrashing out at people, and he's a very, very nice young man, whatever happened to him or whatever his drink was spiked with. I personally am convinced that he'd never taken drugs before, just by having spent a decent amount of time with him since, so quite a sad case actually. (Ian, Interview 3)

Societal reflection involves the application of strategic thinking to address real world problems (Barnett, 1997, p. 99). The Social Work students were reflecting actively on systems and structures, even though much of their reflection concerned their personal powerlessness to influence complex Social Work agencies. Emma showed this type of reflection in respect of a personal care problem:

> And the things that . . . I couldn't give to people that I wanted to, and they wanted most commonly, were baths. Because if somebody could wash themselves but couldn't bath themselves, we could only put in a bath once a week, because they were still able to have a wash. And you know, most people want to have a bath every day. (Emma, Interview 2)

Finally, *reflection as meta-competence* is a more limited, instrumental and technical form of reflection, concerned with getting things done efficiently (Barnett, 1997, p. 97). Despite the competency-based conceptualization of Social Work learning outcomes in official documentation, students were resisting this type of reflection. In interviews they reported tensions between the 'idealism' of their personal projects and the constraints of 'grim reality':

> In reality, you're out there and there isn't the time to do [things], you know, budgets don't allow for certain ways of practising. How you would want to do it is all quite idealistic when you're at university, what services you are providing, what you would do and how much time you would spend with clients, and a lot of it comes down to time constraints and budget restraints. (Jayne, Interview 1)

Overall, we can see that the placement experience promoted active and varied reflection among the students on the self, the practice context, and their interactions with clients. The intensity of practice requirements meant that self-reflection was generally richer than among the Modern Languages students; in the case of Ian at least, it can be suggested that this reflection was developmental for the self, with indications of 'late criticality'.

Development in the World: The Growth of Confidence

Like the Modern Languages students, the Social Work case study students described increased confidence as a result of their practice placements. However, the reasons were somewhat different; while the Modern Languages students solved personal problems and challenges, the Social Work students developed increased skill and success in relating to clients. Ian described his first experience of working with 'excluded' young people:

> [The placement] gave me more confidence because I was involved in face-to-face communication in engaging young people normally with very difficult problems at home and at school and you know, psycho-social problems, problems with deprivation and poverty and social exclusion. . . . It gave me confidence because, for the first time on this course . . . I was trying to be, and hopefully being, a professional in a helping, therapeutic role . . . It was rewarding because I did see a certain amount of success with one particular family that I worked with who were very complimentary of me and my intervention, which again helped my confidence. (Ian, Interview 1)

Jayne, as a mature and experienced person, already had some confidence in her abilities to relate to people, but felt she was building on this:

> I actually think I'm quite well suited to [Social Work] [but the placement had] made me more knowledgeable, more aware of practice . . . I'm learning much more being out on placement. (Jayne, Interview 1)

Development of resources: knowledge and skills

The development of critical thinking skills by Social Work students during the practice placement has already been partly dealt with in Chapter 7, where we reviewed a range of writing arising from the placement. In this section we concentrate on the development of knowledge resources and interpersonal professional skills.

The students started their placements with relatively well-developed knowledge resources, deriving partly from their personal background and partly from engagement with the academic programme during the early period at university.

For example, Jayne started her university studies with personal experience of family breakdown and child rearing: 'my youngest was then 5 and had just started school and . . . my parents were divorced'. Ian, too, had had relevant (and painful) family experiences: 'My father . . . died very young under quite horrible circumstances, having been a very bad alcoholic for at least 10 years previously' (Ian, Interview 1).

Emma came to her course with experience of stressful interactions because she had trained as a Samaritan:

> I started when I was 18 and I was the youngest Samaritan in the branch. . . . Yes, it is kind of unpleasant at times . . . working with situations where you feel you are being slightly abused, which is all good experience, because you are going to go through that as a social worker. (Emma, Interview 2)

From these somewhat different starting points, our case study students had then spent two years in collective academic study of core Social Work theory, developing substantial shared knowledge resources. Overall they were prepared more uniformly for their practice placement than the Modern Languages students, and the close mentoring they received from practice supervisors and university tutors assisted transition and somewhat reduced 'culture shock' in ways unavailable to Modern Languages students.

In Chapter 4 we discussed different kinds of knowledge, including *knowledge that (declarative knowledge), procedural knowledge (knowing how), knowledge why* and *knowledge of what it is to be*. For the practice placement, all four types were needed, including:

- Formal knowledge of theories, approaches, methods, law (general, for example Children Act, 1989; Mental Health Act, 1983; National Health and Community Care Act, 1990). To begin with, this is declarative knowledge, but in practice, it may become procedural knowledge.
- Practice related knowledge – law (relevant to particular practice situations), knowledge of the practice placement agency and related networks. This, too, begins as declarative knowledge but in practice becomes fully transformed to procedural knowledge.
- Procedural knowledge in terms of interpersonal skills (i.e. knowing how to interact with a variety of people, often in very difficult situations, raising complex professional and ethical dilemmas).

- Knowledge of underlying values and ethical principles, which relates to knowing why.
- Personal experience and increasing professional experience. These are both essential but are intangible and cannot be specified precisely. Together with empathy and insight into the lives of others (and in particular, of social work clients), they contribute to relevant knowledge of what it is to be.

Clearly these types of knowledge are interrelated, but one main requirement during the practice placement was for previously acquired declarative knowledge to become proceduralized and transformed into usable guidance in specific professional contexts. Many assessment tasks associated with the placement were intended to promote this development. For example, in a written evidence sheet, Ian wrote about his use of listening skills:

> We met at J's home where only he and I were present. J told me of his problems and we talked openly for about an hour. I used active listening skills with J, and asked open and closed questions. I used several methods of responding dependent on the content of what was said including interpretive, sympathetic and probing responses (Herbert et al., 2002). I also learnt to distinguish between using reflective listening that reflects content, and reflective listening that reflects the emotion or anguish behind the actual words (Hargie, 1998). (Ian, first evidence sheet, second placement)

Here, we see how Ian drew on theoretical knowledge to guide and interpret his interaction with a particular client. The students also referred to this proceduralization process in interview. For example, concerning the study of law, Emma commented:

> The law stuff . . . has been really important, because it is kind of the framework of everything we work on, and it makes you more aware [that] everything you do has got to be justified under some Act. (Emma, Interview 2)

(It is interesting to compare these final-year students' opinions with the more negative views of the first-year students on the formal knowledge imparted in the early part of the programme; see Chapter 6.)

Interpersonal skills in working with clients are an essential part of the procedural knowledge of Social Work. All the case study students described in interview a wide range of interpersonal skills they had developed when on placement, including listening and counselling, intervening diplomatically in highly charged and complex situations, dealing with multiple gatekeepers and audiences, and carrying out assessments. In observed placement supervision sessions, these interpersonal skills were a major focus of discussion, as when Emma picked her supervisor's brains on play therapy techniques in the course of discussing a particular child case. Emma later described enthusiastically what she had learned about working with children:

> I love doing direct work with the children, you know, it's basically therapy through play work with the kids and it's such a lovely approach . . . it's a really creative way to work with children . . . You get to take the kids out for a milkshake and you get to try and build up a good relationship with them and encourage them to talk about how things are for them, and to develop personal strategies of how to manage things. (Emma, Interview 4)

Her confidence about her new skills was evident, and while her language was informal, it was grounded in theoretical constructs ('therapy through play work') which she was able to explain more fully in writing in her placement project.

The issue of values provides a further interesting contrast between Modern Languages and Social Work. In both fields, university education could be expected to challenge students' personal value systems to some degree, and our fieldwork found some instances where, for example, students' religious values conflicted with lecturers' secular liberal views. However, in Social Work students were expected to adopt and demonstrate a particular set of professional values, while in Modern Languages this remained a private matter. On the whole, Social Work students on placement appeared to adopt the consensus values without extensive reflection, with the partial exception of Ian who expressed positive commitment to work with the excluded.

As for knowing 'what it is to be', the students gained substantial insight into their future professional role, through their placement experiences, as could be seen from tutorial discussions as well as interviews (see Chapter 6). They also demonstrated gains in empathy and understanding of client perspectives (see Ian's discussion of client J, presented earlier).

Personal dispositions in Social Work criticality development

In discussing Modern Languages we argued that students' personal dispositions were important for the criticality development they experienced during residence abroad. This was not so much the case for the Social Work students. The dispositions they displayed were generally more closely aligned and relevant to the field (e.g. all declared 'an interest in people' and some form of commitment to social justice, and all were prepared to engage in challenging interactions).

For example, during an observed supervision session, Emma was asked at short notice by her placement supervisor to accompany a vulnerable adult to a police interview. While a little anxious about her lack of relevant knowledge resources (e.g. what lines of questioning were permissible with such a client), Emma felt strongly that the client should be supported and was willing to take on the role; she eagerly quizzed the supervisor about procedure and support techniques.

Without some such set of dispositions it is, of course, unlikely that students would in the first place opt for Social Work training; the strong professional culture and convergent programme structure further reduced the influence of individual dispositions in the course of the practice placement.

Some dispositional differences remained, however. Jayne was the most pragmatic of the case study students, claiming at times that her motivation was purely instrumental: 'I'm going into it for the money' (Interview 1). On the other hand, Ian displayed a strong moral vision and empathy with clients: 'I get very angry that I know there are other people out there in similar situations to me that are having their life chances restricted seriously by things that may be happening at home' (Ian, Interview 1).

It is probably not coincidental that Jayne remained squarely within the level of 'guided criticality', throughout her placement, while Ian at times moved somewhat beyond this.

Connections between domains

Overall, it seemed that Social Work practice placements were sites where students made 'horizontal' connections across the three domains of knowledge, the self and the world; that is, created connections between theory and practice through processes of reflection and self-reflection. One lecturer explained the aims of the programme with a Barnett-style interpretation of reflective practice:

> to encourage and enable students to become reflective and implicitly reflexive practitioners who think about their work, [who] think critically about all kinds of things, about Social Work theory and social policy out there, . . . about themselves as actors in the discourse, and about the

agencies and the people with whom they engage in their practice. (Phillip Brown interview)

The data showed that all the final-year students were able to describe links between theory, the law, the self and related practical action. This linking process was explicitly required from the outset in tutorials, supervision sessions and assessment tasks. As Jayne remarked, 'The theoretical evidence sheets are . . . challenging because you have got to be more analytical, and look at theory behind what you are doing' (Interview 2).

However, the process became more spontaneous over time so that students' practice was informed by formal knowledge, and their formal knowledge was, in turn, enriched by practical knowledge and expertise; in different ways, all three of our Social Work case study students demonstrated this connection making, as we have shown above when discussing the proceduralization of knowledge and the development of interactional skills.

Conclusion: the role of the social work practice placement in criticality development

Overall, we can say that Social Work students on their final-year placements were practising several dimensions of criticality. Their assessment tasks required them to show that they could engage with and act within the real world domain of Social Work practice. Their actions were increasingly informed by a body of relevant knowledge, and they were expected to reflect on that knowledge and on their developing professional selves in action.

But the very use of such words as 'require', 'must' and 'expected' remind us that they were not free agents if they wished to achieve professional qualification. We did not see much evidence of them questioning given frameworks of professional values, knowledge and practice (although we noted Emma's aspirations to do the kind of creative direct work with children that is not often possible within the constrained resources of local authority social services departments).

In summary, our Social Work case study students were operating largely at the level of guided critically, making links across domains but without much challenge to given frameworks, values and ways of working. There was little sign of the advanced professionalism advocated by Barnett, which was unsurprising given the relatively powerless position of students within agencies and the 'grim reality' of resource constraints within these agencies.

But our students showed many of the characteristics of professionals, including the capacity to reflect a clearly articulated value system and take practical actions within a theoretical framework. And some of them showed potential for development to a more transformative professionalism, telling us of their aspirations to rethink professional ethics and to interpret the world through theory.

Conclusion: comparing two placement types

In this chapter we have studied two very different off-campus learning experiences. The main declared purpose of the Year Abroad was the development of knowledge resources (cultural knowledge and linguistic skills), although increased intercultural awareness, self-confidence, maturity and self-reliance were also valued by-products. Supervision of the Year Abroad was light, with little direct contact and only the Year Abroad project as a structured task. Modern Languages students had large discretion as to how they spent their time and as to the kind of resources they actually acquired. The Year Abroad project was an exercise in critical reason with no obligation to reflect on the self or take action in the world. Typically, however, the project represented a level of 'early criticality' only, and the main benefits from the Year Abroad from the point of view of criticality development were seen in the following year, where the gains in knowledge resources (language and culture) and maturity were eventually drawn upon in academic courses.

The Social Work practice placements, on the other hand, were closely supervised and strongly structured with the aim of producing licensed professional practitioners. Development of the professional self and demonstration of the ability to take appropriate professional action in the world were key requirements; declarative knowledge, theory and critical reason were valued insofar as they informed and interpreted professional practice. Assessment was much more all-sided, and made a range of judgements about the professional self, including capacity for self-reflection and real world interaction, as well as about critical reason. The placement project was expected to show theoretical understanding, but the main focus was on linking across domains, drawing on theoretical knowledge to interpret actions in the world.

Other striking differences related to dispositions and to values. Individual dispositions had a large influence on the criticality development of Modern Languages students, but this was much less the case for Social Work due to the more structured nature of the programme and its expectations for professional socialization. As for values, these remained a private affair for Modern Languages students on their Year Abroad, apart from general but unmeasured expectations that they would develop intercultural awareness and a degree of empathy. Social Work students, on the other hand, were expected to provide hard evidence of commitment to a given set of professional values, irrespective of their personal values.

Overall, our analysis of criticality development highlights the significance of the knowledge resources provided before the placement, the support offered during the placement, and the assessment of students during and after the experience. These key factors helped to determine the quality and nature of learning, and explicitly of learning to become critical, that such experiences can provide.

Chapter 9

Conclusions and Implications

The first half of this chapter discusses connections between the empirical data described in Chapters 5 to 8 and the conceptual framework discussed in Chapter 4. The second half explores policy and pedagogic implications of our account.

Conclusions about criticality development

Chapters 2 to 4 explored the questions posed in Chapter 1 about why criticality is desirable in higher education in the twenty-first century and how it can most usefully be conceptualized. In Chapter 4 we argued for a comprehensive and moral vision of criticality, and for the usefulness of a Barnettian framework of domains and types of criticality.

Chapter 5 described policy perspectives on the importance and development of criticality. We noticed policy tensions between, first, discourses of competence, outcomes-based education and employability and, secondly, declarations which acknowledge roles for higher education in the creation of knowledge, in the promotion of social cohesion and ethical behaviour, and in cultural development. The former usually focus on lower levels of criticality development; the latter require the open-ended development of individuals as creative and critical beings. These tensions and variable discourses leave considerable initiative to individual universities and disciplines when conceptualizing criticality goals for the curriculum.

The discussion in Chapter 5 suggests that current curriculum documents capture some, but not all, components of criticality development, partly because of a somewhat one-sided focus on critical reason especially in 'pure' fields, and partly because of a convergent focus on defined learning outcomes. The actuality of criticality development in the classroom and on placement is richer and more complex (see Chapters 6–8).

Chapters 6–8 described criticality development within Westford University. In Chapter 6, we saw how the lecturers articulated values and conceptual priorities within each field which were enacted in their lectures, seminars, tutorials and assignments. They worked implicitly within a liberal education framework. Modern Languages lecturers believed that students could become guided critical beings with regard to critical reason; they hoped that students developed in other domains. Social Work lecturers encouraged student development more broadly across Barnett's three domains, aiming for guided criticality, but talking about further development as Social Work graduates entered their professional career; they hoped to have laid the basis for ongoing reflection.

In Chapter 7 it was clear that even the most effectively critical students were clearly in an apprentice position. For example, they received 'feedback' on assignments from lecturers without the power to respond as might full members of the academic community. Only the lecturer, the student and perhaps a friend read their assignments. The writing, therefore, could not 'act on the world'. Even the most critical students struggled to control field-specific rules of functioning and construct bodies of relevant knowledge, rather than transform the field. They often strove to be more than instrumental, but were hampered by limited resources.

As described in Chapter 8, Modern Languages student development during the Year Abroad was variable, with some students reaching higher levels of intercultural awareness and self-transformation than others, although most increased in self-confidence. In Social Work, students grappled with the (sometimes competing) agendas of social work placement agencies, the higher education institution, and the General Social Care Council. They experienced tensions between their hopes and ideals and reality in challenging placement situations.

Contextual aspects of criticality

We argued in Chapter 4 that context has a crucial role in the exercise of criticality.

Broad context

The criticality enacted in our data is clearly contextualized within twenty-first century higher education. It sat amid the competing critical priorities of the day – personal, civic and creative development for individuals and citizens versus preparation for entry into an increasingly competitive labour market.

Students arrived in this broad context with distinctive individual resources (intellectual, family and personal history), motivations and dispositions.

They may also have arrived with a distinctive personal endowment in terms of intelligence, but our research design did not allow us to tease this possibility apart from other culturally influenced aspects of their personal identity. Students then had different experiences according to their study settings, on and off campus. The detail of these experiences impinged on student critical capacities. Each assignment, for example, was written in a particular context with its own educational, field-specific, emotional and cognitive aspects; and that context was mediated by the student. This was reflected in comments made in student interviews, in lecturer comments, and in the assignment texts themselves.

Student dispositions also influenced their response. Most had clearly chosen their subject because of personal interest. However, a student such as Susie who liked practical approaches with definite answers found the theoretical, 'uncertain' aspects of her Modern Languages degree challenging. Her personal epistemological approach to life was somewhat incongruent with that of her degree programme.

Although the individualized nature of critical development was clear, patterns according to year group, field of study and type of entry qualification were also visible.

Field-specific aspects

In Chapter 4 we emphasized field-specific aspects of criticality in our framework, drawing on descriptions of thinking in specific academic fields; the importance of these field-specific aspects is visible in our empirical chapters.

In Chapter 5, our examination of benchmark statements and programme specifications showed considerable subject differences with regard to criticality and the extent to which criticality is captured explicitly within curriculum frameworks.

In Chapters 6 and 7 we saw how field-specific norms were displayed and modelled through lectures, seminars and readings. In Modern Languages, in the first year, personal response was students' paramount reaction, but they were increasingly required to interpret literature, history and politics through theoretical lenses such as those of race, gender, feminism, psychoanalysis and culture. Students were encouraged to develop largely in the domain of formal knowledge, with some input from the self. The content of courses such as the final-year course 'Narratives of Desire' was challenging to notions of sexuality, a matter at the core of the self. The students were not required to write about critical action, although many aspects of literature, film and history do relate to the domain of the world.

In Social Work, students were increasingly required to link theory, practice and the law within a framework of Social Work values. Even in the first year, they had to reflect on their potential to become critical practitioners, that is, to engage in the domain of the self. In their final two years they were consistently encouraged to make explicit connections across all three domains. This was a formidable challenge, but was seen as necessary for the professional roles they would be undertaking.

Within each field, we saw the emergence of shared patterns as students worked within the same curriculum framework, attended more or less the same classes, and did similar writing assignments over an extended period. Modern Languages dissertations were usually more conceptually analytical than those in Social Work, which focused on practice-related issues. Social Work students had to focus much time and energy in the final year on practice commitments whereas in Modern Languages the dissertation was a major focus. Field-specific norms were promoted and enforced through presentations, writing assignments, feedback and grades. We also saw differences in the practices, priorities and knowledge bases of different sub-fields within Modern Languages and Social Work. Literature differed from History and from Sociolinguistics, and Sociology from Social Work.

Transfer of knowledge and personal resources was complex. Those who entered the university with a relevant academic background coped with field-specific demands more effectively early in their degrees, when university education had not yet compensated for others' lack of knowledge on entry. Students with A levels, but not in relevant subject areas, struggled to acquire field-specific knowledge. Knowledge and skills, for instance in literature or drama, did not automatically transfer to social work or history and politics. Multi-disciplinarity was an aspiration for some Modern Languages lecturers, but the problems caused by disciplinary barriers were acknowledged by others. We suspect that by the final year, the students had largely specialized in particular sub-disciplines, learning the necessary field-specific tools, rather than transferring between disciplines as multi-disciplinary beings.

Certain personal qualities such as confidence did transfer from one domain to another. We saw in Chapter 8 how the confidence developed during the Year Abroad and Social Work practice placements transferred to students' studies. The extent of transfer across Barnett's domains varied, by field, according to how explicitly it was required. For example, Susie did not transfer formal knowledge about gender from her classes at university to her Year Abroad experiences (the world). However, such knowledge did transfer for the Social Work students whose assessments required them to make regular links between theoretical concepts and their placement experiences.

Arguably, the curriculum expected student criticality to remain within certain field-specific parameters. First, a professional course such as Social Work was preparing students for professional qualifications which primarily required adherence to specific professional standards and views. Secondly, in all courses lecturers were inducting students into disciplines, to think and write in particular ways. Thirdly, in some cases lecturers were personally attached to certain approaches and some students believed that alternative ideas would not be welcomed.

By not engaging with the theoretical frameworks propounded by the lecturers, students sometimes resisted conceptualizations and values by which they were unconvinced. Susie and Janet struggled with the socially liberal values of their studies which conflicted with their religious values. Fields enable critique, but they also limit it, especially for novice members in need of accreditation.

Context to encourage critical development

The students in this study were offered a rich learning context through socialization, explicit instruction and practice, with field-specific variations. Often, as described in Chapters 6, 7 and 8, students learned much by undergoing basic processes of socialization through lectures, seminars and reading where criticality was implicitly modelled in the kind of processes described by Wenger (1998) and Lave et al. (1991). Socialization also operated in off-campus experiences, where Modern Languages students learned the ways of a different culture, and Social Work students learned professional roles.

With regard to explicit instruction, Modern Languages teaching focused on the 'joint construction of meaning' with a dialogic, Socratic questioning and modelling of thinking approach. This aligned with descriptions in Chapter 2 of approaches to teaching and learning in soft, pure fields. Social Work students were strongly encouraged to reflect on their practice, listening skills and self in relationship to practice, in line with the recommendations of cognitive psychologists regarding 'meta-cognition', discussed in Chapter 3. In Modern Languages, although reflection was a less prominent element, students were encouraged to reflect systematically on their language learning strategies.

Practice at being critical in class and through writing (as well as in practice placements for Social Work students) enabled active use of different types of knowledge; the need to make connections between the different types facilitated critical development. Writing consolidated knowledge, increased awareness of options, provided frameworks of understanding, necessitated conscious reflection and extended knowledge. Opportunities to develop and practise guided criticality were frequent.

Feedback, of which the students received many types, incorporated elements of the three aspects of the learning context discussed above: socialization, explicit instruction and practice. Formative feedback included lecturer and peer responses to ideas expressed in seminars and language classes. The final-year Social Work students received feedback on their listening skills from lecturers and peers in practical workshops. Extensive individual formative feedback was received from dissertation supervisors and from placement supervisors. Students usually seemed to find such feedback helpful, and it was a major means of socialization into the two academic fields.

In addition, students received written summative feedback on the assignments they completed. The lecturers conscientiously completed feedback forms for the students, often at some length. The influence of this feedback was mixed. At times, the students noted and acted on their lecturer's comments. For example, the first-year Social Work student, Janet, read more widely for her next essay as a result of a lecturer's comments on one essay. Sometimes, however, students misunderstood written comments and were reluctant to ask for clarification. Examples are Janet's misunderstanding of comments about the need for analysis in her writing and Olivia's failure to understand why she received a poor grade for her Latin American history presentation.

The learning context was not always optimal for critical development. In Social Work, the students wrote their dissertations under considerable time pressure and so lacked time for reflection and development of ideas. The Modern Languages students managed their Year Abroad projects with limited support from lecturers and poor access to secondary sources, while writing in a second language; unsurprisingly, levels of competence and criticality fell. A year later, when writing their dissertations, the students had face-to-face contact with supervisors and easy access to secondary sources in the university library; additionally, they wrote the dissertation in their first language. Standards rose dramatically. It may be that some of the Year Abroad conditions are unavoidable and that the major contributions to critical development in that period come from other aspects of the experience which, in turn, feed into achievements in the domain of formal knowledge in the final year.

Resources

Importance of a knowledge base

The curriculum was organized so that knowledge accreted over the years, in response to socialization, specific teaching and out-of-university experiences, and differentially according to individual factors. The final-year students possessed declarative knowledge of field-specific theories, data and (for Social Work students) legal and practice knowledge. They had greater procedural knowledge of how to write critically across a range of genres. They had knowledge of what it is to be, either as apprentice social work practitioners or as students in a specific field. They usually understood the internal logic of the critical systems within which they worked, that is, they had developed knowledge 'why', even if they may have rejected some of that logic. They had internalized a system of beliefs and values, although some disputed those values, which may in itself indicate a degree of criticality.

We can see the importance of the build-up of different kinds of knowledge with the Social Work students where in classes, tutorials, assignments and practice, there was sustained attention to the combination of theory and practice as well as the problematization of social work values. For Modern Languages students, by the final year their improved second language resources enabled them to access and interact with other cultures more effectively through their reading and writing, as well as interpersonally.

The strong Social Work focus on linking across domains, where Social Work students had knowledge in one or more domains, assisted in processing knowledge in the others and eventually promoted overall development. We saw this with Katy, where her personal experiences enabled her to make sense of the theories of grief and loss she was presented with in lectures and vice versa; this was a dynamic, iterative process. Where Modern Languages students had developed knowledge of another culture in their Year Abroad, it was somewhat easier for them to engage with intercultural aspects of their final-year classes, and there were some attempts to integrate self into discussions of literature, for example.

In contrast, where students were new to a particular aspect of study, as with the second-year course 'Studying Spanish Film', much energy had to be devoted to simply mastering the basic critical knowledge resources. The Social Work degree programme, which had no optional courses, moved forward in a more integrated fashion, so individual students did not usually face sudden knowledge gaps. In the first year in both fields, much energy was taken up with learning the basic rules of engagement with secondary literature.

With regard to language knowledge, much energy could initially be focused just on basic decoding and encoding, as with the Modern Languages

Conclusions and Implications

students in their first-year reading or their Year Abroad project. The students needed to learn the conventions and usage of a second or third language, as well as understanding cultural aspects, before they could function critically in that language. Students also had language difficulties if they were unused to the conventions and usage of formal academic English in particular fields, as we saw with the non-traditional Social Work students, Margaret and Katy. First-year students in both fields were often chided for using colloquial language.

Our research design was quasi-longitudinal, so we were unable to follow the progress of first-year students with major writing problems, often mature students from non-traditional educational backgrounds. However, these students were loosely paralleled by those from similar backgrounds in later years of study, all of whom had learned to write more critically in an acceptable fashion, if to different levels of effectiveness.

The mature students might have been expected to possess more 'knowledge of what it is to be' in various situations on entry to university. However, the use they made of this knowledge was variable. The young Social Work student Emma was able to reflect effectively on her practice experience in writing while Jayne, a much older student, invested far less time and effort in her writing because of home commitments.

Personal qualities and values

Various qualities and values such as confidence and an inquiring attitude are important for criticality. As we saw in Chapter 6, the Modern Languages lecturers spoke about the personal qualities they sought to develop among students, including the ability to handle complexity and to enjoy uncertainty, a willingness to take initiative in learning, and an ability to use feedback constructively. Social Work lecturers focused especially on the need for students to develop an ethically aware, creative, independent, reflexive, professional self.

Changes in personal identity as a result of profound educational processes involving knowledge growth, understanding and personal engagement have been suggested by many (Barnett, 1997; Perry, 1968/1999; Peters, 1966). And indeed, an increase in confidence was noticeable as students learned how to function more effectively at university. As reported in Chapter 8, following the Year Abroad Modern Language students returned to their final year feeling more confident, more serious in their approach to work and more focused. It was a common theme among Social Work lecturers and students in later years that first-year students were somewhat 'lost' and that theory and practice connected together after the first practice placement. Social Work students reported a growing sense of personal identity, confidence and completeness as a result of their placement experiences. In both fields, the final-year students were usually more confident about expressing their own views both in class and in writing.

Motivation and engagement are crucial for criticality. However, these are complex phenomena. The students clearly wanted good marks for their assignments, and assessment was regularly discussed in seminars and tutorials at students' requests. However, they also clearly cared about intrinsic qualities of their writing, preparing conscientiously for their assignments, and often producing copious notes and multiple early drafts. Only two students spoke about writing essays at the last minute (as a result of poor time management). After the first year, students also prepared carefully for presentations.

Levels of motivation varied according to context. For example, the first-year Modern Languages students had some motivational problems in reading entire books in a second language for their 'French Culture Today' course. The final-year Social Work students conscientiously completed their assignments, but were often more interested in practice rather than in developing academic criticality through writing.

There is also the vexing issue of how far and in which ways personal qualities are innate, or at least so deeply embedded in personal biography as to be difficult to change, and how far they can be acquired. Our data indicates that at least some qualities and values, for instance confidence, ability to handle complexity, and awareness of various aspects of life, can be enhanced.

There is another vexing question concerning the moral frameworks underpinning individual criticality and the extent to which students can be expected to espouse particular values. As explained in Chapter 4, we expect criticality to be grounded in some form of moral vision and, in the context of the Western university in the twenty-first century, this will generally encompass notions of human rights, impartial justice and fairness in a secular environment. However, lecturers' and students' particular interpretations of these themes can be expected to differ. The logic of a critical approach to student development is that different moral visions need to be open for reflection, analysis and discussion, including those sanctioned by lecturers and, indeed, professional licensing bodies such as the General Social Care Council.

In practice at Westford, Social Work students were required to respect a set of 'human rights' values associated with their professional identity, including, for instance, an acceptance of homosexuality. Parts of this value system were in conflict, for example with Janet's personal religious values. In Modern Languages, students sometimes defended traditional, non-liberal values in seminars. However, in most cases such students remained reticent about their views, which were only intermittently acknowledged and discussed. It seems likely that in the long-term students were stimulated to reconsider their values mainly through processes of implicit socialization and personal reflection.

Developmental aspects of criticality

With regard to our developmental framework and as described in our data analysis, the students worked mainly at the early criticality level, in the early years of their degree programmes, and moved increasingly towards guided criticality. We saw the uncertainty of many first-year students and the effect this had on their academic performance; this aligns with previous research by Perry (1968/1999, p. 116). However, they became increasingly effective at criticality as the degree programmes progressed.

We should question this developmental schema a little. At least some of the first-year students' apparently low level of critical development may be due to motivational difficulties, time management problems, uncertainty about what is expected of them and the nature of assignments, rather than an intrinsic inability to be critical. For example, very short assignments gave first-year students limited scope to develop an argument, even if they had been able to do so effectively at that stage.

Equally, we should remain alert to the possibility, suggested by Perry (1968/1999), of students merely mimicking critical thought, although we do not think this is a general characteristic of the work we analysed. We saw in Chapter 6 how Olivia abandoned her own ideas for an essay title and adopted that suggested by the lecturer without understanding the underlying reasons for using a critical lens, and certainly without agreeing with the critical lens that she used. Susie also complained that students had to come from 'the same angle' as the lecturer to get good grades.

Entry into the critical process

1. Engagement with critical tasks

The first-year students and some second years engaged actively with assignments, although they were sometimes unclear about task purpose. Usually they worked hard, were interested and took pride in their assignments.

The final-year and the other second-year students engaged with tasks more fully, but always within terms of others' understandings.

2. *Control over definition of topic, question and action: question formation and complexity of task*

Usually lecturers defined topics, giving students essay questions or other highly specified writing tasks such as evidence sheets. The Social Work students chose the incidents to include in their evidence sheets and placement projects, but otherwise the genre was strictly controlled. They did, however, choose their own dissertation topics. In Modern Languages, for the final-year course 'Narratives of Desire', students made class presentations on topics set by the lecturer and answered specific essay questions in a timed written examination. Sometimes the Modern Languages students did have the opportunity to pose their own presentation and essay questions, subject to lecturer approval, as in the second-year course, 'Latin America: Nation, Race and Gender', the Year Abroad projects and dissertations for final-year students. In general, the Modern Languages lecturers were more predisposed to encourage creativity and questioning, although Nancy Barron in Social Work also referred to creativity.

Formulating one's own questions, as in the more advanced levels of criticality, is a far more complicated task than answering a pre-set question. It can lead to less sophisticated and critical written products than when using initial questions posed by the expertly critical lecturer. If a student starts without background declarative knowledge and little field-specific knowledge about appropriate and relevant questions, forming questions can be nearly impossible, as we saw with Olivia in Chapter 7. The third-year students also had difficulty developing their own questions in their Year Abroad assignments. The final-year Social Work students, under extreme pressure from placement requirements, developed rather descriptive dissertation topics.

Solution searching

1. *Information location and management*

First-year students often had basic practical problems in using the library to locate information for their writing tasks, and for some these continued even in the second year.

Acquiring, selecting, managing and focusing information in order to exercise criticality is a complex, multi-layered process which involves building links between data, theory and personal understandings. Students may already have relevant knowledge fully or partially at the start of a criticality task or may seek to construct knowledge during the task. Lacking appropriate analytical questions, Olivia found it difficult to focus and manage her information search for her 'Latin America: Nation, Race and Gender' presentation.

2. Use of explanatory frameworks or theory

The first-year students and some second-year students were uncertain how to relate field-specific theories to empirical data, to other texts or to pre-existing knowledge. The final-year students were considerably more proficient at this, although they employed explanatory theoretical frameworks with differential sophistication and effectiveness, as we saw with the final-year French literature students. In evidence sheets, the Social Work students frequently related their own actions on placement to theoretical frameworks. However, their comments were related to application, rather than critiques, of frameworks. Even in their final-year dissertations, the Social Work students reflected and described, but did not really evaluate and certainly did not produce an alternative view of the world.

3. Engagement with data/evidence/other voices in the field

Most first-year students gave little evidence of engaging with the substance of the secondary literature, of knowing how to enter in the academic conversation of written texts, or of understanding texts as 'social exchanges to be understood' (Wineburg, 1991, p. 83). The non-traditional Social Work students experienced particular difficulty.

The first-year Modern Languages students could express critical opinions of literary texts through personal response; however, engagement with connected secondary literature was more challenging, although Isobel was making valiant, if somewhat uncertain, attempts to do so in the unfamiliar field of history. The first-year students and some second years struggled to integrate evidence in their writing.

The second-year students knew that they should engage with the secondary literature and could do so to varying degrees if working within a guided question. When Olivia moved outside the guiding question set by the lecturer and her recommended texts, she became lost when seeking relevant material. Katy at times regurgitated theories from lecture notes and readings without critical appraisal or integration.

By the final year, students generally understood how to engage with the secondary literature. The 'Narratives of Desire' students used evidence largely from primary and secondary texts presented to them in class and drew on interpretations which were part of the currency of the class to make fine-tuned personal interpretations of particular literary texts. The final-year Social Work students could relate their practice experiences and the law to existing literature.

Within both fields, students had to build a coherent argument and acknowledge their engagement with others in the field through correct referencing. Considerable class time in the first year was devoted to explanation of referencing rules, with both verbal and written feedback on referencing in writing. These conventions are among the precursors to criticality in an academic sphere, in the sense that until writers have control over them, they will not be recognized as players in the critical game. By the second year, the students had realized what was expected and endeavoured to produce appropriately referenced texts. By the final year, students were much more in control.

4. Making links between domains of formal knowledge, the self and action

The Modern Languages students were encouraged to make links between the self and the varied texts they were exposed to in their courses, and did so with varying degrees of effectiveness. The students had considerable difficulty, as we have seen, in making links between their formal class knowledge to situations in their Year Abroad, but had some success in transferring intercultural knowledge to the classroom after their Year Abroad.

The second- and final-year Social Work students could all make connections between their own actions (domains of self and action), social work theory and legal aspects (domain of formal knowledge) with varying sophistication and intellectual engagement. All the second-year students seemed interested in reflecting on practice and theory in their writing, but Sarah and Mark seemed more able to do so, she perhaps because of her relevant A level background, and he because of time and effort invested. Of the final-year students, Emma and Ian were more successful than Jayne in making connections between domains, again possibly because of higher effort invested.

5. Reflection (including reflection on formal knowledge, the self and action)

In interview, all the students could describe their writing processes, difficulties faced and achievements gained. They articulated their thoughts about the formal knowledge with which they were expected to engage – in some cases with great respect and in some cases raising questions – with differential effectiveness and sophistication.

For the first-year students, self was expressed in specific ways in their writing, through personal responses to literary texts for the Modern Languages students and a personal reflective assignment for the Social Work students. Rita, in her first-year agonies, seemed to be engaged in a constant process of reconstruction of herself. However, this was a draining, rather than a productive process, and affected her work negatively. In some assignments, second- and final-year students were specifically required to reflect on personal capabilities, and students of all ages could do so, often insightfully.

Practice placements were a strong focus of reflection for Social Work students who reflected formally on their practice in written assignments. In interview, they offered further reflections on matters such as their limited impact in difficult placement situations and the usefulness or otherwise of their university training as preparation for their placement. Modern Languages students reflected on their experiences during their Year Abroad, undergoing considerable personal change as a result of their experiences.

6. Constructing a case (process – 'solution searching')

Increasingly, students developed routines and understandings of what was expected of them and their capacity to articulate disciplinary arguments, both in writing and in presentations, developed as writing tasks became longer and writing processes more complex. Some students operated under severe time restrictions, especially the mothers, who managed their time in rather different ways, Rebecca worked through the night and Jayne completed her work within strictly allotted daytime slots.

Rationale building

The first-year students and some in their second year had variable control over acceptable forms of writing. Isobel, for example, was far ahead of her fellow first-year Modern Languages students in terms of building an argument while integrating secondary sources. Margaret and Janet, two non-traditional Social Work students, struggled more than Rita, who had traditional entry qualifications, with constructing academic arguments and integrating sources into their writing. It was mainly in the strategies related to 'rationale building' that Katy had problems; these were of a technical and structural nature and related to spelling, grammar, referencing and appropriate structuring of paragraphs. All the final-year students had greater control over 'rationale building'.

At times, a written product suggested a low level of criticality, but had emerged from a sophisticated 'solution searching' process. For example, although Katy produced a poorly argued essay on grief, from her interview it was clear that she had undertaken a thorough knowledge building process, including synthesizing different viewpoints and had clearly learned much from all this preparation. It is, of course, difficult to determine whether Katy's basic problem was with presenting a written argument appropriately, or whether the interview talk without the detailed linear construction required in a written argument disguised a wider range of problems in the 'solution searching' process.

Understanding of the territory (including power relationships)

In their writings and in seminars, the students rarely challenged the power structures, theories and evidence with which they were expected to work, whether they accepted these personally or not. They acknowledged their position as apprentice members of their fields and strove to become more proficient at applying given theoretical frameworks, presented by their lecturers.

Moving through the levels

The students often did not move smoothly through the different levels of development, from 'early' to 'guided' criticality. For example, we have seen that Katy was progressing well with many aspects of the 'solution searching' process, but appeared to be having problems with 'rationale building'. Other students appeared to cope well when the analytical question was set for them but, when developing their own question, criticality levels in their writing apparently diminished (as with Olivia, the Year Abroad students and the final-year Social Work students). These apparent retrogressions were part of the complex developmental process.

Students could evaluate theory against data, but only sporadically and not with sophistication. The Modern Languages students did not attempt this until the final year, which may be a result of the particular students and assignments we selected or because critiquing theory rather than simply making connections between theory and practice is an inherently more difficult task.

Students often appeared at different levels of critical development, according to the context in which they were working. In class, when speaking spontaneously, students might speak hesitantly and show reluctance to use academic terminology. In prepared presentations, they showed more advanced criticality, and in writing they made academic language much more their own.

Perry (1968/1999) suggested that students at lower levels of development needed more structured input than those at higher levels. Our students, however, continued to receive structured input, although it changed in nature. In Social Work, fourth-year input related to professional competences while in Modern Languages, after the relatively unstructured Year Abroad, final-year students returned to structured classes with topics and texts selected by the lecturers and presentations and essays assigned by them. Apart from selection of their dissertation topic, students normally did not negotiate about the content and direction of their courses. A framework organized around predetermined learning outcomes clearly constrains the extent to which curricula can be 'open' and student-led.

Implications of our account

Policy implications

We now discuss some national and institutional policy implications of our conceptualizations and data analysis.

National policy

The first issue relates to the use of learning outcomes as a key foundation for curriculum design. Learning outcomes are aimed primarily at a relatively low level of criticality where it is thought possible to specify what is learned. Curricula based around learning outcomes are therefore unlikely to be compatible with students exercising 'late' criticality as this type of critical activity is difficult to conceptualize in terms of pre-specified outcomes. Although we think it unlikely that undergraduates will routinely exercise late criticality, if we wish to foster the possibility a strict 'learning outcomes' approach to curriculum design may be unhelpful.

This is a complex issue, however. We saw in our data that Social Work lecturers, for example, were able to promote quite sophisticated levels of reflection and professional development within a framework of defined competences, although largely within 'guided' criticality. We should also remember the 'wild' experience of the Year Abroad which incorporated many elements related to survival in an unfamiliar cultural and linguistic context, encouraging development of the self, of confidence and of intercultural understanding. This experience was managed by the university with a very light touch, with students having widely varying experiences; the only assessment of their cultural and linguistic development took the form of the Year Abroad Project, and there was no systematic measurement, for example, of students' resulting intercultural understanding. Correspondingly, students' response to the Year Abroad experience was more variable than that of Social Work students to their structured placement. Lack of control in the curriculum does not always lead to better critical learning experiences.

Secondly, our conceptualizations of contexts and resources are relevant to current debates in higher education on internationalization and widening participation. The twenty-first century is witnessing a large growth in the numbers of students travelling internationally for higher education (Wildavsky, 2010). Simultaneously, there are moves on the part of governments to widen participation beyond traditional groups of students (Osborne, 2003). Both these policies have greatly increased the range of cultural, biographical and learning contexts, knowledge resources and value systems from which students come. Inevitably, questions will arise about how far students with more varied profiles should fit into their new educational contexts and perform criticality on its terms and how far the new educational context should adapt to them and the resources they bring. (See Levin, 2010 for a discussion of such issues.) The contextualized nature of criticality itself, as discussed in Chapter 1, should be borne in mind.

Thirdly, as discussed in Chapter 5, policy documents often talk about transfer of skills as desirable and unproblematic; transferability of graduate-level skills is one reason why governments have been willing to fund mass higher education. The literature reviewed in Chapters 2 and 3 problematized such transfer, and our conceptual framework in Chapter 4 acknowledged this. As discussed earlier in this chapter, our data analysis chapters raised various examples where transfer was difficult (conceptualization from sociology to social work, literature to history, classroom theory to Year Abroad real life situations) and some examples where it worked (confidence from the Year Abroad to classes in the final year; Social Work concepts to practice situations). Qualities such as confidence seem to be at least transferable. Transfer of knowledge between Barnett's domains seems to be possible where such transfer is explicitly encouraged, discussed and assessed as in Social Work; as argued in Chapter 3, 'thorough and diverse practice' of transfer assisted in development (Perkins et al., 1992). However, where such transfer is not explicitly encouraged and assessed, as with formal classroom theorization to situations in the Year Abroad, it is less likely to take place. So we should be wary of policy claims about transferable skills for graduates. It probably does not matter so much whether a student can function effectively in more than one academic field while at university, but how far and in what ways they can transfer what they learn from their higher education to their lives beyond graduation is important. It also matters that appropriate, effective policies at higher educational levels can be developed to encourage transfer of criticality to the postgraduation experience.

Finally, school level education, in any country, should contribute to student criticality development and address Barnett's three domains. It should prepare students for a variety of 'soft' fields by encouraging recognition of the uncertainty of knowledge, curiosity and creativity, as well as fostering qualities such as independence and confidence. It should encourage development of the range of knowledge resources described in our conceptual framework in Chapter 4. Extended writing and spoken activities are likely to be especially useful for encouraging the development of sustained critical thought. It is likely that criticality will decline temporarily on transfer to higher education because of the change in context and resulting uncertainty about what is expected and how to achieve it. Coping with such changes is a normal part of the criticality developmental process and can be supported by more consistent 'transition' activities with school leavers.

Institutional policy

Institutional policies on assessment have a key role in the type and nature of criticality developed. Assessment at Westford was typical of higher education internationally in various aspects: summative assessment within modules focused on coursework, with some timed written examinations; variable amounts of peer, self or formative assessment; and explicit assessment criteria aligned with learning goals in formal documents. These methods favour particular types of critical development. Students are unlikely to take risks with formal assignments which count toward the final degree grade. Assignments, typically submitted at the end of a semester where they are subject to summative assessment, may be of limited value as formative assessment for future assignments, where these relate to different academic fields. There is little formal training in self-evaluation of assignments for students, which keeps the power of assessment squarely in teachers' hands. Explicit assessment criteria may raise similar issues for criticality development to specified learning outcomes; there may be a danger that explicitness encourages students to focus only on what is specified as some research suggests (e.g. Gibbs et al., 2007; Torrance, 2007). Other assessment patterns are possible (e.g. an increased focus on formative assessment or on self and peer assessment, or an increased focus on final examinations) with different implications for critical development.

The choice between more modular and more unitary degrees also has implications for the type of criticality developed. Hirst (1974/1998), among others, has advocated that students should sample knowledge across different academic fields, not aiming for comprehensive understanding or specialist knowledge, but instead for initiation into various disciplines and so a broader knowledge; in Chapter 5, we briefly examined the 'Melbourne model', a current example of this type of curriculum thinking. However, Barnett argues that if students are not engaged in the habitus of one particular discipline, they may seem free to form their own models of thinking but in reality will only bank unconnected knowledge and be unable to engage in a meaningful dialogue with any of the big knowledge holders in the disciplines (1994, Chapter 9). Our data indicated some problems in functioning across fields and suggest that the extent of this cross-field functioning should be managed and the difficulties recognized, perhaps in explicit discussion for students of field-specific differences and awareness raising among teachers of the issues involved.

If more financial resources were available for certain aspects of study, more could be achieved. Policy makers have to ask how much resource they wish to allocate to providing experiences for students which may enhance their criticality. For example, more active management of Modern Language students during their Year Abroad experience could promote more consistent engagement with the target community and development of intercultural understanding. However, this would require more university resources to organize. In Social Work, placements were organized and funded as an essential requirement for professional accreditation, but organization of these placements in the local area was far easier and less resource heavy than providing similar opportunities and levels of support internationally for Modern Languages students.

The exact focus of the curriculum will vary according to field, as the shape of criticality in each field (e.g. organizing concepts, logical structure) differs. For example, 'pure' subjects may find it hard to offer development in the domain of the world, and in such cases care should probably be taken to offer extra-curricular opportunities in a manner likely to encourage critical development. Similarly, in applied fields which facilitate the development of horizontal linkages across domains, care should be taken also to provide opportunities for vertical development to higher levels of criticality.

Pedagogic implications

This section will highlight key principles related to the coherence and transparency of the teaching/learning of criticality arising out of our conceptual framework in Chapter 4. Pedagogic issues relating to institutional policy have been addressed in the foregoing section, 'Policy Implications', p. 219; here we focus on the micro level of individual teachers, students and classes.

We have suggested that various aspects of learning context (e.g. content and nature of classes, nature of the academic field and the nature of assignments) influence students' critical capacity, in addition to their personal biography. Past and present contexts, as well as some unknowable factors such as intelligence and dispositions, affect the nature and level of knowledge and personal resources available to students. Students may appear uncritical not because they are fundamentally ill-disposed or unintelligent, but because they lack one or more of the knowledge or personal resources necessary to practise criticality. Teachers concerned with fostering criticality should consider how students can most effectively develop particular resources, focusing on the contextual factors over which they have control.

As teachers initiate students into academic fields, they should remain aware of their empowering yet restricting influence. Students who are 'resisting' initiation may lack the requisite resources to function in the field or, alternatively, may be unconvinced by the worth of what is asked; that is, by the knowledge 'why' which has been presented to them.

Informal aspects of the curriculum are important. For example, the underlying tone of the initiation process is as important as what is formally said or written. If students receive messages through the nature of classroom interaction and formative feedback that views different from those of the teacher will be unwelcome, they will probably align themselves with their teacher's opinions, regardless of their own personal views If the students receive the message that their own views are truly valued, they are more likely to develop and express those. Students cannot be forced to become critical in a particular way, however desirable that way might seem to their teachers, without removing the students' right to independent criticality. Additionally, care is needed to assure as close an alignment as possible between non-formal aspects of assessment and a context encouraging to criticality development.

We have explored the concrete means through which students are encouraged to develop critical resources. We saw *modelling* of criticality and *co-construction of critical understandings* in lectures, seminars and other small group interactions; *practice activities and assessment* affected the particular shape of criticality development. All these activities can be related to the three different approaches to learning (social constructivism, communities of practice and cognitivist understandings of transfer) discussed in Chapter 4 (see 'How People Acquire the Resources Necessary for Criticality' p. 93). Teachers should be aware of the complexities involved in these activities, and some examples follow.

First, formal lectures, where students passively receive information, often have a bad press, with small group sessions where students have more chance to talk and construct understandings enjoying more favour. However, one cannot assume unproblematically that seminars are more beneficial for students. Lectures offer opportunities to model lively, critical arguments in an engaging way (on this, see also Biber, 2006). Seminars sometimes offer little more than low-level anecdotal talk as we saw in Chapter 6, although this is perhaps a necessary developmental stage where students struggle to express basic pre-critical ideas.

Promoting criticality in classroom interaction is challenging, as we showed in Chapter 6. The talk should be engaging and constructive so that people are motivated and empowered to contribute. However, people have to be willing and able to challenge one another. We saw examples of such interaction in our data, but we also saw examples of what Mercer (1995) has called 'cumulative talk' (Mercer, 1995) where 'speakers build positively but uncritically on what the other has said. Partners use talk to construct a "common knowledge" by accumulation. Cumulative discourse is characterized by repetitions, confirmations and elaborations' (p. 104). Preferable is what Mercer calls 'exploratory talk' where:

> partners engage critically but constructively with each other's ideas . . . Statements and suggestions are offered for joint consideration. These may be challenged and counter-challenged, but challenges are justified and alternative hypotheses are offered . . . in exploratory talk *knowledge is made more publicly accountable and reasoning is more visible in the talk*. Progress then emerges from the eventual joint agreement reached. (p. 104)

Thirdly, practice is an important element of critical development, often most visible through associated assignments and resulting assessment. However, the focus of practice activities, for example, will differ and teachers should reflect on the priorities for criticality development when setting assignments in their field. In Social Work, our example of a soft, applied field, we saw how assignments focused on the development of critical links across domains, rather than on tasks focused on theoretical challenge as Social Work students were led towards their role as early-stage professional practitioners.

With regard to developmental levels, we saw in Chapter 7 the kinds of support that students may require before being able to exercise advanced levels of criticality. For example, as argued in Chapter 4, question formation is a late-developing critical skill, so allowing students to set their own question for assignments can be problematic. Initiation into appropriate question posing through means such as modelling of questions or sustained practice and guidance on question formation is likely to support students. However, this may present practical dilemmas for teachers faced with heavy workloads and time constraints. Should they design simpler and less challenging assignments? It also presents dilemmas for a teacher who sees a student proposing an inappropriate question about how forceful controls over students should be. There are also likely to be issues relating to student confidence and trust; students may be nervous about speaking to a lecturer if they feel their ideas are not sufficiently developed, and they may be unaware that talking to a lecturer might help them develop and focus their ideas.

The use of model answers was not observed at Westford, but could provide useful support for developing rationale building skills, as suggested for history by Coffin (2004). For example, a lecturer could construct a model answer for a presentation or essay in a different topic area from that of students' actual assignments, with a thesis and various supporting arguments, and highlight various aspects of this in class. The students would then be clear about the nature of the final product expected of them. If students are to move between academic fields during their degree programme and typically may have only one or two assignments in a particular field, this type of specific guidance may be especially useful and necessary so that students may become attuned more readily to genre expectations. This may involve development of a greater awareness on the part of teachers about the particular nature of their expectations in written work.

With regard to assessment, one cannot unproblematically assume that written examinations are undesirable while un-timed coursework essays are good. Students will often prepare ideas before examinations so examination answers are often a product of the quality of this preparation, rather than the ability to think on one's feet. However, timed examinations generally favour those able to work under pressure, to memorize and to predict questions rather than those who may prefer time to reflect and to work on subtleties in response to novel questions.

It is necessary to prioritize pedagogic effort because of time and resource limitations. The teachers in our study were hugely concerned with correct referencing. The rules for referencing are arcane, and it is worth asking how important the minutiae are for students who are not planning to continue in academia. Arguably, this relates to the larger problem of students engaging effectively with primary and secondary literatures and serious thought has to be given to which are the important underlying issues to address in this regard and which are less so.

Long-term criticality development

Throughout this book we have consistently argued that higher education should be preparing critically capable citizens able to function in a transformatory critical way across the three domains that Barnett (1997) suggests. In conclusion, therefore, we have to ask what evidence we can see that the students at Westford were being prepared appropriately and what longer term contribution their higher education had made to their criticality. The answers to these questions are complex and largely speculative.

The students functioned mainly at the 'guided' criticality level by their final year. All the students had developed in all three of Barnett's domains to some extent, although in field-specific ways as discussed previously. It might be considered disappointing that they had not reached the 'advanced' level, but this may be as far as one could realistically expect an undergraduate education to take students. Arguably a firm base had been provided for graduates to go on to develop more advanced criticality as they move on through life, though much is likely to depend on the personal and professional contexts in which they functioned after graduation. The Social Work lecturers especially had tried to provide the students with a strong base for post-graduation critical development, for instance through encouraging strong peer relations with a professional focus during the degree programme.

There are issues about the transfer of criticality from higher education to a post-graduation context. When required to move to a new arena of criticality (perhaps a new sub-discipline or a new field in the world), a person may operate at a lower level of criticality than before as they may lack some of the necessary critical resources. However, if the person has previously undergone development in one area, they are likely to start with some advantage in the new field, as certain relevant resources can be transferred, such as life experience, knowledge of how to manage learning, knowledge of what it is to be critical in another area, and so on. Some aspects of declarative knowledge are also likely to transfer. Presumably, for example, the Modern Languages students will watch films and read literature differently from before. The students will have developed the ability to write logically, to engage with the ideas of others, to apply explanatory frameworks, even if in field-specific ways. Confidence from the Year Abroad and practice placement experiences transferred to other aspects of studying. This confidence is likely to transfer to other aspects of life.

In Chapter 4 we drew attention to the idea of group tendencies, in line with the issues raised in the social emancipatory literature discussed in Chapter 2. We suggested that if members of one social group consistently fail to reach the highest levels of criticality and become societal leaders, then we have to question underlying social dynamics and issues of equity. In some ways, our data is encouraging on this point. Through sustained effort, some students with non-traditional entry qualifications were able to achieve well at university in the end. However, not all did, and entry via traditional qualifications clearly conferred an initial advantage in terms of preparedness for university assessment practices. We should also remember that these non-traditional students graduated in Social Work, and that it is probably in such a professional field that students with this type of qualification find it easiest to enter a research-intensive university. Students from non-traditional, typically poorer backgrounds may still be largely excluded from many fields within an elite criticality education and so from later societal leadership roles.

Ways forward

In this book we have proposed a principled conceptual framework useful for understanding the development of criticality, especially as it manifests itself at the undergraduate level in an elite research university in 'soft' academic fields. We have tested this framework against a large qualitative database in Modern Languages and Social Work and believe it has survived the test, providing explanatory accounts of the development of real students in real learning contexts. The principles underlying the framework need to be further investigated in different settings such as 'hard' disciplinary fields, at postgraduate levels, in institutions which focus more on non-traditional students, and with student bodies from different cultural backgrounds. Given the increasing importance of higher education in the twenty-first century world, a fuller understanding of criticality and its development is vital for ongoing development of curriculum policies, assessment strategies and higher education pedagogies in increasingly diverse settings.

References

ACNielsen Research Services (2000), *Employer Satisfaction with Graduate Skills: Research Report*, Department of Education, Training and Youth Affairs. Commonwealth of Australia, February.

Altbach, P. G. (1998), *Comparative Higher Education: Knowledge, the University, and Development*. Ablex: Westpoint.

Anderson, L. W. and Krathwohl, D. R. (eds.) (2001), *A Taxonomy for Learning, Teaching and Assessing: A Revision of Bloom's Taxonomy of Educational Objectives*. New York: Longman.

Annette, J. (2000) 'Education for citizenship, civic participation and experiential and service learning in the community', in D. Lawton, J. Cairns and R. Gardner (eds.), *Education for Citizenship*. London: Continuum.

Association of American Colleges and Universities (2002), *Greater Expectations: A New Vision for Learning as a Nation Goes to College*, Report of AACU, available online at www.aacu.org.

Association of Commonwealth Universities (2001), *Engagement as a Core Value for the University: A Consultation Document*. London: ACU.

A Test of Leadership: Charting the Future of U.S. Higher Education (2006). A Report of the Commission Appointed by Secretary of Education, Margaret Spelling, Pre-publication Copy, September.

Australian Qualifications Framework Advisory Board (2007), *Australian Qualifications Framework: Implementation handbook*. 4th edn. Available online at http://www.training.com.au/aqtf2007.

Axelrod, P. (2002), *Values in Conflict: the University, the Marketplace, and the Trials of Liberal Education*. Quebec: McGill-Queen's University Press.

Bailin, S., Case, R., Coombs, J. R. and Daniels, L. B. (1999a), 'Conceptualizing critical thinking', *Journal of Curriculum Studies*, 31 (3), 285–302.

Bailin, S., Case, R., Coombs, J. R. and Daniels, L. B. (1999b), 'Common misconceptions of critical thinking', *Journal of Curriculum Studies*, 31 (3), 269–83.

Barber, B. (1992), *An Aristocracy of Everyone: The Politics of Educators and the Future of America*. Oxford: Oxford University Press.

Barnes, G. G., Thompson, P., Daniel, G. and Burchardt, N. (1998), *Growing up in Step-Families*. Oxford: Clarendon Press.

Barnett, R. (1990), *The Idea of Higher Education*. Buckingham: SRHE and Open University Press.

Barnett, R. (1994), *The Limits of Competence: Knowledge, Higher Education and Society*. Buckingham: SRHE and Open University Press.

Barnett, R. (1997), *Higher Education: A Critical Business*. Buckingham: SRHE and Open University Press.

Barnett, R. (2003), *Beyond all Reason: Living with Ideology in the University*. Buckingham: SRHE and Open University Press.

Barrow, R. (1999), 'The higher nonsense: some persistent errors in educational thinking', *Journal of Curriculum Studies*, 31 (2), 131–42.

Bartholomae, D. (1985), 'Inventing the university', in M. Rose (ed), *When a Writer Can't Write: Studies in Writer's Block and Other Composing – Process Problems*. New York: Guilford Press.

Baxter Magolda, M. (1992), *Knowing and Reasoning in College: Gender-related Patterns in Students' Intellectual Development*. San Francisco: Jossey-Bass.

Bazerman, C. (1988), *Shaping Written Knowledge: the Genre and Activity of the Experimental Article in Science*. Madison: University of Wisconsin Press.

de Beauvoir, S. (1966), *Les Belles Images*. Paris: Gallimard.

Becher, T. (1989), *Academic Tribes and Territories: intellectual enquiry and the cultures of disciplines*. Milton Keynes: SRHE and Open University Press.

Becher, T. and Trowler, P. (2001), *Academic Tribes and Territories: Intellectual Enquiry and the Culture of the Disciplines*, London: SRHE and Open University Press.

Beck, U. (1994), 'The reinvention of politics: towards a theory of reflexive modernisation', in U. Beck, A. Giddens and S. Lash (eds.), *Reflexive Modernisation: Politics, Tradition and Aesthetics in the Modern Social Order*. Cambridge: Polity Press.

Becker, H., Geer, B. and Hughes, E. (1968), *Making the Grade: The Academic Side of College Life*. New York: John Wiley & Sons.

Belenky, M. F., McVicker Clinchy, B., Rule Golberger, N. and Mattuck Tarule, J. (1986), *Women's Ways of Knowing: The Development of Self, Voice, and Mind*. New York: Basic Books.

Bereiter, C. and Scardamalia, M. (1987), *The Psychology of Written Composition*. London: Lawrence Erlbaum Associates.

Berg, C. A. (2000) 'Intellectual development in adulthood', in R. Sternberg (ed), *Handbook of Intelligence*. Cambridge: Cambridge University Press.

Berlin, I. (1980), *Against the Current: Essays in the History of Ideas* (ed H. Hardy). New York: The Viking Press.

Bernstein, D. A. (1995), 'A negotiation model for teaching critical thinking', *Teaching of Psychology*, 22 (1), 22–4.

Biber, D. (2006). *University Language*. Amsterdam: John Benjamins.

Biglan, A. (1973), 'The characteristics of subject matter in different academic areas', *Journal of Applied Psychology*, 57 (3), 195–203.

Black, P. and Wiliam, D. (1998), 'Assessment and classroom learning', *Assessment in Education*, 5 (1), 7–74.

Bloom, B. S., Englehart, M., Furst, E., Hill, W., and Krathwohl, D. (1956), *Taxonomy of Educational Objectives: The Classification of Educational Goals: Cognitive and Affective*. New York: David McKay Company, Inc.

Bologna Working Group on Qualifications Frameworks (2005), *The framework for qualifications of the European Higher Education Area*. Denmark: Ministry of Science, Technology and Innovation. Available online at http://www.bologna-bergen 2005.no/Docs/00-Main_doc/050218_QF_EHEA.pdf.

Bourdieu, P. (1996), *The State Nobility: Elite Schools and the Field of Power* (trans. L. C. Clough). Cambridge: Polity Press.

Bourdieu, P. and Wacquant, L. (1992), *An Invitation to Reflexive Sociology*. Chicago: University of Chicago Press.

Braxton, J. (1995), 'Disciplines with an affinity for the Improvement of undergraduate education', in N. Hativa and M. Marincovich (eds.), *Disciplinary Differences in Teaching and Learning: Implications for Practice*. San Francisco: Jossey Bass.

Brookfield, S. (2003), 'Critical thinking in adulthood', in D. Fasko (ed), *Critical Thinking and Reasoning: Current Research, Theory and Practice*. Cresskill, NJ: Hampton.

Broudy, H. S. (1977), 'Types of knowledge and purposes of human education', in R. Anderson, R. Spiro and W. Montague (eds.), *Schooling and the Acquisition of Knowledge*. Hillsdale, NJ: Lawrence Erlbaum Associates.

Brown, A. (1987), 'Metacognition, executive control, self-regulation, and other more mysterious mechanisms', in F. E. Weinert and R. H. Kluwe (eds.), *Metacognition, Motivation and Understanding*. Hillsdale, NJ: Lawrence Erlbaum Associates.

Brown, J. S., Collins, A. and Duguid, P. (1989), 'Situated cognition and the culture of learning', *Educational Researcher*, 18 (1), 32–42.

Brown, S. and Knight, P. (1994), *Assessing Learners in Higher Education*. London: Kogan Page.

Browne, M. N. and Keeley, S. M. (2007), *Asking the Right Questions: a guide to Critical Thinking*. Upper Saddle River, NJ: Pearson, Prentice-Hall.

Brumfit, C., Myles, F., Mitchell, R., Johnston, B. and Ford, P. (2005), 'Modern languages and the development of criticality', *International Journal of Applied Linguistics*, 15 (2), 145–68.

Bruner, J. (1963), *The Process of Education*. New York: Vintage Books.

Burbules, N. C. and Berk, R. (1999), 'Critical thinking and critical pedagogy: relations, differences and limits', in T. Popkewitz and L. Fendler (eds.), *Critical Theory in Education: Changing Terrains of Knowledge and Politics*. New York: Routledge.

Burden-Leahy, S.M. (2009), 'Globalisation and education in the postcolonial world: the conundrum of the higher education system of the United Arab Emirates', *Comparative Education*, 45 (4), 525–44.

Byram, M. S. (1997), *Teaching and Assessing Intercultural Communicative Competence*. Clevedon: Multilingual Matters Ltd.

Ceci, S., Rosenblum, T., de Bruyn, E. and Lee, D. (1997), 'A bio-ecological model of intellectual development: moving beyond h^2', in R. Sternberg and E. Grigorenko (eds.), *Intelligence, Heredity and Environment*. New York: Cambridge University Press.

Chacun Cherche Son Chat (1996), [Film]. Writer/Director Cédric Klapisch. France: Vertigo Productions.

Chase, W. G. and Simon, H. A. (1973), 'Perception in chess', *Cognitive Psychology*, 4 (1), 55–81.

Chi, M. T. H., Feltovich, P. J. and Glaser, R. (1981), 'Categorization and representation of physics knowledge by experts and novices', *Cognitive Science*, 5 (2), 121–52.

Clinchy, B. M. (1994), 'On critical thinking and connected knowing', in K. S. Walters (ed), *Re-Thinking reason: New perspectives on critical thinking*. Albany, NY: State University of New York Press.

Coffin, C. (2004), 'Learning to write with history: the role of causality', *Written Communication*, 21 (3), 261–89.

Coleman, J. A. (1996), *Studying Languages: A Survey of British and European Students. The Proficiency, Background, Attitudes and Motivations of Students of Foreign Languages in the United Kingdom and Europe*. London: CILT.

Commonwealth of Australia (2008), *Review of Australian Higher Education: Final Report (Bradley Report)*. Available online at www.deewr.gov.au/he_review_finalreport.

Costa, A.L. (2000), 'Describing the habits of mind', in A. L Costa and B. Kallick (eds.), *Discovering and Exploring Habits of Mind (Habits of Mind, Book 1)*. Alexandria, VA: Association for Supervision and Curriculum Development.

Cottrell, S. (2005), *Critical Thinking Skills: Developing Effective Analysis and Argument*. Basingstoke: Palgrave Macmillan.

Coulshed, V. and Orme, J. (1998), Social work practice: an introduction, 3rd

Council of Europe (2001), *Common European Framework of Reference for Languages*. Cambridge: Cambridge University Press. Also available online at http://www.coe.int/t/dg4/linguistic/Source/Framework_EN.pdf.

Darling, L. F. (2001), 'Portfolio as practice: the narratives of emerging teachers', *Teaching and Teacher Education*, 17 (1), 107–21.

Dauer, F. W. (1989), *Critical Thinking: An Introduction to Reasoning*. Oxford: Oxford University Press.

De Corte, E. (1999), 'On the road to transfer: an introduction', *International Journal of Educational Research*, 31 (7), 555–59.

Delanty, G. (2001), *Challenging Knowledge: The University in the Knowledge Society*. Buckingham: SRHE and Open University Press.

Department for Business Innovation and Skills (2009), *Higher Ambitions: The Future of Universities in a Knowledge Economy*. Available online at http://www.bis.gov.uk/assets/biscore/corporate/docs/h/09-1447-higher-ambitions.pdf (accessed 21 May 2010).

Department of Education and Skills (2003), *The Future of Higher Education*. London: The Stationery Office.

Devlin, M. (2008), 'An international and interdisciplinary approach to curriculum: the Melbourne model', in Universitas 21, U21 Conference. Glasgow, February.

Dewey, J. (1902), *The Child and the Curriculum*. Chicago: University of Chicago Press.

Donald, J. (1985), 'Intellectual skills in higher education', *La Revue Canadienne d'Enseignement Supérieur*, XV (1), 53–68.

Donald, J. (1986), 'Knowledge and the university curriculum', *Higher Education*, 15 (3), 267–82.

Donald, J. (1995), 'Disciplinary Differences in Knowledge Validation', in N. Hativa and M. Marincovich (eds.), *Disciplinary Differences in Teaching and Learning: Implications for Practice*. San Francisco: Jossey Bass.

Dreyfus, H. L. and Dreyfus, S. E. (1986), *Mind over Machine: The Power of Human Intuition and Expertise in the Era of the Computer*. New York: The Free Press.

Elder, L. and Paul, R. (2006), *The Thinker's Guide to Analytic Thinking, The Foundation for Critical Thinking*. Dillon Beach, CA: Foundation for Critical Thinking.

Elliott, R. K. (1998), 'Education and human being', in P. Hirst and P. White (eds.), *Philosophy of Education: Major Themes in the Analytic Tradition, Volume II: Education and Human Being*. London: Routledge.

Ellsworth, E. (1989), 'Why doesn't this feel empowering? Working through the repressive myths of critical pedagogy', *Harvard Educational Review*, 59 (3), 297–324.

Elton, L. and Laurillard, D. (1979), 'Trends in research on student learning', *Studies in Higher Education*, 4 (1), 87–102.

Ennis, R. H. (1962), 'A concept of critical thinking', *Harvard Educational Review*, 32 (1), 81–111.

Ennis, R. H. (1969), *Logic in Teaching*. Englewood Cliffs, NJ: Prentice-Hall.

Ennis, R. H. (1987), 'A taxonomy of critical thinking dispositions and abilities', in J. B. Baron and R. Sternberg (eds.), *Teaching Thinking Skills: Theory and Practice*. New York: W. H. Freeman and Company.

Ennis, R. H. (1989), 'Critical thinking and subject specificity: clarification and needed research', *Educational Researcher*, 18 (3), 4–10.

Ernaux, A. (1991), *Passion Simple*. Trans Tanya Leslie, 1993. Paris: Gallimard.

Facione, P. A. (1990), *Critical Thinking: A Statement of Expect Consensus for Purposes of Educational Assessment and Instruction: Executive Summary*. California: California Academic Press.

Farrell, E. (2005), 'N.J. Court rejects gay student's bias suit against Seton Hall', *Chronicle of Higher Education*, 51 (44), A30.

Feuerstein, R., Rand, Y, Hoffman, M. B. and Miller, R. (1980), *Instrumental Enrichment: An Intervention for Cognitive Modifiability*. Baltimore, MD: University Park Press.

Fisher, A. (1988), *The Logic of Real Arguments*. Cambridge: Cambridge University Press.

Fisher, A. and Scriven, M. (1997), *Critical Thinking. Its Definition and Assessment*. California, USA: Edgepress and Norwich, UK: Centre For Research in Critical Thinking.

Flower, L., Stein, V., Ackerman, A., Kantz, M. J., McCormick, K. and Peck, W. C. (eds.) (1990), *Reading-to-Write: Exploring a Cognitive and Social Process*. New York: Oxford University Press.

Foertsch, J. (1995), 'Where cognitive psychology applies: how theories about memory and transfer can influence composition pedagogy', *Written Communication*, 12 (3), 360–83.

Ford, G. W. and Pugno, L. (eds.) (1964), *The Structure of Knowledge and the Curriculum*. Chicago: Rand McNally.

Ford, P., Johnston, B. and Mitchell, R. (2004), 'How does the practice placement experience affect the development of social work students as "critical practitioners"?', 6th Joint Social Work Education Conference. University of Glasgow, Scotland, July.

Ford, P., Johnston, B. and Mitchell, R. (2006), 'Skills Development and theorising practice in social work education', *SWAP Funded Projects 2005–2006*, no. 3, Subject Centre for Social Policy and Social Work.

Freire, P. (1981), *Education for Critical Consciousness*. New York: Continuum.

Freire, P. (2000), *Pedagogy of the Oppressed*. New York: Continuum.

Fuchs, M. (2004), 'At one Catholic college, crucifixes make a comeback', *New York Times*, 12 June.

Fulkerson, R. (1996), *Teaching the Argument in Writing*. Urbana, IL: NCTE.

Gallagher, J. J. (1994), 'Teaching and learning: new models', *Annual Review of Psychology*, 45, 171–95.

Gallo, D. (1994), 'Educating for empathy, reason and Imagination', in K. S. Walters (ed), *Re-thinking Reason: New Perspectives in Critical Thinking*. Albany: State University of New York Press.

Gardner, H. (1993), *Multiple Intelligences: The Theory in Practice*. New York: Basic.
Gardner, H. (2006), 'Developmental psychology after Piaget: an approach in terms of symbolisation', in *The Development and Education of the Mind: The Selected Works of Howard Gardner.* Abingdon: Routledge.
Gazon Maudit (1995) [Film – 'French Twist'] Director Josiane Balasko. France: Pathe.
Gibbons, M., Limoges, C., Nowotny, H., Schwartzman, S., Scott, P. and Trow, M. (1994), *The Production of Knowledge: The Dynamics of Science and Research in Contemporary Societies*. London: Sage.
Gibbs, G. and Dunbar-Goddet, H. (2007), *The effects of programme assessment environments on student learning*. Report to the Higher Education Academy. York: Higher Education Academy.
Giddens, A. (1984), *The Constitution of Society: Outline of the Theory of Structuration*. Berkeley, CA: University of California Press.
Giroux, H. A. (1983), *Theory and Resistance in Education*. South Hadley, MA: Bergin and Garvey.
Giroux, H. A. (1988), *Teachers as Intellectuals: Towards a Critical Pedagogy of Learning*. Massachusetts: Bergin and Garvey.
Glaser, R. (1984), 'Education and thinking: the role of knowledge', *American Psychologist*, 39 (2), 93–104.
Glevey, K. E. (2006), *Thinking and Education*. Leicester: Troubadour.
Goals 2000: Educate America Act (1994), Pub. L. 102–227. Available online at http://www2.ed.gov/legislation/GOALS2000/TheAct/index.html.
Gobet, F. and Simon, H. A. (2000), 'Five seconds or sixty? Presentation time in expert memory', *Cognitive Science*, 24 (4), 651–82.
Goldberg, E. M., Walker, D. and Robinson, J. (1977). 'Exploring the taskcentred casework method, *Social Work Today*, 9 (2), 9–14.
Goodwin, C. and Duranti, A. (1992), 'Rethinking context: an introduction', in A. Duranti and C. Goodwin (eds.), *Rethinking Context: Language as an Interactive Phenomenon*. Cambridge: Cambridge University Press.
Gore, J.M. (1993), *The Struggle for Pedagogies*. New York: Routledge.
Graham, G. (2005), *The Institution of Intellectual Values: Realism and Idealism in Higher Education*. Exeter: Imprint Academic.
Grant, B. (1997), 'Disciplining students: the construction of student subjectivities', *British Journal of the Sociology of Education*, 18 (1), 101–14.
Grigorenko, E. L. (2007), 'Hitting, missing and in between: a typology of the impact of western education on the non-western world', *Comparative Education*, 43 (1), 165–86.
Grossman, P.L. (1990), *The Making of a Teacher: Teacher Knowledge and Teacher Education*. New York: Teacher College Press.
Grotzer, T. A. and Perkins, D. (2000), 'Teaching intelligence: a performance conception', in R. Sternberg (ed), *Handbook of Intelligence*. Cambridge: Cambridge University Press.
Guilford, J.P. (1950), 'Creativity', *The American Psychologist*, 5 (9), 444–54.
Habermas, J. (1987), *The Theory of Communicative Action, Volume 2: Lifeworld and System: A Critique of Functionalist Reason* (trans. T. McCarthy). Boston: Beacon.
Habermas, J. (1991), *The Theory of Communicative Action, Vol. 1: Reason and the Rationalisation of Society* (trans. T. McCarthy). Cambridge: Polity.

Haggis, T. (2003), 'Constructing images of ourselves? a critical investigation into 'approaches to learning' research in higher education', *British Educational Research Journal*, 29 (1), 89–104.

Halonen, J. S. (1995), 'Demystifying critical thinking', *Teaching of Psychology*, 22 (1), 75–81.

Halpern, D. F. (1997), *Critical Thinking Across the Curriculum: A Brief Edition of Thought and Knowledge*. Mahwah, NJ: Lawrence Erlbaum Associates.

Halpern, D. F. (2003), *Thought and Knowledge: An Introduction to Critical Thinking* (4th edn). Mahwah, NJ: Lawrence Erlbaum Associates.

Halpern, D. F. and Nummedal, S. G. (1995), 'Closing thoughts about helping students improve how they think', *Teaching of Psychology*, 22 (1), 82–3.

Halstead, J. M. (2004), 'An Islamic concept of education', *Comparative Education*, 40 (4), 517–29.

Hanley, G. L. (1995), 'Teaching critical thinking: focussing on metacognitive skills and problem solving', *Teaching of Psychology*, 22 (1), 68–72.

Harris, K.-L. (2009) *International Trends in Establishing the Standards of Academic Achievement in Higher Education: An Independent Report and Analysis*. Melbourne: Centre for the Study of Higher Education, University of Melbourne.

Herrnstein, R. J. and Murray, C. (1996), *The Bell Curve: Intelligence and Class Structure In American Life*. New York: Free Press.

Higgins, S., Baumfield, V., Lin, M., Moseley, D., Butterworth, M., Downey, G., Gregson, M., Oberski, I., Rockett, M. and Thacker, D. (2004), 'Thinking skills Approaches to effective teaching and learning: what is the evidence for impact on learners', in *Research Evidence in Education Library*. London: EPPI-Centre, Social Science Research Unit, Institute of Education, University of London.

Hirst, P. H. (1998) 'Liberal education and the nature of knowledge', in P. H. Hirst and P. White (eds.), *Philosophy of Education: Major Themes in the Analytic Tradition, Volume II: Philosophy of Education*. London: Routledge.

Jaspers, K. (1960), *The Idea of a University* (ed K. Deutsch). London: Peter Owen.

Johanson, A. (1987), 'Can informal logic courses teach critical thinking: reflections on McPeck and Paul', paper presented at the Conference on Critical Thinking (Newport News, VA, April), ERIC depository.

Johnston, B. and Elton, L. (2005), 'German and UK higher education and graduate employment: the interface between systemic tradition and graduate views', *Comparative Education*, 41 (3), 351–73.

Kerr, C. (1972), *The Uses of the University – with a Postscript – 1972*. Cambridge, MA: Harvard University Press.

King, A. (1995), 'Inquiring minds really do want to know: using questioning to teach critical thinking', *Teaching of Psychology*, 22 (1), 13–17.

King, P.M. and Kitchener, K. (1994), *Developing Reflective Judgement: Understanding and Promoting Intellectual Growth and Critical Thinking and Adolescents and Adults*. San Francisco: Jossey Bass.

Kinginger, C. (2008), 'Language learning in study abroad: Case studies of Americans in France', in *Modern Language Journal Monograph 1*. Oxford: Blackwell.

Kolb, D. A. (1981), 'Learning styles and disciplinary differences', in A. W. Chickering & Associates (eds.), *The Modern American College*. San Francisco: Jossey-Bass.

Kuhn, T. S. (1962), *The Structure of Scientific Revolutions*. Chicago: University of Chicago Press.

Kuhn, T. S. (1970), *The Structure of Scientific Revolutions* (2nd edn). Chicago: University of Chicago Press.

Lattuca, L. and Stark, J. S. (1994), 'Will disciplinary perspectives impede curricular reform?', *The Journal of Higher Education*, 65 (4), 401–26.

Lave, J. and Wenger, E. (1991), *Situated Learning: Legitimate Peripheral Participation*. Cambridge: Cambridge University Press.

Lea, M. and Street, B. (1998), 'Student writing in higher education: an academic literacies approach', *Studies in Higher Education*, 23 (2), 157–72.

Learning for Life: Final Report (1998), Review of higher education financing and policy, Commonwealth of Australia: Department of Employment, Education, Training and Youth Affairs, April.

Leighton, J. A. (1895), 'Fichte's conception of God', *The Philosophical Review*, 4 (2), 143–53.

Lesgold, A. M., Robinson, H., Feltovich, P., Glaser, R., Klopfer, D. and Wang, Y. (1988), 'Expertise in a complex skills: diagnosing x-ray pictures', in M. T. H. Chi, R. Glaser and M. J. Farr (eds.), *The Nature of Expertise*. Hillsdale, NJ: Lawrence Erlbaum Associates.

Levin, R. (2010), 'The rise of Asia's universities', in Higher Education Policy Institute, *Seventh Annual Lecture*. London: Royal Society, February.

Livingston, K., Soden, R. and Kirkwood, M. (2004), *Post-16 Pedagogy and Thinking Skills: An Evaluation*. London: Learning and Skills Research Centre.

Lodahl, J. B. and Gordon, G. G. (1972), 'The structure of scientific fields and the functioning of university graduate departments', *American Sociological Review*, 37 (1), 57–72.

Lubart, T. I. (1994), 'Creativity', in R. J. Sternberg (ed), *Thinking and Problem Solving*. San Diego: Academic Press.

Lyotard, J.-F. (1984), *The Postmodern Condition: A Report on Knowledge*. Trans. Geoff Bennington and Brian Massumi. Manchester: University of Manchester Press.

Macedo, D. (2000), 'Introduction', in P. Freire, *Pedagogy of the Oppressed: Thirtieth Anniversary Edition*. New York: Continuum.

Markman, A. and Gentner, D. (2001), 'Thinking', *Annual Review of Psychology*, 52, 223–47.

Martin, J. R. (1998), '(ii) Needed: a new paradigm for liberal education', in P. H. Hirst and P. White (eds.), *Philosophy of Education: Major Themes in the Analytic Tradition, Volume I: Philosophy and Education*. London: Routledge.

Marton, F. and Säljö, R. (1997), 'Approaches to learning', in F. Marton, D. Hounsell and N. Entwistle (eds.), *The Experience of Learning*. Edinburgh: Scottish Academic Press.

Mattson, K. and Shea, M. (1997), 'The selling of service-learning to the modern university: how much will it cost?', Civic Practices Network. Walt Whitman Centre, Rutgers University, available at http://www.cpn.org/topics/youth/highered/selling_service.html (accessed 27 February 2007).

de Maupassant, G. (1883/2006), *Une Vie* ['A Woman's Life']. New York: Adamant Media Corporation.

Mayer, R. (2000), 'Intelligence and education', in R. Sternberg (ed), *Handbook of Intelligence*. Cambridge: Cambridge University Press.

Mayer, J. D., Salovey, P. and Caruso, D. (2000), 'Models of emotional intelligence', in R. Sternberg (ed), *Handbook of Intelligence*. Cambridge: Cambridge University Press.

McBride, R., Xiang, P., Wittenburg, D. and Shen, J. (2002), 'An analysis of pre-service teachers' dispositions toward critical thinking: A cross-cultural perspective', *Asia-Pacific Journal of Teacher Education*, 30 (2), 131–40.

McBurney, D. H. (1995), 'The problem method of teaching research methods', *Teaching of Psychology*, 22 (1), 36–8.

McCarthey, S. and Raphael, T. E. (1992), 'Alternative research perspectives', in J. W. Irwin and M. A. Doyle (eds.), *Reading/Writing Connections: Learning from Research*. Newark, Delaware: International Reading Association.

McDonald, D. (1989), *The Language of Argument* (6th ed). New York: Harper and Row.

McGuinness, C. (1993), 'Teaching Thinking: new signs for theories of cognition', *Educational Psychology*, 13 (3 and 4), 305–316.

McGuinness, C. (1999), *From Thinking Skills to Thinking Classrooms*. Report for Department of Education and Employment. London: HMSO.

McGuinness, C. (2005), 'Teaching thinking: theory and practice', in P. Tomlinson, J. Dockrell and P. Winne (eds.), *British Journal of Educational Psychology Monograph Series II, No. 3 – Pedagogy – Teaching for Learning*, 1, 107–26.

McPeck, J. E. (1981), *Critical Thinking and Education*. Oxford: Martin Robinson.

McPeck, J. E. (1990a), 'Critical thinking and subject specificity: a reply to Ennis', *Educational Researcher*, 19 (4), 10–12.

McPeck, J. E. (1990b), *Teaching Critical Thinking: Dialogue and Dialectic*. New York: Routledge.

Mercer, N. (1995), *The Guided Construction of Knowledge*. Clevedon, UK: Multilingual Matters.

Mercer, N. (1996), 'Language and the guided construction of knowledge', in G. Blue and R. Mitchell, *Language and Education*. Clevedon: Multilingual Matters.

Miles, M. B. and Huberman, A. M. (1994), *An Expanded Sourcebook: Qualitative Data Analysis* (2nd edn). London: Sage.

Miller, C. and Parlett, M. (1974), *Up to the Mark: A Study of the Examination Game*. London: SRHE.

Molyneux, M. (2000), 'State gender and institutional change: the *Federación de Mujeres* Cubanas', in M. Molyneux and E. Dore (eds.), *Hidden Histories*. Durham, NC: Duke University Press.

Moseley, D., Baumfield, V., Elliott, J., Gregson, M., Higgins, S., Lin, M., Newton, D. and Robson, S. (2004), *Thinking Skills Frameworks for post-16 Learners: An Evaluation*. London: Learning and Skills Research Centre.

Moseley, D., Elliott, J., Gregson, M. and Higgins, S. (2005), 'Thinking skills frameworks for use in education and training', *British Educational Research Journal*, 31 (3), 367–90.

Murphy-Lejeune, E. (2002), *Student Mobility and Narrative in Europe: The New Strangers*. New York: Routledge Studies in Anthropology.

National Committee of Inquiry into Higher Education (1997), *Higher Education in the Learning Society* (*Dearing Report*). Available online at http://www.leeds.ac.uk/educol/ncihe/ (accessed 23 February 2010).

Neave, G. (2002), 'The stakeholder perspective historically explored', in J. Enders and O. Fulton (eds.), *Higher Education in a Globalising World: International Trends Mutual Observations*. Dordrecht: Kluwer.

Neumann, R. (2001), 'Disciplinary differences and university teaching', *Studies in Higher Education*, 26 (2) 135–46.

Neumann, R., Perry, S. and Becher, T. (2002), 'Teaching and learning in their disciplinary contexts: a conceptual analysis', *Studies in Higher Education*, 27 (4), 405–17.

Newman, J. H. (1899/1996), *The Idea of a University*. New Haven and London: Yale University Press.

Nokes, J., Dole, J. A. and Hacker, D. J. (2007), 'Teaching high school students to use heuristics while reading historical texts', *Journal of Educational Psychology*, 99 (3), 492–504.

Les Nuits Fauves (1992) [Film – 'Savage Nights'. Writer/Director: Cyril Collard. France: Banfilm.

Nusche, S. (2008), 'Assessment of learning outcomes in higher education: a comparative review of selected practices', OECD Education Working Paper No. 15. OECD Publishing.

Nussbaum, M. C. (1997), *Cultivating Humanity: A Classical Defence of Reform in Liberal Education*. Cambridge, Mass. and London: Harvard University Press.

Oakeshott, M. (1989), *The Voice of Liberal Learning*. London: Yale University Press.

Organisation for Economic Cooperation and Development (OECD) (2008), *Tertiary Education for the Knowledge Society*, OECD Thematic Review of Tertiary Education: Synthesis Report. Available online at http://www.oecd.org/dataoecd/20/4/40345176.pdf

Osborne, M. (2003), 'Increasing or widening participation in higher education? a European overview', *European Journal of Education*, 38 (1), 5–24.

Palinscar, A. S. (1998), 'Social constructivist perspectives on teaching and learning', *Annual Review of Psychology*, 49, 345–75.

Parker, J. (2001), 'Humanities higher education: new models, new challenges', in E. A. Chambers (ed), *Contemporary Themes in Humanities Higher Education*. London: Kluwer.

Parkes, C. Murray (1986), *Bereavement: Studies of Grief in Adult Life*, 2nd edn. London: Tavistock Publications.

Passmore, J. (1980), *The Philosophy of Teaching*. London: Duckworth.

Paul, R. (1982), 'Teaching critical thinking in the 'strong' sense: a focus on self-deception, world views and a dialectical mode of analysis', *Informal Logic Newsletter*, 4 (2), 2–7.

Paul, R. (1990), 'McPeck's mistakes', in J. McPeck, *Teaching Critical Thinking: Dialogue and Dialectic*. New York: Routledge.

Paul, R. (1994), 'Teaching critical thinking in the strong sense: a focus on self-deception, world views and a dialectical mode of analysis', in K. S. Walters (ed) *Re-thinking Reason: New Perspectives in Critical Thinking*, Albany: State University of New York Press.

Paul, R. W. (1984), 'Critical thinking: fundamental to education for a free society', *Educational Leadership*, 42 (1), 4–14.

Paul, R.W. (1987), 'Dialogical thinking: critical thought essential to the acquisition of rational knowledge and passions', J. B. Baron and R. Sternberg (eds.), *Teaching Thinking Skills: Theory and Practice*. New York: W. H. Freeman and Company.

Pellegrino Aveni, V. A. (2005), *Study Abroad and Second Language Use: Constructing the Self*. Cambridge: Cambridge University Press.

Perkins, D. (1985), 'General cognitive skills: why not?', in S. F. Chipman, J. Segal and R. Glaser (eds.), *Thinking and Learning Skills, Vol 2: Research and Open Questions*. Hillsdale, NJ: Lawrence Erlbaum Associates.

Perkins, D., Jay, E. and Tishman, S. (1993), 'Beyond abilities: a dispositional theory of thinking', *Merrill-Palmer Quarterly*, 39 (1), 1–21.

Perkins, D. and Salamon, G. (1992), 'Transfer of learning', in *International Encyclopedia of Education* (2nd edn), Oxford: Pergamon, September. Available online at http://learnweb.harvard.edu/alps/thinking/docs/traencyn.htm (accessed 15 November 2009).

Perkins, D. and Salamon, G. (2001), 'Teaching for transfer', in A. Costa, *Developing Minds: A Resource Book for Teaching Thinking* (3rd edn). Alexandria, VA: Association for Supervision and Curriculum Development.

Perkins, D., Tishman, S., Ritchhart, R., Donis, K. and Andrade, A. (2000), 'Intelligence in the wild: a dispositional view of intellectual traits', *Educational Psychology Review*, 12 (3), 269–93.

Perry, W. G. (1968/1999), *Forms of Intellectual and Ethical Development*. New York: Holt, Rinehart and Winston.

Peters, R. (1966), *Ethics and Education*. London: Allen and Unwin.

Phillips, V. and Bond, C. 'Undergraduates experiences of critical thinking', *Higher Education Research and Development*, 23 (3), 277–94.

Piaget, J. and Inhelder, B. (1969), *The Psychology of the Child*. New York: Basic Books.

Quality Assurance Agency for Higher Education (2006), *Guidelines for Writing Programme Specifications*. Available online at http://www.qaa.ac.uk/academicinfrastructure/programSpec/guidelines06.pdf (accessed 19 May 2010).

Quality Assurance Agency for Higher Education (2007), 'Languages and related studies', Subject benchmark statement. The Quality Assurance Agency for Higher Education, available online at http://www.qaa.ac.uk/academicinfrastructure/benchmark/statements/languages07.pdf (accessed 19 May 2010).

Quality Assurance Agency for Higher Education (2008), *The framework for higher education qualifications in England, Wales and Northern Ireland (FHEQ)*. Available online at www.qaa.ac.uk.

Quality Assurance Agency for Higher Education (2009), *An introduction to QAA* (2nd edn). Available online at http://www.qaa.ac.uk/aboutus/IntroQAA.pdf (accessed 18 May 2010).

Quellmalz, E. S. (1987), 'Developing reasoning skills', in J. R. Baron and R. J. Sternberg (eds.), *Teaching Thinking Skills: Theory and Practice*. New York: Freedman Press.

Raufaste, E., Eyrolle, H. and Marine, C. (1998), 'Pertinence generation in radiological diagnosis: spreading activation and the nature of expertise', *Cognitive Science*, 22 (4), 517–46.

Readings, B. (1996), *The University in Ruins*. London: Harvard University Press.

Reed, J. (1998), 'Effect of a model for critical thinking on student achievement in primary source document analysis and interpretation, argumentative reasoning, critical thinking dispositions, and history content in a community college history course', unpublished thesis. University of South Florida.

Reich, R. (1992), *The Work of Nations: Preparing Ourselves for Twenty-First Century Capitalism*. New York: Vintage Books.

Reid, J. M. (1998), *The process of composition* (2nd edn.). Englewood Cliffs, NJ: Prentice Hall.

Reid, W. J. and Epstein, L. (1972), *Task-Centered Casework*. New York: Columbia University Press.

Reimer, B. (1998), 'What knowledge is of most worth in the arts', in P. Hirst and P. White, *Philosophy of Education: Major Themes in the Analytic Tradition, Volume IIII: Problems of Educational Content and Practices*. London: Routledge.

Riley, N. S. (2004), 'A struggle over mind and soul', New York Times, September 8.

Roberts, C., Byram, M., Barro, A., Jordan, S. and Street, B. (2001), *Language Learners as Ethnographers*. Buffalo, NY: Multilingual Matters.

Romero de Mills, P. (2008), 'The development of criticality amongst undergraduate students of Spanish', unpublished thesis, School of Humanities, University of Southampton.

Rouet, J.-F., Britt, M. A., Mason, R. A. and Perfetti, C. A. (1996), 'Using multiple sources of evidence to reason about history', *Journal of Educational Psychology*, 88 (3), 478–93.

Rudy, W. (1984), *The Universities of Europe, 1100–1914*. Rutherford: Fairleigh Dickinson Press.

Ruggeiro, V. R. (2003), 'Neglected issues in the field of critical thinking', in D. Fasko (ed), *Critical Thinking and Reasoning: Current Research, Theory and Practice*. Cresskill, NJ: Hampton Press.

Runco, M. (2004), 'Creativity', *Annual Review of Psychology*, 55, 657–87.

Rutter, M. and Quinton, D. (1977), 'Psychiatric disorder: ecological factors and concepts of causation', in M. McGurk (ed), *Ecological Factors in Human Development*. Amsterdam: North Holland Press.

Ryle, G. (1949), *The Concept of Mind*, London: Hutchison's University Library.

Saito, N. and Imai, Y. (2004), 'In search of the public and the private: philosophy of education in post-war Japan', *Comparative Education*, 40 (4), 583–94.

Sartre, J. P. (1944), *Huis Clos [No Exit]*. Paris: Gallimard, 1945.

Schneider, C. G. (2001), 'Toward the engaged academy: new scholarship, new teaching', *Liberal Education*, Winter, 87 (1), 18–27.

Schön, D. (1991), *The Reflective Practitioner: How Professionals Think in Action*. Aldershot: Arena.

Schuller, T. (1996), 'Relations between human and social capital', in F. Coffield (ed), *A National Strategy for Lifelong Learning*, based on papers presented at Close House, University of Newcastle.

Scott, P. (1995), *The Meanings of Mass Higher Education*. Buckingham: SRHE and Open University Press.

Scriven, M. (2003), 'The philosophy of critical thinking and informal logic', in D. Fasko (ed), *Critical Thinking and Reasoning: Current Research, Theory and Practice*. Cresskill, NJ: Hampton Press.

Shaull, R. (2000), 'Foreword', in P. Freire, *Pedagogy of the Oppressed*. New York: Continuum.

Shearer, B. (2004), 'Multiple intelligence after 20 years', *Teachers College Record*, 106 (1), 2–16.

Shenghong, J. and Dan, J.-W. (2004), 'The contemporary development of the philosophy of education in mainland China and Taiwan', *Comparative Education*, 40 (4), 571–81.

Shils, E. (1997), *The Order of Learning: Essays on the Contemporary University*. New Brunswick: Transaction Publishers.

Shulman, L. S. (1986), 'Those who understand: knowledge growth in teaching', *Educational Researcher*, 15 (2), 4–14.

Siegel, H. (1988), *Educating Reason*. London: Routledge.

Skills Development in Higher Education: Full Report (1998): London: The Committee of Vice-Chancellors and Principals of the Universities of the UK (CVCP), DfEE and HEQE.

Smalley, R. and Ruetten, M. (1986), *Refining Composition Skills: Rhetoric and Grammar for ESL Students*. New York: Macmillan.

Snyder, B. R. (1970), *The Hidden Curriculum*. Cambridge, MA: MIT Press.

Spiro, R. J., Vispoel, W., Schmitz, J., Samarapungavan, A. and Boerger, A. (1987), *Knowledge Acquisition for Application: Cognitive Flexibility and Transfer in Complex Content Domains. Technical Report No. 409*. Champaign, IL: University of Illinois, Centre for the Study of Reading.

Stern, H. H. (1964), 'The future of modern languages in the universities', *Modern Languages*, 45 (3), 87–97.

Sternberg, R. (1985), *Beyond IQ: A Triarchic Theory of Human Intelligence*. Cambridge: Cambridge University Press.

Sternberg, R. (2000), 'The concept of intelligence', in R. Sternberg (ed), *Handbook of Intelligence*. Cambridge: Cambridge University Press.

Swales, J. M. (1990), 'Discourse analysis in professional contexts', *Annual Review of Applied Linguistics*, 11, 103.

Tierney, W. (1997), *Academic Outlaws: Queer Theory and Cultural Studies in the Academy*. Thousand Oaks, CA: Sage.

Torrance, H. (2007), 'Assessment as learning? How the use of explicit learning objectives, assessment criteria and feedback in post-secondary education and training can come to dominate learning', *Assessment in Education: Principles, Policy and Practice*, 14 (3), 281–94.

Toulmin, S. (1958), *The Uses of Argument*. Cambridge: Cambridge University Press.

Tulving, E. (1972), 'Episodic and semantic memory', in E. Tulving and W. Donaldson (eds.), *Organisation of Memory*. New York: Academic Press.

University of Melbourne (2007) 'Attributes of the Melbourne graduate'. Available online at http://www.unimelb.edu.au/about/attributes.html (accessed on 18 April 2010).

Van den Brink-Budgen, R. (2000), *Critical Thinking for Students: Learn the Skills of Critical Assessment and Effective Argument* (3rd edn.). Oxford: How To Books.

Volet, S. (1999), 'Learning across cultures: appropriateness of knowledge transfer', *International Journal of Education Research*, 31 (7), 625–43.

Voss, J. F. and Wiley, J. (1995), 'Acquiring intellectual skills', *Annual Review of Psychology*, 46, 155–81.
Vygotsky, L. S. (1962), *Thought and Language*. Cambridge: MA Institute of Technology.
Vygotsky, L. S. (1978), *Mind in Society: The Development of Higher Psychological Processes* (eds. M. Cole, V. John-Steiner, S. Scribner, E. Souberman). Cambridge, MA: Harvard University Press.
Walker, P. and Finney, N. (1999), 'Skill development and critical thinking in higher education', *Teaching in Higher Education*, 4 (4), 531–47.
Walters, K. S. (1994), 'Introduction: beyond logicism in critical thinking', in K. S. Walters (ed), *Re-thinking Reason: New Perspectives in Critical Thinking*. Albany: State University of New York Press.
Walvoord, B. E. and McCarthy, L. P. (1990), *Thinking and Writing in College: A Naturalistic Study of Students in Four Disciplines*. Urbana, IL: National Council of Teachers of English.
Warren, K. (1994), 'Critical thinking and feminism', in K. S. Walters (ed), *Re-thinking Reason: New Perspectives in Critical Thinking*. Albany: State University of New York Press.
Wenger, E. (1998), *Communities of Practice: Learning, Meaning and Identity*. Cambridge: Cambridge University Press.
White, R. W. (1999), 'Foreword', in W. G. Perry, *Forms of Intellectual and Ethical Development*. New York: Holt, Rinehart and Winston.
Whitehead, A. N. (1932a), 'The aims of education', in A. N. Whitehead, *The Aims of Education and Other Essays*. London: Williams and Norgate.
Whitehead, A. N. (1932b), 'Universities and their function', in A. N. Whitehead, *The Aims of Education and Other Essays*. London: Williams and Norgate.
Wildavsky, B. (2010), *The Great Brain Race: How Global Universities are Reshaping the World*, Oxford: Princeton University Press.
Wineburg, S. (1991), 'Historical problem-solving: a study of the cognitive processes used in the evaluation of documentary and pictorial evidence', *Journal of Educational Psychology*, 83 (1), 73–87.
Wineburg, S. (1998), 'Reading Abraham Lincoln: an expert/expert study in the interpretation of historical texts', *Cognitive Science*, 22 (3), 319–46.
Ylijaki, O.H. (2000), 'Disciplinary differences and the moral order of studying', *Higher Education*, 39 (3), 339–62.

Index

A Test of Leadership 1–2, 97–9
adolescents 63
adult learners 61–3
argument 22–6, 117–18
   construction 167, 172, 176
   fallacy theory 21–5
   Toulmin's model 22
assessment 95–6, 110, 117–22, 130, 198–203, 221–8

background
   educational 207
   student 27, 55–8, 158, 166, 169, 176, 196, 197, 217, 227–8
   theoretical 11, 152, 175
Barnett, R. 2, 18–20, 26, 38, 51, 69–74, 101, 182–3, 193–5, 200, 222
benchmark statements
   Modern Languages 104–6
   Social Work 106–9
Bildung 16
Bologna Process 101
Bradley Report 97–102

care–control dilemma 144, 171
citizenship 17, 36–9, 65
cognition 40–52
   Piagetian 43, 59–63
communities of practice 35, 72, 93, 224
competence 30, 43, 101, 111, 204, 209
   intercultural 112–15, 118–19, 182
   linguistic 111
   professional 39, 192–4, 219
   Social Work 121–5
confidence 80–1, 211–12, 220
conformity 94, 161, 163
constructivism
   cognitive 48, 59–60, 224
   social 60–1, 93, 95, 224

contextualization and criticality 68, 220
   broad context 71–2, 205–6
   encouraging the development 73–4, 208–9
   field-specific aspects 72–3, 206–7
   historic and geographic 3–8, 81
conventions
   academic 165, 176
Cornell Critical Thinking tests 22
courage 53, 62, 81
critical being 18–20, 65, 69, 73, 81, 89, 205
   Barnett's three domains 18–20, 26, 39, 69–73, 83
criticality approaches
   embedded in specific fields 28–36
   philosophical approaches 15–39
      critical being 18–21
      liberal academic 16–18
      resources 26–8
      skills and dispositions 21–6
   political engagement 36–9
      citizenship education 38–9
      social emancipatory engagement 36–8
   psychological approaches 40–67
      cognitive psychology 40–52
      creative thinking 52–6
      intellectual development 59–64
      intelligence 56–9
   twenty-first century 1–3
criticality development *see* development
culture shock 179, 183–4, 197
curriculum 95–126, 136, 210, 223
   models 95, 107

Dearing Report 97, 99, 100–3, 110, 113
de-contextualization 51

definition
  of criticality 70–1, 127–8, 138–9
  learning outcomes 101, 110–15
desirability of criticality 7–9, 14, 64–5
development
  adults 61–3
  classes
    Modern Languages 128–38
    Social Work 138–51
  cognitive constructionists 59–60
  of criticality 8–9, 14, 64–5, 73–4, 81–96, 190, 202, 204–9, 213–19
  levels of criticality 19, 82–92
  out-of-university experiences
    practice placements 193–202
    residence abroad 182–90
  pedagogy encouraging 73–4, 95–6, 223–6
  policies encouraging 219–23
  professional 92–3
  social constructivist 60–1
  vertical 223
  writing
    Modern Languages 134–66
    Social Work 166–77
disabilities 147, 173
disciplines *see* fields
dispositions 15, 21–2, 25, 41–4, 48–51, 128, 187–8, 199–206 *see also* resources, personal
  approach 41, 49–51, 83
diversity 7, 17
domains
  criticality 11, 18–20, 38, 65, 69–70, 73, 83, 101, 220, 226
    connections between 190, 200
    lack of linkage 190
  formal knowledge 17, 27, 35, 39, 73–9, 83
  self 18–20, 69–71, 74, 80–92, 105–9, 112–25, 137–9, 152, 177, 181–4, 188–96, 200–3, 206–8, 210–11, 216–17, 220–2
  world 18–20, 22, 38–9, 69, 74, 85, 89–90, 108, 113, 118, 137, 184–5, 189, 196, 200–2, 216
Donald, J. 31–3

emancipation
  social 36–8, 87–8, 90, 92
empathy 17, 38, 56, 181–2, 193, 198–200, 203
engagement 86–8
  civic 110
  political 36–9, 49, 69
  social 127
  student 10, 50, 86–9, 153, 160, 180–5, 212–16
Engagement as a Core Value for the University 1
Enlightenment 4, 16
equity 38, 82, 227
evidence sheets 192, 198–201
expertise 40–3, 57, 75

feedback response 129, 165–73, 205, 209, 216
feminism 14, 160, 162, 266
fields 28–36, 72–3, 206–8, 221, 225, 227
  hard 31, 46, 72, 227
  soft 31–4, 72–3, 99, 106, 152, 208, 221, 225, 227
framework
  National Qualifications 103, 115
  thinking skills 47–52
framework for criticality
  development 68, 71–96, 227
  acquisition of resources 93
  aspects of criticality 83–92
  assessment aspects 95–6
  contextual matters 95
  curricular matters 95
  developmental processes 93–6
  knowledge types 74–80
  levels of development 82–93
  nature of criticality 69–71
  personal qualities 80–1
  resources 74–81
  qualifications 103, 115
  theoretical 11–12, 215
    critiquing 152
Freire, P. 36–7, 151
Future of Higher Education, The 1

Index

gender theory 188, 207
genres
   academic 78–9, 116, 153, 210, 225
   literary 76, 78, 118, 128, 136–7, 214

Harvard 6, 62
Higher Ambitions 98–9
Higher Education: A Critical Business 18
Higher Education in the Learning Society
    see Dearing Report

intelligence 54, 56–60
intercultural awareness 105, 118, 179–81, 202–5
international trends 97–102
   higher education policies 97–102

judgement 20, 23, 27, 32, 41, 50–3, 76, 101–9
   refraining from 123, 183

knowledge 14–19, 23–62, 74–80, 96–7, 112, 114, 124–8, 141, 175, 196, 202–3, 210, 220
   background 26, 74, 117, 129, 135, 214
   declarative 75
   de-contextualized 51
   destabilization 140, 169
   economy 97–9
   frameworks 27, 35, 48, 62–3, 69, 74, 80, 81
   linguistic 78–9, 181–9, 192
   of what it is to be 77–8
   passive 47, 81
   patterns 63, 80
   procedural 75–6
   resources 139, 202, 210
   types 74, 197, 198
   why 76–7
Kolb, D. A. 33–5

language 66, 78
   academic 164
   colloquial 116, 158, 163, 168, 211
   fluency 128, 180–6, 210–11
language-game 28
Learning for Life 1

lectures 144–6, 224
legislation 170
liberal education 16–18, 21, 40, 99, 110, 205
library 156, 159, 167, 214
life span 58–9, 63, 66
literacy *see also* reading
   academic 129, 141
logic 15, 21–32, 43–5, 59, 69, 89, 210

massification 6, 110
maturity 180–5, 189, 202
Melbourne model 17, 222
memories 43–4
metacognition 50, 66, 93, 208
mimicry 94–5, 213
Modern Languages
   benchmark statements 104–6
   curricular documentation 116–20
   institutional documents 111–14, 178
   languages classes 136–8
   lecturers 126–30, 181–91
   lectures and seminars 130–6
   perceptions of criticality 126–8
   residence abroad 178–90
   students 154–66, 181–90
motivation 41–8, 51–5, 70–3, 79–83, 153, 212–13

narratives 131, 134, 157–9, 173, 185–6, 214
national context 102–25
National Qualifications Framework 103, 115

OECD *see* Organization for Economic and Cultural Development
of what it is to be 77–8
oppression 35–8, 114, 120, 171
Organization for Economic and Cultural Development 100–1
outcomes
   approach 97, 100–2, 109–11, 204, 219–21
   language course 116, 120
   Social Work 114–15, 121, 192

pedagogic implications 223–6
pedagogy 14–15, 24–5, 37–8, 223–8
perceptions of criticality
    final year classes
        Modern Languages 134–6
    first-year classes
        Modern Languages 131–3
        Social Work 142–6
    lecturers
        Modern Languages 126–30
        Social Work 138–42
    second-year classes
        Modern Languages 133–4
        Social Work 146–7
    seminars 149
personal change 94, 169, 182, 217
Peters, R. 78
policies 1–3, 39, 97, 219–21
    criticality and
        undergraduates 101–25
    encouraging criticality
        institutional level 221–3
        national level 219–21
    goals for higher education 97–100
    institutional 109–24
politics 3, 6, 26, 36, 91
positivism 40, 51
postmodernism 14, 17–19
practice 107, 154
practice placements 121, 122, 149, 178–209, 217, 222
    fitness for purpose 193
    project 124
pressures 53, 60–4, 143, 156, 176, 195, 207–9, 214, 217, 225
problem-solving 180, 184
professional development 92
professionalism 201, 208
programme specification
    Modern Languages 111–14
    Social Work 114–15
psychology
    cognitive 24, 40, 44, 47–51, 65, 66

questions
    control of definition 86, 179, 214
    formation 214–15, 225

rationale building 83, 85, 91–2, 217–18, 225
reading *see also* literacy
    academic 155–6, 170
    difficulties 212
    fluency 156
referencing 157–62, 167–8, 172, 216, 226
reflection
    critical 182–3
    strategic 46, 50
reflective thinking 49, 193, 200
relationships 15, 91, 169, 174, 218
religion 4–5, 162, 184, 213
research methodology 9–12
residence abroad 118–20, 178–90, 220
resources
    acquiring 93, 96 *see also* library
    confidence 80–1, 211–12, 220
    courage 53, 62, 81
    criticality 20, 26–7, 65–9, 74, 83, 210–13, 223–7
    knowledge 74–80, 96–7, 112, 114, 124–8, 141, 175, 196, 202–3, 210, 220
        declarative 75
        of what it is to be 77–8
        procedural 75–6
        why 76–7
    linguistic 78–9, 181–9, 192
    personal 73, 80–1, 94, 187–9, 223
Review of Australian Higher Education see Bradley Report

scholarship 37, 100–2
    ancient Greek 3, 16
    Islamic 3–5
    non-Western 3–5
    Socratic tradition 17
    Western 24
self *see also* domains, self
    -actualization 53
    -realization 183, 184, 194
    -regulation 50
skills 196–7
    criticality 21, 26
    essay-writing 129, 141, 153–77

thinking 23–6, 41–3, 47–52, 59, 75–6, 185–6
Social Work
  benchmark statement 106–9
  curricular documentation 120–4
  institutional documents 114–15, 190–3
  lecturers 138–42
  lectures, seminars and tutorials 142–51
  perceptions of criticality 138–9
  practice placements 190–202
  students 166–76, 192–202
sociology 71, 140–1, 168, 220
solution-searching processes 87, 214–18
sources
  primary data 11, 68, 175
  secondary 164–7, 172, 186, 209, 215

thinking
  collectivist 17
  creative 52, 54, 65, 214
  deficiencies 21–2
  domain-specific 42–4
  field-specific 27, 30, 72
  historical 42
  knowledge-based 30
  patterns 46
  skills frameworks 47–52
  style 54–5
  value-grounded 39–41, 49, 149
transfer
  across domains 27, 35, 63, 83, 124, 154, 172, 188, 207
  horizontal 177, 200, 222
  intellectual and professional 192
  knowledge types 209
  theory–practice 149, 170–1, 173–7, 189, 218
  vertical 223
transferability 15, 18, 23, 43–5, 93, 220, 226
  cultural 63
Triarchic Theory of Intelligence 56
tutorials
  Modern Languages 141
  Social Work 147

types of criticality
  instrumental 69–70, 205
  transformatory 69–70, 226

university
  Humboldtian 16
  neohumanist 16
uses
  of criticality 20
  of knowledge 65

values
  conflicting 70, 162–3, 169, 199, 208, 212–13
  human rights 212
  internalization of 206–13
  Modern Languages 152, 183, 203, 208
  personal 74, 80–1, 120–5, 145, 152, 169, 183–4, 199–203, 206, 211–13
  professional 15, 99, 107, 121, 151, 191, 201, 203, 210, 212
  questioning 70, 201, 214–18, 227
  Social Work 107–9, 114, 120–2, 142–5, 149–52, 175, 191–8, 201–3, 207, 211–13
  systems 37, 76, 183–4, 199, 202–3, 210
  underlying criticality 70, 169, 210–13
video workshops 147–8
Vygotsky, L. S. 48, 60–4, 71–3, 93

Watson-Glaser critical thinking test 22
Wittgenstein, L. 28
women 5, 37–8, 62–3, 145, 160, 184
writing *see also* literacy
  final year
    Modern Languages 162–5
    Social Work 173–6
  first year
    Modern Languages 155–8
    Social Work 167–70
  second year
    Modern Languages 158–62
    Social Work 170–3

year abroad *see* residence abroad

Zapatista movement 134, 161

Printed in Great Britain
by Amazon.co.uk, Ltd.,
Marston Gate.